CRIME PREVENTION WITHDRAWN

PRINCIPLES, PERSPECTIVES AND PRACTICES

Second edition

Crime Prevention: Principles, Perspectives and Practices is a concise, comprehensive introduction to the theory and practice of crime prevention. The authors contend that crime prevention strategies should include both social prevention (programs addressing social causes of delinquency) and environmental prevention (reducing crime by minimising opportunities). It embraces these strategies as a policy alternative to policing, criminal justice, and 'law and order'.

This book examines a range of Australian examples within an international context. Part 1 presents an overview of the history and theory of crime prevention, featuring chapters on social prevention, environmental prevention and evaluation. Part 2 explores the practice of crime prevention and the real life challenges of implementation, including policy making, prevention in public places, dealing with social disorder and planning for the future.

Fully revised and updated, this edition features a new chapter on emergent issues in crime prevention (including cyber-crime, environmental crime and counter-terrorism) as well as expanded content on crime prevention partnerships and key knowledge bases. Case studies, discussion questions, further reading exercises and a glossary of key terms highlight the links between the development and application of crime prevention approaches.

Crime Prevention provides readers with an understanding of the political dimension of crime prevention and the ability to critically analyse prevention techniques. It is essential reading for undergraduate students of criminology, crime prevention and public policy.

Adam Sutton was Associate Professor in the Department of Criminology at the University of Melbourne. He passed away in 2010.

Adrian Cherney is Senior Lecturer in Criminology in the School of Social Sciences at the University of Queensland.

Rob White is Professor of Criminology in the School of Social Sciences at the University of Tasmania.

CRIME PREVENTION

PRINCIPLES, PERSPECTIVES AND PRACTICES

Second Edition

Adam Sutton

Adrian Cherney

Rob White

CAMBRIDGE
UNIVERSITY PRESS

CAMBRIDGE
UNIVERSITY PRESS

477 Williamstown Road, Port Melbourne, VIC 3207, Australia

Cambridge University Press is part of the University of Cambridge.

It furthers the University's mission by disseminating knowledge in the pursuit of education, learning and research at the highest international levels of excellence.

www.cambridge.org
Information on this title: www.cambridge.org/9781107622470

First published 2008
Reprinted 2012 (twice)
Second edition 2014

Cover designed by Zo Gay

A catalogue record for this publication is available from the British Library

A Cataloguing-in-Publication entry is available from the catalogue of the National Library of Australia at www.nla.gov.au

ISBN 978-1-107-62247-0 Paperback

Adam Sutton passed away shortly after the publication of the first edition of this book. We would like to dedicate this edition to Adam's memory. Adam's legacy endures within the crime prevention field in many different ways and within the present pages. His ongoing contribution is also permanently acknowledged by the Adam Sutton Crime Prevention Award, which is awarded each year by the Australian and New Zealand Society of Criminology. The Award is presented to the person whose report or paper (a) demonstrates pragmatic and workable solutions to Australasian crime problems; (b) reflects the values of a tolerant and inclusive society; and (c) which is founded in theory and research on crime prevention. Our thanks go once again to a wonderful friend and colleague.

Adrian Cherney and Rob White

CONTENTS

PART 2 PRACTICE

PREFACE AND ACKNOWLEDGMENTS

The first edition of this book was in gestation for a long time, and was the product of lengthy and at times demanding discussions and debates among the authors. The central figure during this process was our late colleague Adam Sutton. Adam passed away in the time between editions. For the first edition he was instrumental in writing chapters 1, 3, 5 and 9; however, with respect to the changes and additions to this edition, there is no doubt that his presence endures both within the field and within the present pages. Adam was inspirational in every sense of the word, especially when it came to crime prevention matters, and was a much valued friend, confidant and connecter. The first edition, and now the second edition, of this book could not have occurred without his wisdom, vision and enduring legacy. For this Adrian and Rob are particularly grateful.

Over the course of the two editions a number of people have provided constructive feedback and encouraging suggestions, including Zoe Hamilton and Jessica Pearce from Cambridge University Press. We remain grateful to Jill Henry, who preceded Zoe as Commissioning Editor, for coming up with the idea of a book on crime prevention. Finally we wish to thank our partners, Lorraine and Sharyn, for their encouragement and support, and to acknowledge the ongoing interest of Alessandra in this book project.

PART

1

THEORY

1

CRIME PREVENTION AND COMMUNITY SAFETY IN AUSTRALIA

Introduction

Crime prevention has a long history in Australia, and in other parts of the world. In all societies, people have tried to protect themselves and those close to them from assaults and other abuses. Every time someone locks the door to their house or their car, they practise a form of prevention. Most parents want their children to learn to be law abiding and not spend any period of their lives in prison. In this country, at least, most succeed. Only a small minority of young people become recidivist offenders. In a functioning society, crime prevention is part of everyday life. While prevention can be all-pervasive at the grassroots, it is oddly neglected in mass media and political discourses. When politicians, talkback radio hosts and newspaper editorialists pontificate about crime and possible remedies, it is comparatively rare for them to mention prevention. Overwhelmingly, emphasis is on policing, sentencing and other 'law and order' responses.

One aim of this book is to understand, and explore ways to overcome, this apparent conspiracy of silence. At various times over the last four decades governments in Australia and other Western countries have 'rediscovered' crime prevention and committed resources to its development and implementation. Many jurisdictions still have schemes in place. Despite these efforts, prevention and community safety remain background tasks, as far as the mass media and government crime policy are concerned. Police and other criminal justice reactions to crime continue to command the lion's share of attention and budget allocations.

Throughout this volume, we focus on arguing that prevention is 'do-able'; that it works, and that it can be far more cost effective than criminal justice responses. We will show how prevention theory, properly applied, not only reduces offending but can help make cities, towns, suburbs, streets, shopping centres and homes more liveable. We also argue that principles of prevention can be applied to emerging problems that face society, such as terrorism and environmental threats.

However, we also acknowledge that ensuring prevention captures the public imagination will require more than building the evidence base through identifying 'what works'. One of the key arguments of this book is that there is a political dimension to the development and implementation of strategies. Making crime prevention 'work' in political contexts entails more than ensuring that it is practically effective. It must also succeed at the symbolic – or, as Freiberg (2001) terms it, 'affective' – level (also see Ekblom 2010). Law and order dominates policy and media discourses and helps political parties garner votes because of the powerful messages that the apprehension, trial, punishment and other associated shaming of offenders conveys. Durkheim (1912) argued that punishment rituals redefine and reinforce a society's 'collective consciousness': the shared values and rules that help bind its members together. Crime prevention policy makers and practitioners in Australia have tended to gloss over the symbolic dimensions, treating prevention as purely an instrumental task. We try to rectify this deficiency, and discuss ways prevention programs and practices might both feed into and help reshape the ways governments and communities respond to crime.

The realities of crime prevention policy and practice in Australia and abroad

When examining Australian experience it is important to locate it in an international context (see chapter 6). As a number of researchers (e.g. Crawford 1997; Hughes 1998; Sutton 1997; Homel 2005, 2009a, 2009b) have made clear, Australia was not the first country to endeavour to introduce crime prevention to the policy mix. Attempts by Australian state and commonwealth governments to develop and implement prevention strategies in the late 1980s and 1990s were inspired by, and drew upon, experience in the US, the UK, and France, the Netherlands and other parts of Europe during the early 1970s and 1980s.

As highlighted by Homel (2009, 2010), there are a number of consistent features that characterise modern crime prevention initiatives. These are based upon the experiences of many jurisdictions and can provide guidance for future policy developments in this area (see, for instance, the Victorian Drugs and Crime Prevention Committee 2012). The common programmatic features include:

- centrally developed and driven policies
- a commitment to evidence-based approaches (the professed commitment does not always equal reality, though – see chapters 5 and 6)
- strategies built upon multi-agency or partnership approaches (e.g. whole-of-government/whole-of-community approaches)
- emphases upon local delivery (e.g. via local government – see Case study 1.1)
- crime prevention/community safety plans (also see Case study 1.1 and chapter 6)
- a mix of social and environmental prevention (see chapter 3 and 4).

(See also Sutton & Cherney 2002; Crawford 1997; Homel 2006, 2009a, 2009b; Shaw 2001, 2009.)

Given this commonality in how crime prevention has been designed and delivered by state and local government, it is not surprising there are also consistent problems that plague the implementation of crime prevention strategies (Clancy, Lee & Crofts 2012; Homel 2006, 2009; Homel & Homel 2012; Shaw 2009 – see chapter 5). However, when considering how countries have developed crime prevention programs and the lessons that might be learnt from these efforts, it is important to be mindful of broader pressures affecting governments and how they may influence the emphasis placed on any particular approach to strategy design and implementation.

It is no accident that in Western democracies crime prevention began to emerge as a distinct policy theme during the final third of the 20th century. This was when 'welfare' models of governance came under pressure, with central states urged to rein in taxation and public sector expenditure in order to ensure that national and regional economies could compete globally. Theorists such as Garland (2000, 2001) and O'Malley (1994) in fact see crime prevention as part of attempts by central authorities to divest themselves of direct social control roles, and shift more and more of the community safety burden to individuals and groups at the local level. Drawing on Foucault (1991), they see this trend towards individual and community 'responsibilisation' as characteristic of the indirect and dispersed ways power is exercised in the late-modern era.

It is true that, in most Western jurisdictions, a key factor prompting governments to explore crime prevention has been the hope that it will help curb escalating outlays on police, prisons and other criminal justice institutions. However, Garland and O'Malley go too far when they imply that there is no more to contemporary crime prevention than an attempt by the centre to back away from aspects of its protective role and compel individuals, organisations and communities to take greater responsibility for their own safety and security. We argue that such an account ignores the fact that, rather than crime prevention being something entirely new, the 'rediscovery' of crime prevention involves belated acknowledgment of an ongoing reality.

Part of this reality involves the realisation that crime prevention is about reforming and augmenting how agencies and groups go about their daily duties and routine activities (see chapter 2). It requires that governments and police alter and re-think how they have traditionally gone about addressing crime, and involves efforts to enhance the existing capacities of third parties – constituted of individuals, families, businesses and communities (who always have had a role in this sphere) – to operate and function in ways that preclude crime. This means that some sections of society are far more likely to benefit from prevention than others. Australian data consistently reveals disproportionately high rates of violence and other victimisation among the economically and socially disadvantaged, in particular many Indigenous communities. Governments that genuinely want these groups to be more effective in prevention need to find ways to ensure that they are not deprived of the material and cultural resources and skills they need to make their lives more secure and their communities more liveable. At various points in this book we argue that this requires reassessment of the classic neo-liberal doctrine that competitive market forces invariably generate the best social outcomes.

Crime prevention as an alternative to law and order

Law and order attracts people because it seems to tackle crime at its most direct and obvious source, the offender. In chapter 2 we point out, however, that factors contributing to the occurrence of any single offence are multiple and complex. One of the advantages of prevention policy is that it moves beyond a fixation with deviants and deviance and begins to address all the contributing elements. This is why, as criminologists, we are convinced that governments would be well advised to spend more of their resources on prevention. However, our commitment is based on more than technical assessment. Democratic societies that devote excessive resources to the 'tough on crime' approach risk more than wasting money. They also risk damaging the social fabric.

In our view, law and order's domination of contemporary policy and media discourses threatens a 21st century equivalent of the 'tragedy of the commons' fable: the tendency for 'rational' choices made by individuals in isolation to combine to destroy an invaluable and irreplaceable collective resource (Hardin 1968). In the crime policy case, however, the collective resource is social as well as physical. In many parts of the world there is a growing tendency for citizens to live in gated communities (Atkinson & Blandy 2005), work in secured office blocks and find leisure and recreation in similarly controlled and patrolled enclaves (Davis 1990); while their governments rely more and more on aggressive policing tactics to maintain order in what remains of the public domain. For individuals exposed to the benefits and disciplines of the market and with access to economic and other resources, physical segregation from – and lack of tolerance for – potentially disruptive 'outsiders' might well seem a rational choice. For some members of the stigmatised and excluded 'communities of fate' generated by such choices, however, an equally rational response may be to strike out through crime and other predatory behaviour (Jordan 1996; Wilkinson 2005). The burgeoning of private security and increased emphasis on law and order in market-based democracies characterised by significant levels of inequality can lead, therefore, to heightened levels both of unease and fear (Atkinson 2006, p. 180; Low 2003) and of crime itself (see chapter 8).

Crime prevention can help break this cycle. This is one reason why, throughout this book, we follow the Dutch researchers Van Dijk and de Waard and define crime prevention as:

> The total of all private initiatives and state policies, other than the enforcement
> of criminal law, aimed at the reduction of damage caused by acts defined as
> criminal by the state. (Van Dijk & de Waard 1991, p. 483)

Readers should be aware that in defining crime prevention this way we make a value judgment. Not all criminologists and policy makers accept our view that crime prevention should be treated as a conscious alternative to policies that emphasise the privatising of policing and other security and harsher criminal justice responses to crime. As noted, Garland and O'Malley's responsibilisation thesis assumes that prevention simply will complement increased punitiveness in late-modern states. At a more pragmatic level, researchers such as Ekblom (1994) and Weatherburn (2002) point out that the Van Dijk and de Waard approach ignores research evidence that arrest, imprisonment and other criminal justice based initiatives also deter and reduce offending.

A problem with these objections is that they fail to locate the renaissance of crime prevention and community safety policy in relevant historical, cultural and political contexts. As chapter 6 will point out, one of the key reasons governments in Western democracies, such as France and the Netherlands, began to develop relevant strategies during the 1980s – and Australian state governments began to emulate them – was concern about the economic and human costs of over-reliance on law and order. Policy makers who advocated crime prevention in these countries were not simply looking for forms of social control that would 'work' better in a pragmatic sense; they were striving to develop policies and programs that were more compatible with their ideals of a good society. Experience over the last three decades has shown, moreover, that once the vision faded, and governments in these and other countries began to treat crime prevention as a purely administrative challenge, even the most generously-funded programs lost impetus and direction (Hough 2006; Homel 2010).

It is possible for crime prevention to be deployed as an adjunct to law and order. Indeed, the Republic of Singapore has been pursuing just this approach since the mid-1960s (Quah 1992; Clammer 1997; Singh 2000). This includes, for example, punitive measures (e.g. caning) for a wide range of offences, such as vandalism and graffiti, and significant investment in social infrastructure, such as housing and education (Clammer 1997). Few would debate that Singapore's long-term strategy of combining major penalties and humiliations for those who break the law with high levels of state intervention to promote social integration has succeeded in producing an extremely law-abiding society. However, its citizens have paid a price for this success, not just in terms of individual rights and liberties but politically and culturally.

Our point, however, is that criminologists who want to assess prevention purely on an instrumental basis and ignore its expressive and political dimensions gloss over the fact that decisions relating to social control are critical for determining the quality of life any community enjoys (see also chapters 7 and 8). For high-crime areas in particular, commitment to crime prevention and community safety also involves recommitment to investing in physical infrastructure and social capital.

Throughout this book, relationships between prevention and other dimensions of social control policy are treated as more than technical. In advising on and devising ways for human behaviour to be restrained and redirected, it is not just appropriate but obligatory that researchers and policy makers always also consider the types of communities that might result (Hughes 2007). Singapore's elites have used both crime prevention and law and order to produce and sustain a society that is highly prosperous and consumerist, but at the same time distrustful of outsiders and with minimal tolerance even for comparatively minor deviance. We do not see such an approach as appropriate for other countries.

Our view is that when governments make prevention part of their crime control repertoire, they should avoid doing it in ways that simply try to suppress every symptom of difference, diversity, surprise and disorder. Our preference for defining prevention as a distinct alternative, rather than as a mere supplement, to law and order should be understood in this context.

Chapter themes and outline

In the field of crime prevention there has been much debate about whether it would be better to focus on environmental – or as Clarke (1997) terms it 'situational' – or social prevention. Situational prevention, which in essence focuses on reducing opportunities for crime rather than trying to change the disposition to offend, has long been criticised by advocates of social prevention as 'commodified control' (Garland 2001, p. 200), more likely to simply displace crime than eliminate it (Halsey 2001). After reading our summary of relevant approaches and frameworks in chapter 2 and our more detailed assessment of various schools in chapters 3 and 4, we hope readers will realise that taking sides in this debate is neither necessary nor helpful. 'Common-sense' assumptions that social prevention schemes are more likely to generate outcomes that are consistent with ideals of social justice simply are not supported by the research evidence. In fact, unless carefully managed, even the best intended social programs are likely to have stigmatising and damaging effects (see chapter 3), while situational initiatives can be implemented in ways that avoid these problems and generate broad social benefits (chapter 4).

Throughout the book we use the general term 'environmental' to refer to any approach to prevention that focuses on modifying the physical environments in which offences can occur (e.g. by making targets less accessible or by improving guardianship – see chapters 2 and 4). However, we reserve the specific term 'environmental crime prevention' to refer to attempts to reduce offences against the environment (e.g. air or water pollution). As indicated in chapter 9, the principles reflected in crime prevention generally can also be applied to the specific area of environmental threats and harms.

A key theme of this book is that crime prevention is simply not a technical task. Hence a key emphasis in chapter 5, on implementation and evaluation, is that not only do we need to know whether a prevention strategy or program 'has worked' we also need to ask and answer a series of sub-questions, such as: 'Worked for whom?'; 'Worked in what circumstances and in relation to what problems?' and 'Worked in what ways?' Evidence-based approaches to crime prevention and community safety involve systematically unpacking and responding to each of these demands.

In deciding on ways to improve crime prevention and community safety, context is as important as technique. This is the principle informing chapter 6, which moves from crime prevention and community safety theory to politics and practice. We commence by reflecting on experience since the 1970s in the US, the UK and other European countries, and of course, Australia. Various lessons can be drawn from this history. One is the need for prevention to be implemented through local or regional plans rather than as discrete projects. Another is that to avoid problems such as program drift, large-scale crime prevention and community safety strategies require more than technical expertise. They also must be informed by a strong sense of vision and purpose, and must facilitate dialogue between central and local agencies about priorities and resource allocations. In the absence of such vision and dialogue, local implementation invariably becomes dogged by conflict and division.

Chapters 7 to 10 discuss ways our vision of inclusive crime prevention and community safety might translate into grassroots practice. The key is to embrace difference, spontaneity, the unexpected and the ambiguous rather than to reject every apparent symptom of disorder as 'threatening'. Chapter 7, on the social dynamics of public spaces (including cyberspace), focuses on ways these principles can revitalise how authorities and businesses respond to activities by people whose urge to use these environments in particular ways (e.g. through social networking, graffiti writing, skateboarding or simply 'hanging around') often makes them both the object of exclusion and criminal victimisation.

Chapter 8 analyses ways that notions of 'danger', 'disorder' and 'harm' are constructed at the local level, and how our preferred approaches to prevention and safety might help reconfigure these concepts. Consistent with our view that crime prevention should be treated as a distinct policy alternative to current tendencies to 'commodify' security services and promise tough 'law and order' responses to crime, this chapter gives comparatively little attention to private policing. However, it acknowledges that in shopping centres, entertainment precincts and other venues private sector based guards and other officers can help develop and implement programs that are consistent with crime prevention's emphasis on more inclusive social control (e.g. through acting as effective place-managers).

Chapter 9 aims to apply some of the principles outlined in this book to recent (but not necessarily new) threats that have gained attention within the public consciousness (e.g. terrorism and eco-crime), and examine whether our vision of crime prevention is applicable to these 'new' emerging problems.

We end in chapter 10 by discussing ways that the approaches to crime prevention and community safety planning developed and analysed in this book might be employed by a (not-so-hypothetical) 'city of the future', and discuss the new notions of community that relevant practices might draw upon and help forge.

CASE STUDY 1.1   **THE ROLE OF LOCAL GOVERNMENT IN CRIME PREVENTION**

A number of Australian and overseas crime prevention policies have identified local government as important to the delivery of crime prevention initiatives (Anderson & Homel 2005; Clancy, Lee & Crofts 2012; Shaw 2009; Sutton & Cherney 2002; also see chapter 6). Policies in Victoria (Sutton & Cherney 2002), Western Australia (Anderson & Tresidder 2008) and New South Wales (Anderson & Homel 2005; Clancy, Lee & Crofts 2012) have all allocated significant responsibility to local government to develop and implement crime prevention plans, and form multi-agency partnerships with local agencies (such as the police) and stakeholders (such as businesses and residential groups). One key justification for this approach is the argument that local government is in the best position to identify relevant local crime issues – which vary from community to community – and develop responses that are tailored to local needs. However, the problem with such an approach is that local government often lacks the capability to effectively plan, develop and implement long-term crime prevention programs, with it being difficult to generate and sustain community and agency input and participation in crime prevention initiatives. Also, local government has limited resources to adequately address key causes of crime and delinquency (e.g. alcohol, drugs or dysfunctional families). This is not to say that local government should not have a role in crime prevention; to the contrary, it is a central player. Rather, it points to the need for capacity building to be a key component of any crime prevention program (see chapters 5 and 6).

2

KEY
APPROACHES
AND
FRAMEWORKS

Introduction

This chapter will discuss the following topics:

- disputes and controversies in the crime prevention field
- assessing the value of crime prevention through technical and critical paradigms
- broad crime prevention classifications
- understanding crime in context
- the importance of crime prevention problem solving.

In attempting to prevent or reduce crime, it is essential that policy makers and practitioners be prepared to confront two fundamental questions: 'What are the underlying causes of offending?' and 'Which of these causes are most relevant to the crime or crimes currently being addressed?' Providing answers to these questions is never straightforward. Almost invariably, therefore, crime prevention policy and practice will be contested.

It is important to recognise that the topic of crime prevention is linked to broader discourses about the nature of society and preferred approaches to social control. Crime prevention theories are not neutral in the assumptions they make about individuals and society. For instance, situational crime prevention assumes that if the opportunity presents itself, people will commit crime (see chapter 3). Social prevention, though, regards crime as the result of particular social deficits and argues that prevention should focus on aiding individuals, families and communities to act in ways that preclude crime (see chapter 4). The fact that every theory about crime prevention is nested in broader sets of assumptions about society and social control helps explain why – despite the fact that most criminologists endorse prevention in principle – they differ widely in their views on ways it should be approached in practice. What follows is a review of key analytical perspectives and frameworks that have informed developments in theory, policy and practice. These frameworks and models are useful for introducing the reader to the myriad ways crime prevention has been conceptualised and understood as a distinct policy approach. Our aim is to canvass a range of perspectives. We do not claim to be exhaustive, but simply to complement crime prevention classifications and theories developed in other texts (e.g. Crawford 1998; Ekblom 2010; Hughes 1998; Laub 2013). It is a summary of what we see as the most productive ways to understand and operationalise crime prevention.

Prevention of crime as disputed terrain

To the layperson, crime, by definition, is bad, and any attempt to prevent it is therefore to be applauded. Within criminology, however, there is significant division over the merits and meanings of contemporary approaches to crime prevention. Some have welcomed the tendency for Western governments to 'rediscover' crime prevention over the last three or four decades, seeing this as a long-overdue opportunity for the discipline to exert greater influence in the policy arena. Other criminologists have been sceptical about this shift, and are less sanguine about the prospect of becoming involved in the development and implementation of strategies and programs. Many criminologists who have welcomed the apparent renaissance of prevention in the policy field endorse what has been termed the 'what works', 'administrative' paradigm. Those who are more sceptical tend to subscribe to 'critical' schools. Both sets of perspectives have made important contributions, and throughout this book we refer to ways they have coloured approaches to specific themes and topics. Before doing so, however, we will discuss in more general terms how and why they have helped make crime prevention contested terrain.

The 'what works' paradigm also has been described as a technicist perspective (Hughes 1998; Hope 2011). Its key goal is to identify the most effective methods of crime reduction and to ensure that such knowledge guides policy and practice. Proponents of the 'what works' approach criticise mainstream criminology for failing to furnish governments with practical guidance on methods to reduce crime. Sociologically-based theories have been portrayed as particularly deficient in this respect. To be translated into policy, theories that explain crime purely in terms of inequality or other structural 'root causes' would require fundamental social transformations that are seen as impossible for governments to achieve, unrealistic and costly, and whose promised pay-offs are uncertain (Clarke 1980; Tilley 2004a; Wiles 2002).

A key argument of this school is that policy-relevant criminology needs to be underpinned by a scientific agenda that uses experimental methods and empirical investigation to identify 'what works'. Such a rigorous, evidence-based approach is seen as the best way to overcome successive government failures to implement successful programs (e.g. see Campbell Collaboration). This has led to the emergence of what has been termed 'experimental criminology' and 'crime science': schools that are concerned less with sociological understanding (e.g. with locating Western governments' renewed interest in crime prevention in broader socio-political contexts) than with developing and documenting successful crime prevention projects and programs using experimental methods and meta-evaluations (see chapter 5) that focus on scientifically measurable outcomes. Such procedures are seen as providing a basis for the development of evidence-based policy (Laycock 2005a; Farrington & Petrosino 2001; Welsh & Farrington 2011, 2012a, 2012b; Sherman 2011; Wiles 2002). As McLaughlin (2002, p. 49) points out, this framework – which understands crime prevention purely in instrumental terms – is underpinned by a 'high modernist' faith in the capacity for science to ensure human progress. Not all criminologists share this faith (see also Hope 2011).

Confidence in science often is aligned with a belief that one of the keys to making government more effective against crime is to adopt more sophisticated techniques of administration, and in particular to move towards a 'whole of government' approach. The argument here is that strategies and programs to address causes of crime generally require input from a range of agencies (e.g. education, human services, urban planning and police) located at different levels of government (e.g. both central and regional). Achievement of 'joined up outcomes' around crime prevention therefore must involve more effective coordination between these levels of administration and spheres of specialisation (Cherney 2004b; Homel 2006). In this context, achievement of crime prevention outcomes is understood as part of a broader managerial challenge to reform the ways in which central and local agencies work to achieve identified goals, by ensuring that they break out of their narrow operational 'silos' and cooperate in new partnership arrangements and policy structures. The whole-of-government paradigm has informed policy developments both in Australia and overseas (Homel & Homel 2012; Laycock & Webb 2003 – see also chapter 5 and below).

Advocates of the new administration paradigm see the advent of crime prevention as offering opportunities for rationality to prevail in a policy field which historically has been the prisoner of political ideology, anecdotal evidence, media-inspired panics and program fads rather than being guided by empirical data on efficacy and cost-effectiveness (Sherman et al. 2002; Welsh & Farrington 2012a; Wiles 2002). The basic premise is that due to 'system overload' on the part of criminal justice institutions and a shrinking tax base, governments no longer can afford to waste funds on policies that cannot demonstrate they are achieving intended outcomes. In this context empirical research is seen as the key to helping policy makers and practitioners achieve consensus on strategies and programs to be pursued. Approaches that claim to be guided by evidence-based principles and 'best practice models' include situational prevention (see chapter 4) and targeted interventions which draw on detailed research on developmental pathways that can lead into delinquency (see chapter 3). In developing strategies, governments should first use meta-evaluations (i.e. reviews of existing evaluations – see chapter 5) to identify promising approaches, then test these approaches in controlled demonstration projects that are rigorously assessed using experimental or quasi-experimental methods and, finally; implement the 'success stories' jurisdiction-wide using a whole-of-government style of administration.

Arguments that governments should opt for more rational, cost-effective crime policies are difficult to contest, and a number of Western countries – Australia included – have paid lip-service to the 'what works' philosophy. The most ambitious attempt to translate these principles into working policy has been the UK's Crime Reduction Programme, which was announced in 1999 and initially intended to run for 10 years. Policy makers in the UK's Home Office played major roles in the design and initial implementation of the strategy, and the government's decision to allocate £250 million to the program in its first three years seemed a breakthrough for a more evidence-based approach (see Homel & Homel 2012). As chapter 5 will show, however, translating the evidence-based philosophy into working projects and programs proved far more difficult than anticipated. The Crime Reduction Programme was wound up after its initial three-year trial and, in light of this experience, criminologists associated with the program have begun advocating a more 'realistic' approach to issues such as program evaluation (Pawson & Tilley 1997) and whole-of-government administration (Homel 2006).

'Critical' criminologists argue, however, that even these modified attempts to make criminology a policy-relevant science are misconceived. They see the applied focus as diminishing the discipline: depriving it of the capacity to locate government initiatives in broader social contexts. 'Crime science' is dismissed as mere 'administrative' criminology, subservient to the dictates of government (Hope 2011; Walters 2003). Rather than being accepted at face value, critical theorists argue that prevention policies need to be located in the context of broader economic and political forces reshaping late-modern societies. Specifically, the late 20th century renaissance of crime prevention in the UK, other parts of Western Europe, and Australia, is symptomatic of a fundamental shift in forms of governance and in power relations between the state and the populations it seeks to govern.

For governmentality theorists, these underlying changes are more relevant to an understanding of the nature, causes and likely effects of contemporary crime prevention than are declared objectives in policy documents and ministerial statements. Specifically, crime prevention should be understood as part of a 'responsibilisation' strategy aimed at ensuring that individuals and communities accept more of the burden of dealing with safety and security problems (Crawford 1997; Garland 2001; Phoenix & Kelly 2013; Rodger 2008). The resurgence of crime prevention policies and practices since the late 20th century has been driven by a neo-liberal government agenda in which the state recognises it no longer has the capacity to provide full crime control, and private citizens, commercial firms, community groups and agencies are drawn together, in the context of government exhortations that 'crime prevention involves the whole community', to become active partners in the co-production of safety and security (Garland 2001; Hughes 1998; Koch 1998; Rodger 2008). The key function of crime prevention strategies and programs, therefore, is to help dismantle the notion that the central state is the primary insurer against risks of criminal victimisation, and to encourage and instruct citizens and organisations at the grassroots on the use of situational (see chapter 4) and other techniques to reduce their own risk status (see Garland 2001; Hughes 1998; Pavlich 1999; Phoenix & Kelly 2013; Rodger 2008).

Governmentality theorists argue that resurgence of interest in crime prevention also should be seen as part and parcel of managerialist reforms of the public sector. Managerialism – with its language of 'cost-benefits', 'best value' and 'fiscal responsibility' – is part of an agenda to restrict the size and the cost of public sector agencies in the late-modern era but at the same time improve their efficiency, effectiveness and economy (Crawford 1997). Managerialism has provided a foothold for the 'what works' crime prevention paradigm but also has affected practices in other spheres, such as policing, youth justice, imprisonment and parole (Garland 2001; McLaughlin, Muncie & Hughes 2001; Phoenix & Kelly 2013). Once again, the re-emergence of crime prevention should not be seen simply as evidence of the persuasiveness of 'rational' criminology but as part of a broader socio-political trend.

How to understand and respond to the emergence of crime prevention on government policy agendas clearly has divided criminologists. Advocates of the 'what works' approach have been optimistic – probably too optimistic in that they have failed to acknowledge possible problems and been too prepared to accept policy pronouncements at face value. On the other hand, we see the governmentality thesis as too pessimistic. As noted in chapter 1, this rather one-dimensional account is not consistent with the diverse ways crime prevention policy has been developed and practised in various jurisdictions (see also chapter 6), and refuses to acknowledge that there may be more to this movement than a simple reconfiguration of forms of governance (for other critiques along these lines see Hughes 2002b, 2004; Stenson 2005). Specifically, this school ignores evidence that in countries such as France and the Netherlands and in some Australian states, prevention was initially conceptualised as a distinct alternative to 'law and order'.

Both crime science and the governmentality theory also make the mistake of treating prevention as a purely instrumental exercise. Throughout this book we argue that crime prevention has, and should have, a symbolic or expressive dimension. Successful policy development in this field requires that governments signal their preferred approach to (or 'vision of') social control (see chapter 6). Despite the pessimism of governmentality theorists, we therefore see crime prevention as offering unique opportunities to overcome the strict division between applied and critical approaches that has characterised the discipline. Throughout this book we will discuss and draw on the theories and knowledge bases that the 'what works' approach has helped generate. At the same time, we will assess crime prevention policies and practices in terms of what they might signify in broader political and social contexts. As chapters to follow will make clear, responding to the practical challenge of helping develop and implement crime prevention schemes should not preclude assessment of their normative and political significance.

Crime and everyday life

Good prevention requires good theory. Chapters 3 and 4 of this book therefore provide detailed summaries of the concepts underpinning two key approaches: social (chapter 3) and environmental prevention (chapter 4). Before doing so,

Figure 2.1   Felson's crime triangle

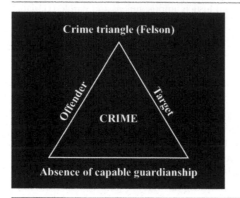

however, we want to canvass a more general perspective: Marcus Felson's 'routine activity' thesis. Other scholars, such as Ekblom (2010), have developed similar conceptual models. We have selected Felson's (1995, 2002) framework because we believe that, for all the criticisms made of it, routine activity does provide a very accessible heuristic guide to link prevention theory and action. Felson's model also is useful for highlighting the limitations of policies that focus purely on punitive responses to crime.

Felson argues that any crime must be the product of three factors: the coming together at a particular time and place of a motivated offender, a potential target, and the absence of capable guardianship (see Figure 2.1). Targets can include both people and inanimate objects. Guardianship can be defined in terms of both human actors and security devices: parents, security guards, store people, teachers, cameras and alarms. Guardianship can take the form of formal surveillance or more informal social controls (e.g. the presence of bystanders in a busy street). Absence of capable guardianship of whatever type (formal or informal) will exacerbate the likelihood of a crime occurring in a specific context (Hollis-Peel et al. 2011; Tillyer & Eck 2011).

Felson's framework highlights how population growth, urbanisation and the sprawling nature of modern cities, mass production, consumerism and the advent of the motor vehicle, all can help explain major increases in crime in many parts of the world over the last century. Consumer society is characterised by a proliferation of attractive targets (cars, laptop computers, digital cameras, mobile phones, DVD players, etc.), while mass vehicle ownership and improved public transport have made guardianship more difficult because people are more mobile. Demographic trends – for example, the post-war baby boom during the 1960s, 1970s and 1980s that resulted in a higher proportion of males in the 16–24 age group (a segment of society that Felson sees as more prone to offending) – can also lead to increased crime rates. Hence, rather than always being viewed as evidence of social decline, crime also can be seen as the unwanted and unintended side effect of changes that have brought positive benefits (Tilley 2004a).

The routine activity model acknowledges that victimisation will not occur in the absence of a person or persons motivated to, and capable of, offending. However, in exploring its prevention implications Felson puts less emphasis on this aspect than on target and guardianship issues. Like Ron Clarke, the pioneer of situational prevention with whom he has collaborated (Clarke & Felson 1993 – see chapter 4), Felson tends to assume that 'changing human nature' is an uncertain and expensive enterprise, and that initiatives that focus on manipulating physical environments (i.e. on target and guardianship aspects) are far more likely to be cost-effective. As a result, Felson's 'crime triangle' approach has been strongly criticised by feminist criminologists (see also Hollis-Peel et al. 2011 for a critical review of the framework). They argue that for some crimes, such as family violence and sexual assault, society has a moral obligation to try to change (mainly male) offender motivations, rationalisations and behaviours rather than seeming to accept them as unalterable. They also point out that police and other programs that impose too much of the prevention burden on potential targets (e.g. by advising young women to reduce their chances of being sexually assaulted by avoiding being out alone at night) can unfairly restrict women's behaviour and verge on blaming the victim when an offence does occur.

Such criticisms are legitimate. They reinforce a point made throughout this book: that crime prevention always involves moral and political as well as technical decisions. Nonetheless we see Felson's 'crime triangle' as useful for highlighting the limitations of traditional criminal justice based crime policies. No matter how vigorously it is pursued, 'law and order' can only address one aspect of the triangle – the potential offender – and does so using a comparatively limited range of techniques (i.e. deterrence through the threat of police detection and punishment).

Felson's approach to crime and its prevention also can be developed in ways that put less emphasis on the immediate (or 'proximal') roles of offenders, victims and guardians and more on the indirect (or 'distal') influence of broader social institutions. Eck (2003), for example, has modified Felson's model to include an outer triangle which emphasises factors that can influence both offending behaviour and target vulnerability (also see Hollis-Peel et al. 2011; Tillyer & Eck 2011). Eck argues that crime problems arise when offenders and targets come together in contexts where key 'controllers' fail to act to prevent crime, or where their capacity to assert control is restricted (see Hollis-Peel et al. 2011; and Tillyer & Eck 2011 for a more recent discussion).

Figure 2.2   Eck's modification of Felson's crime triangle

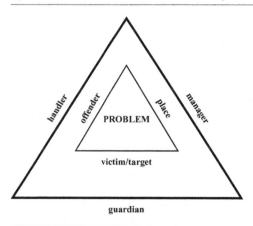

Controllers include, but are not restricted to, guardians. They also include what Eck terms 'handlers' – whose main influence is over potential offenders – and 'managers' whose control is over places or sites where crime can occur (Figure 2.2). 'Handlers' may be parents, siblings, peers, employers or teachers: anyone who can regulate, supervise and affect some restraint over the actions of a potential offender (Tillyer & Eck 2011).

Managers are people responsible for overseeing behaviour in particular environments and securing them from crime and harm (Hollis-Peel et al. 2011). Managers therefore can include concierges, bar staff, private security personnel and property managers. Eck uses the term 'guardian' in a way similar to Felson's original definition: a guardian is any person or technology assigned or used to look after specific potential targets (e.g. CCTV or someone who has been asked to keep an eye on a friend's belongings). Guardians should not be confused with place managers. The latter's responsibilities are fixed and limited to particular places or locations, whereas a guardian's role can vary over time. The influence of handlers also can wax and wane (Felson 2006). As an individual progresses along his or her distinctive pathway from infancy to childhood, adolescence and adulthood, different handlers – whether they be family members, peers or spouses – will assert influence.

Eck's modification of Felson's original model helps highlight the ways crime is a product of social processes as well as of specific interactions at particular times and places. Such processes include the ways 'handlers' interact with people who might, in some circumstances, offend (e.g. parents socialising and supervising their children); the ways third parties – like public and private sector organisations – design and manage environments for which they are responsible; and the ways ordinary citizens organise their daily routines in order to reduce exposure to criminal victimisation. It highlights that, in addition to using situational and other techniques to try to modify the 'inner triangle' of immediate (or proximal) contributors to the criminal event (e.g. by strengthening guardianship or removing targets), prevention also can work on the 'outer triangle' of social processes that indirectly affect whether people become capable of offending and are able to locate victims or targets that are not adequately protected. Relevant 'outer triangle' interventions can include social programs aimed at strengthening positive attachments between potential offenders and their 'handlers', as well as place-management initiatives to deter offending through better surveillance and guardianship.

Policy makers and practitioners who understand this model should be prepared to be flexible in their approaches to policy and to recognise the wide variety of ways in which crime victimisation can be reduced. They should never dismiss out of hand the possibility of trying to affect more remote (or distal) 'social' factors. As chapter 3 will show, there is now significant evidence that developmental crime prevention, which aims to influence distal causes of crime by strengthening relationships between young people identified as being at risk of becoming offenders and their various so-called handlers (within family, educational and other contexts), can be effective.

While concentrating prevention resources on the immediate situations where crime occurs (i.e. addressing proximal causes – see Ekblom 2010) may seem the most obvious course of action, payoffs from addressing distal social causes may be more long-term and significant. The key lesson arising from Felson and Eck's analyses is that before intervening, politicians, researchers, policy makers and practitioners need to devote resources to assessing all the factors underlying relevant patterns of offending. In other words, before selecting and implementing initiatives they need to understand thoroughly the contexts in which relevant behaviour is occurring.

Of course, this is an ideal position. What generally occurs is that rather than investing time and resources on detailed analysis of the processes contributing to specific patterns of offending and victimisation, then using this information to implement and evaluate remedies, agencies and governments opt for 'solutions' (e.g. police crackdowns, installation of CCTV systems, and 'restorative justice' schemes) that have become part of their routine and seem politically safe. It is important not to reject such responses out of hand as 'irrational'. Throughout this book, we argue that to win the recognition and resources it needs and deserves, crime prevention must 'work' at a symbolic and political as well as a purely instrumental level. Decisions about the design of crime prevention policies and the implementation of interventions cannot simply be reduced to debates about the most effective techniques. Invariably, such decisions also reflect value positions relating to the sort of society we want to live in, and what sorts of social controls should predominate. However, even from the simple models summarised in this section, it should be clear that prevention offers a much wider range of options for dealing with crime than most governments seem prepared to adopt, and that within this array it should be possible to identify approaches that achieve both instrumental and political and expressive goals.

Classifications of crime prevention

Hughes (1998) warns against trying to force all prevention approaches into a single, unproblematic classification scheme. We agree. However, given the range of activities covered by the term 'crime prevention', there is utility in summarising and commenting on typologies already in use. While not perfect, these frameworks and associated terminologies can be useful for understanding the theories and assumptions informing particular program types and can help 'envisage, distinguish between, articulate, teach and communicate the range of possibilities for preventive action' (Ekblom 1994, p. 187). Various classification systems have been formulated (see Brantingham & Faust 1976; Crawford 1998; Ekblom 2010; Hughes 1998; Laub 2013; Tonry & Farrington, 1995; Van Dijk & de Waard 1991), but two tend to dominate. One has emerged from, and been shaped by, debates within criminology. The other draws on experience in public health.

The 'criminological' classification divides prevention into two broad approaches: *social* and *environmental*. These are distinguished on the basis of their focus of intervention. Social prevention tries to reduce the likelihood that individuals or groups will include crime in their repertoire of behaviours by strengthening informal (e.g. immediate and extended family, neighbourhood networks and peer group) and institutionally based (e.g. in education, work, culture and sport) incentives to be law abiding. Specifically, social prevention aims to identify and address 'risk' and 'protective' factors manifest in individual, family, peer, school, neighbourhood, community and other contexts that can affect whether people are likely to become involved in, or continue, offending. Social prevention frequently focuses on the early or 'formative' stages of life (i.e. infancy through to the late teenage years). Theoretically, however, schemes can encompass all the life stages, and can include known offenders as well as individuals who have not been found breaking the law (see chapter 3).

Environmental prevention, by contrast, concentrates on addressing the target and guardianship aspects of crime. It aims to modify the physical (and, in the cyber era, virtual) contexts in which crimes can occur and potential offenders can operate and, in particular, to minimise the extent to which such environments give rise to criminal opportunities. It encompasses two techniques:

- broad-based planning and design, which is concerned with ensuring that the settings in which people work, live and find recreation are not 'built' in ways that undermine capacities for surveillance and guardianship (e.g. that large-scale housing estates do not include walkways or open spaces that are impossible for residents to defend, and that city centres provide ample opportunities for formal and informal surveillance)

- focused situational prevention, which concentrates on manipulating specific environments or environment types (e.g. banks, cars, airport terminals and transport interchanges) in ways that will increase the risks and efforts associated with offending and reduce associated rewards and excuses (chapter 4 provides a summary).

Epidemiology has provided the inspiration for classifications that draw on public health theory. Developed by Brantingham and Faust (1976), this model divides programs into three categories – primary, secondary and tertiary – on the basis of the stage and target of the intervention. Primary prevention addresses factors or conditions relevant to crime that can affect an entire populace. Such conditions can be both physical and social. Examples include early interventions with socioeconomically disadvantaged infants to improve their legitimate life opportunities in education and other fields (see chapter 3) and adoption by cities and shires of planning and design rules to ensure that the built environment does not inadvertently include features that exacerbate opportunities for crime. Secondary prevention involves interventions in environments or with populations deemed 'at risk', with the aim being to preclude the onset of offending.

Examples include situational interventions in locations where statistical or other data indicate that crime is likely to occur (e.g. CCTV outside licensed premises and throughout entertainment districts); measures to reduce the accessibility of certain targets (e.g. engine immobilisers in motor vehicles); and school-based programs to reduce truancy (a number of studies have indicated that truants are more likely to drift into offending). Tertiary prevention targets known offenders and environments already affected by crime. The objective here is to reduce future offending and the re-victimisation of people or places already affected by crime. Examples include prison-based treatment programs for convicted sex offenders and post-release schemes to help offenders resettle in the community, as well as the use of situational techniques to improve guardianship at crime hot spots or in premises that have recently been burgled.

As noted, the key value of both the 'criminological' and the 'public health' schemas is that they can help locate specific crime prevention practices in a more general context. However, neither is without weaknesses. For example, Ekblom (1994) argues that the distinction between social and environmental prevention is conceptually sloppy. To be adopted and operate successfully, environmental prevention invariably relies on social processes: owners and managers of relevant facilities need to commit resources to relevant physical changes (e.g. the installation of better lighting), and employees or other users need to be prepared to undertake a guardianship role. While the public health analogy can help raise awareness of the diversity of practices that can fall under the ambit of crime prevention (Crawford 1998), compared to the situational and social dichotomy, it says little about the key theoretical assumptions informing these practices. It is mainly concerned with identifying the level and scope of intervention, which is important when developing strategies and allocating budgets, but does not provide insight into how and why programs are expected to work in particular contexts (Ekblom 2000, 2010). Such understanding is essential for adequate policy implementation and review (Cherney 2006a; Eck 2005; Pawson 2006). These issues are discussed further in chapter 5 on evaluation.

Readers should note that both of the systems summarised above would acknowledge traditional police and other criminal justice responses as part of crime prevention. Few criminologists dispute that arrest, imprisonment and other forms of punishment have at least some deterrent and incapacitative effects, and can help reaffirm and reinforce mainstream values. To the extent that they achieve these outcomes, such activities could be regarded as social prevention applied at the tertiary phase (i.e. after an offence has occurred – see Table 2.1).

These points notwithstanding, our approach to crime prevention will continue to emphasise initiatives and policies *other than* those associated with, or stemming from, enforcement of criminal law. As explained in chapter 1, our endorsement of Van Dijk and de Waard's (1991) definition reflects a desire to treat prevention as a distinct crime policy option rather than as a mere set of techniques.

Our decision has significant implications for the remainder of the book. Rather than making it a textbook-style 'grand tour' of all the types of interventions – environmental and social, primary through to tertiary – that might conceivably have potential to reduce crime (see, e.g. Table 2.1), we focus on those that might also help constitute a distinct policy alternative to law and order. Readers should note that our decision to define crime prevention in a way that excludes traditional criminal justice responses does not mean that we consider that police, corrections and other personnel based in justice agencies cannot contribute to prevention. In this book, however, focus will be on contributions that involve police and other justice personnel *stepping out of*, rather than remaining in, traditional roles. One example would be a police department taking officers off routine patrols in order to work with local schools in developing and implementing programs aimed at reducing truancy.

Table 2.1   Crime prevention: A typology and examples

	Primary	Secondary	Tertiary
Social	Programs to give all children a 'headstart' before they encounter formal school systems Early school programs to reshape concepts of masculinity Initiatives to support parents	Wilderness programs for 'at risk' teenagers School truancy reduction schemes	Tougher sentences for selected crimes Initiatives to help released prisoners secure paid jobs Behaviour-change programs for recidivist sex offenders
Environmental	Incorporation of prevention principles into urban planning and design of residential complexes General prevention advice for householders and businesses	Installation of alarms Use of routine patrols or other special surveillance Neighbourhood watch	Closure of high-risk crime areas Installation of bulletproof glass and CCTV in banks with records of repeat victimisation

Crime prevention and problem solving

The final key perspective to be covered is the problem-solving aspect of crime prevention. As Ekblom (2010) has pointed out, any attempt to develop a crime prevention program needs to be underpinned by systematic planning which requires a problem-solving approach. The fact that prevention involves identifying, then finding ways to solve, crime problems may seem blindingly obvious – it is surprising how often the problem-solving process is neglected. The pressure on policy makers and practitioners generally is to get programs and projects 'up and running', rather than to set aside time and resources for systematic analysis of problems and for the selection, implementation and evaluation of appropriate interventions. The core element of this perspective is that crime prevention should be problem-oriented rather than practice-oriented, meaning that preconceived notions should not determine how to tackle the crime problem under investigation (Gilling 1996).

Rather than adopting interventions 'off the shelf' and transplanting them to a given location, strategies need to be tailored to the specific nature of crime and safety problems within particular localities (Clarke & Eck 2005; Ekblom 2010). The nature of the problem should determine solutions. Such a process should follow a systematic approach via in-depth collection of relevant data on the crime problem(s) and the selection of strategy objectives and interventions based upon this research, and accumulated evidence on what has been successful in reducing the particular crime problem. What is helpful during this problem analysis phase is for practitioners to use the crime (or problem analysis – see Clarke & Eck 2005) triangle models outlined above. These models can help understand why a crime problem is occurring (e.g. non-existent or inadequate place management) and which factors need to be addressed. The next step is to identify and mobilise agents responsible for implementation and put in place evaluation procedures to assess impact. Problem solving also should incorporate a response loop whereby evaluation outcomes can feed back into preceding stages, with re-assessment of the crime problem and re-selection of interventions both being possible.

Situational crime prevention (Clarke & Eck 2005; Tilley 2004a – see chapter 4) also is built around a problem-solving approach, which again is seen as the key to effective crime prevention planning. Strategies emanating from the UK (Hough and Tilley 1998; Hough 2004; Hope 2005), Canada (Canada, National Crime Prevention Centre 1998), New Zealand (New Zealand Crime Prevention Unit 1994), Australia (Panton 1998; Sutton & Cherney 2002) and Sweden (Wikstrom & Torstensson 1999) all have endorsed this methodology. A number of problem-solving models have been formulated: some rudimentary, others more complex. Box 2.1 gives examples. They are all underpinned by a similar logic.

Readers should not assume that problem-solving methods such as those outlined in Box 2.1 can be applied in a simple linear fashion. Hough (2004) and Ekblom (2010) in particular are critical of this version of 'scientific rationalism'. Most advocates of the problem-solving approach warn against assuming that once the identification and analysis phase has been completed it can be dispensed with and not revisited (Clarke & Eck 2005). Problem identification and solving should be understood as iterative, with practitioners needing constantly to reassess the conclusions drawn from their analysis, to ensure that responses implemented are relevant to the crime problem in question. Also the problem-solving method as outlined in Box 2.1 does not necessarily have a definitive end point, whereupon the process ceases following the evaluation stage. Rather, the process of evaluation, when done correctly (see chapter 5) may indicate a program needs modification or even abandonment. Hence the process may begin all over again and ongoing monitoring can be necessary to ensure a strategy remains effective.

Given the alluring simplicity of popular problem-solving models like SARA (see Box 2.1) it can be very easy for police and other crime prevention professionals

BOX 2.1:   MODELS OF CRIME PREVENTION PROBLEM SOLVING

Scanning   **Analysis**   **Response**   **Assessment**

SARA model – see Eck & Spelman 1988 & Clarke & Eck 2003.

Routine scanning and analysis of problems

Devising strategies to address problems

Implementing attempted solutions to problems

Monitoring of strategy and crime problem and evaluation of effectives of solution

Problem solving process – see Hough & Tilley (1998 p. 7)

'5Is' MODEL

The aim of the 5Is model is to provide a framework for distilling good practice in the process of crime prevention problem solving. For more detail about the model see Ekblom (2010).

INTELLIGENCE – gathering and analysing information on crime and disorder problems and their consequences, diagnosing the causes of crime and identify any existing risk or protective factors associated with criminality.

INTERVENTION – consider the full range of techniques that could be applied to blocking, disrupting or weakening those causes (Clarke & Eck 2003).

IMPLEMENTATION – converting the intervention principles into practical methods that are:

1. Customised for the local problem and context
2. Targeted on offenders, victims, buildings, places and products, on an individual or collective basis
3. Planned, managed, organised and steered by relevant stakeholders
4. Monitored, with documentation of inputs of human and financial resources, outputs and intermediate outcomes
5. Assessed for ethical considerations.

INVOLVEMENT – mobilising agencies, companies and individuals to play their part in implementing the intervention, or acting in partnership. Roles and responsibilities need to be specified and methods found to alerte, motivate, empower or direct responsible stakeholders.

IMPACT – Identify evaluation design; assess cost-effectiveness, coverage of crime problem and timescale for implementation; and conduct process (i.e. did agencies/individuals do what was recommended?) and impact evaluation (were intended reductions in crime achieved?). Consideration also needs to be given to replicability (i.e. identify which contextual conditions and infrastructure were helpful and necessary to successfully replicate project). What are the key learning points both positive and negative (what to do, what not to do next time)?

to claim they are 'solving problems', but whether they are doing so in a systematic manner is often open to question (Bullock, Erol & Tilley 2006; Clarke 1998a; Ekblom 2010). Problem solving should never be broad-brush: its very nature requires collection and detailed analysis of empirical data that will enable practitioners to dissect relevant problems and break them down into subcategories. Examples include the division of car thefts into opportunist and professional, and analyses of graffiti and vandalism according to locations targeted, with each target type potentially requiring a uniquely tailored response. Such micro analysis underpins situational crime prevention, which will be covered in chapter 4.

In summary, while the problem-solving methodology seems deceptively easy on paper, in practice it can be extremely difficult. Barriers to effective implementation include lack of access to good-quality data, resource constraints, difficulties in securing cooperation from relevant agencies and poor take-up of interventions by target groups (Bullock, Erol & Tilley 2006; Clarke & Eck 2005; Cherney 2004a, 2006a; Ekblom 2010; Gilling 1996; Hope 2003, 2005; Sutton 1996). In some circumstances this methodology requires a level of creative adaptation (Cherney 2006a; Ekblom 2010). Chapters to follow elaborate on the relevance of a flexible problem-solving approach to crime prevention policy and practice. As Hough (2004) points out, systematic problem solving tends to sit uncomfortably with a law-and-order politics that favours simplifying the complexity surrounding crime rather than engaging in in-depth analysis of offending patterns and relationships between crime and the environment.

Conclusion

Our aim in this chapter has been to give the amorphous concept of crime prevention structure and content, and to review key analytical perspectives. Within criminology the very meaning of this term has been hotly contested and there have been widely differing explanations for its resurgence as a policy theme. Some see crime prevention as a purely technical and administrative challenge, with the criminologist's key role being to accumulate expert knowledge on 'what works' and ensure that such knowledge and expertise are applied more generally (Hope & Karstedt 2003). Others, however, have been less enthusiastic and committed, seeing prevention policies and programs as symptomatic of a broader – and not necessarily benign – shift in modes of governance that is reshaping late modernity.

Researchers and practitioners need to be aware of differences between the 'what works' advocates and more critical schools, but in our view taking sides in this debate is neither necessary nor helpful. While critical perspectives can alert policy advocates to possible unintended outcomes from prevention, they tend to underestimate the wide variety of ways in which strategies have been conceived and implemented in different countries and eras. For its part, a narrow focus on identifying and documenting 'success stories' and ensuring that crime prevention is evidence-based can lead to neglect of its important political and symbolic dimensions. Crime prevention is a complex process: far more complex than 'law and order'. A range of prior conditions needs to be satisfied before relevant philosophies and principles can begin to have an effect on mainstream crime policy. Most importantly, a shift to prevention requires that political leaders and policy coordinators articulate a clear and powerful vision capable of coordinating and guiding the wide range of players who must be involved in strategy and program implementation. Such vision is just as important as detailed knowledge about what types of interventions tend to be successful in what contexts.

Whenever prevention practitioners apply a specific prevention technique they make certain assumptions about the causes of the crime or crimes they are addressing. Most important among these is whether the most significant causal factors relate to ways potential offenders are socialised (social prevention) or whether aspects of the environment trigger offending (environmental prevention).

Chapter 3 explores social prevention in detail, while chapter 4 reviews and assesses environmental approaches.

From these chapters and others it will be clear that both social and environmental prevention have seen further sub-specialisation. Before plunging into a detailed exploration of these dimensions, this chapter has drawn on Felson's 'routine activity' model, with its 'triangle' of offender, target and absence of capable guardianship, to help locate crime prevention techniques in a broader framework.

Of course, routine activity itself has been criticised, for seeming to downplay or disregard offender motivations. Drawing on Eck's (2003; also see Hollis-Peel et al. 2011) work, however, we have argued that the 'crime triangle' framework can be adapted to incorporate the ways institutional settings and social contexts, as well as individual and community risk frameworks, help determine how often there will be a convergence of a motivated offender, an available target, and an absence of capable guardianship and other controls (see also Felson 2006; Brantingham, Brantingham & Taylor 2005; Hollis-Peel et al. 2011; Tillyer & Eck 2011). Whatever its weaknesses, Felson's model – as refined by Eck – also helps highlight limitations inherent to conventional 'law-and-order' based policies, which address only one constellation of causal factors (i.e. the possibility that potential or actual offenders will be deterred by the risk of being caught and punished) using a very limited array of techniques.

At a very practical level Felson's perspective also reminds practitioners that it is important to be flexible in approaching crime problems, and that they should always be prepared to contemplate a mix of approaches rather than pursuing a single line, regardless of cost-effectiveness. Of course, choices can never be made purely on a cost basis: they must also involve value judgments and political decisions. Nonetheless we should always be open-minded to possibilities.

This chapter has also reviewed ways of categorising crime prevention. This exercise has made clear that, at least in theory, coercive approaches (e.g. tougher sentences or youth curfews) can be classified as prevention. In a literal sense they may well reduce crime. Our decision not to dwell on them in the context of this book reflects the view that in the late-capitalist democracies, renewed interest in crime prevention has been part of attempts to develop policies that are less socially divisive and exclusionary than law and order (see chapter 6).

One of the few issues that most criminologists agree on is that problem identification and solving constitute key elements of crime prevention policy and practice. Effective crime prevention is about being informed, systematic and flexible. While the problem-solving model may seem straightforward, its practical application can be beset by obstacles. How to overcome these challenges will be a major theme of chapters to follow. We start by exploring social prevention.

CASE STUDY 2.1 ADOPTING A PROBLEM-SOLVING APPROACH TO CRIME PREVENTION

Despite the benefits of a problem-solving approach to the development and implementation of crime prevention strategies, adopting such a systematic method is not straightforward (see also chapter 5). Crime prevention practitioners in local government and in the police, for instance, can often ignore problem analysis and diagnoses, and instead focus on the pragmatic task of implementation. To some degree this is understandable given that there is intense pressure on policy makers and practitioners to immediately 'do something' about crime problems, which does not provide space for more in-depth and systematic examination of why certain crimes are occurring. There is also the need for flexibility when responding to crime, particularly when implementing strategies, because often implementation rarely follows a sequential path (Cherney 2006a; Ekblom 2010 – also see chapter 5). Some of the biggest barriers to crime prevention problem-solving are a lack of adequate and reliable data, a lack of knowledge about crime prevention theory, a fixation with delivering programs, low awareness of successful interventions, poor evaluation skills and a tendency among policy makers and practitioners to default to pre-existing practices or programs that have political appeal, e.g. wilderness camps and boot camps (Cherney 2006a, Clancey, Lee & Crofts 2012; Ekblom 2010; Wikstrom 2007).

QUESTIONS

Questions for further exploration

1. Is it fair for governments or the police to argue that people should take reasonable precautions to reduce their risk of criminal victimisation and take responsibility for their own security?

2. Select a particular type of crime and analyse why it occurs through applying Eck's crime triangle (see Figure 2.2).

3. When conducting crime prevention problem solving what key issues do crime prevention practitioners need to consider at each stage of the process?

EXTENSION TOPICS AND REFERENCES

1. It is argued that crime prevention should be evidence-based. What is meant by the term evidence-based policy? Is it naive to argue that crime control policy should simply be based on science and research evidence about 'what works'?

References

Bullock, K. & Tilley, N. (2009) 'Evidence-based policing and crime reduction', *Policing*, vol. 3, no. 4, pp. 381–387.

Pawson, R. (2006) *Evidence-based policy: a realist perspective*. London: Sage Publications.

2. Data collection and analysis is an important feature of various problem-solving models (see Box 2.1). To obtain a comprehensive understanding of a crime problem what types of data should be collected? Are there any patterns or trends one should look for?

References

Clarke, R. & Eck, J. (2005) *Crime analysis for problem solvers in 60 small steps*. Office of Community Oriented Policing Services, Centre for Problem Oriented Policing, US Department of Justice, www.cops.usdoj.gov/Publications/.

3. Guardianship is an important component of Felson's routine activity theory. How can the term be conceptualised to include different forms or types of guardianship?

References

Hollis-Peel, M.E., Reynald, D.M., Bavel, M.V., Elffers, H. & Walsh, B.C. (2011) 'Guardianship for crime prevention: a critical review of the literature', *Crime, Law and Social Change*, vol. 56, no. 1, pp. 53–70.

3

SOCIAL
PREVENTION

Introduction

This chapter will discuss the following topics:

- approaches to social prevention
- developmental prevention
- structure and agency
- theory to policy
- the limits to social prevention.

In the early 1960s, educationists in the US designed an intriguing experiment. They had noted that during the initial year at school, children from severely disadvantaged backgrounds often struggled to keep up in class, and that many failed to bridge the gap in subsequent years. As a result, these youngsters were far more likely to drop out, or be expelled for disruptive behaviour. The aim of the Perry Preschool Project, as it became known, was to see what happened when infants deemed 'at risk' due to gross socio-economic disadvantage received additional support before they encountered the formal education system. Between 1962 and 1967, 123 African American children aged three and four and living in poverty in inner-city Detroit were randomly assigned to an experimental or a control group. The experimental group were enrolled in a high-quality preschool program aimed at enhancing their problem-solving and planning skills. Teachers also made weekly home visits. Those in the control group received no special assistance.

Results for the two groups now have been compared over 40 years. Differences are striking. Individuals who had taken part in the preschool program were much more likely to graduate from high school, had higher incomes at ages 27 and 40, and were less likely to have been arrested for a criminal offence than the non-program group. They also were less likely, as adults, to have relied on welfare. Sponsors estimate that for every dollar invested in the program, US governments saved $12.90 in criminal justice and welfare expenditures. A further $4.17 in benefits accrued to the participants themselves (Schweinhart, Barnes & Weikart 1993; Schweinhart et al. 2005).

The Perry Preschool is one of a number of experiments that provide dramatic illustration of the advantages of a preventive approach to social problems. Others include the New York-based Elmira Prenatal and Early Infancy Project, the Montreal Prevention Project and the Seattle Social Development Project. The Elmira program enabled trained nurses to pay regular prenatal and postnatal home visits to grossly disadvantaged teenage first-time mothers. Evaluations indicated that infants born to mothers in the program experienced less physical abuse and neglect during their first two years, and that at 15 these children had less than half as many arrests as those in a control group (Olds et al. 1998, 1999; Olds 2013). The Montreal scheme involved boys identified by preschool teachers as 'disruptive' being trained in social skills and self-control, while their parents received support aimed at enhancing their skills in monitoring and applying appropriate forms of discipline and encouragement. Follow-up at age 12 indicated that, compared with controls, boys in the intervention group were performing better at school, had lower rates of self-reported offending and were less likely to have been found fighting or engaging in other anti-social behaviour (Tremblay & Craig 1995; Homel 2005a).

The Seattle Project focused on entire classes of primary schoolchildren. The children, their teachers and parents were all enrolled in programs. Interventions with the children concentrated on enhancing problem-solving skills and peer-group interactions, while work with the adults focused on behaviour management and group supervision abilities. Follow-up studies indicated that at age 18, young people who had been in the program were less likely than a comparison group to report deviant behaviour, such as violence and heavy drinking, and to have greater levels of school attachment and achievement (Hawkins & Catalano 1992; Hawkins et al. 1999; Hawkins, Catalano & Arthur 2002).

For administrations battling to contain budget outlays and confronted with the prospect of ever-increasing expenditure on policing, corrections and other criminal justice activities, experiments such as these could hardly fail to excite interest. However, for criminologists and policy makers concerned about the impacts of inequality and the economic and social costs of the 'new punitiveness', social prevention has special attractions. One of the key (albeit often unstated) rationales for law and order is belief that the public shaming and social exclusion of perpetrators (e.g. the imposition of lengthy prison sentences) is the only assured mechanism for reducing crime. Programs like Perry Preschool are evidence that more effective inclusion in institutions such as family, community and education can lead to lower rates of offending. If governments are not moved by social justice and equity arguments in favour of family, educational, vocational training and other support for the most disadvantaged, perhaps they will respond to evidence that redistributive policies can play key roles in achieving and maintaining a more law-abiding and secure society.

What progress, however, have Australia and other countries made in recent decades in translating the crime prevention promise apparent in these experiments into effective and sustainable programs? This chapter argues that the process has proven difficult. Part of the problem is at the political level: the 'law and order' message, with its connotations of tough leadership, is far easier to sell to mass media and the public than social prevention. However, difficulties don't just relate to politics and communication. Even among criminologists who agree, in principle, that investment in human capital and infrastructure can have significant prevention benefits, there is little consensus on how such understanding should translate into policy and even whether, at the grassroots level, it is wise to draw too close an association between social interventions and the reduction of crime. These debates have important implications, not just for the ways strategies and programs are designed and implemented, but for the ways they are reviewed and evaluated.

Cambridge-Somerville: the perils of social prevention

Outcomes from the well-known Cambridge-Somerville Youth Study, a US initiative which began in the late 1930s and which, like Perry Preschool, was systematically followed up over decades, help explain why theorists and practitioners can be wary about rushing into social prevention. Study subjects were boys under 10 years from disadvantaged backgrounds living in inner-city Massachusetts. Those deemed on the basis of family background and school records to be at risk of delinquency were assigned to matched groups. Individuals in the experimental group received a range of supports over several years. Interventions included counselling from qualified social workers, academic tutoring, and financial assistance to attend summer camps during school vacations. Control group members received no special assistance.

To the disappointment of program sponsors, follow-up studies indicated that on most measures the experimental group in fact fared worse than the controls. Not only were their criminal records more extensive, they had achieved less educational success and were more likely to have experienced mental illness. Suicide rates also were higher (McCord & McCord 1959; McCord 2003).

What went wrong with Cambridge-Somerville? Interview data indicated that most study subjects appreciated the counselling, tutoring and other support they had received, and saw it as beneficial. Nonetheless, the very process of singling out some disadvantaged youngsters for special attention and support seems to have had unintended negative consequences. Specifically, it helped cause these young males to begin to see themselves as potential delinquents, and to act out this identity. Involvement in summer camp programs was particularly problematic. Because such camps generally were the prerogative of more privileged (i.e. middle-class and upper-class) youngsters, participants sponsored by the Cambridge-Somerville scheme encountered constant pressures to 'explain their presence' – not just to others but to themselves (McCord 2003).

An important lesson from Cambridge-Somerville is that in social prevention, the way schemes are implemented is as important as their content. The point is reinforced when we compare Cambridge-Somerville with the Perry Preschool. The latter avoided adverse labelling, partly because it was not conceived as crime prevention. For those who designed and implemented Perry Preschool, the concern was to improve educational outcomes. The fact that participants were less likely to have had trouble with police was discovered later, and was a collateral benefit.

These observations are also entirely consistent with everyday practice. Researchers have identified a range of factors that can help reduce the incidence of offending at local or neighbourhood levels. They include higher family income, greater parenting competence and diligence (Weatherburn & Lind 1998, 2001), enhanced neighbourhood cohesion and 'collective efficacy' (Sampson 1997; Vinson 2004), positive peer relations, enhanced levels of school achievement and more constructive use of leisure time by young people (Caldwell & Smith 2007). Almost invariably, however, these 'protective' activities and goals are pursued for their own sake, not because they might have crime prevention benefits. Relabelling them as crime prevention will not necessarily render them more effective, or attractive to those involved at the grassroots.

Structure and agency

Another key question is whether social prevention should focus on individuals or social structures and institutions. Demographic studies consistently have revealed significant correlations between arrest and imprisonment rates and more general indicators of disadvantage, such as unemployment, low income, early school-leaving, and physical and mental illness (for Australian data see Vinson 2004; Vinson & Homel 1975). Such findings have led theorists such as Merton (1938), Bourgois (1995), Wilkinson (2005), Hagedorn (2008) and Wacquant (2008) to portray violent and other offending as strategies that males, in particular, tend to pursue when more legitimate avenues to power, wealth and status are blocked.

Their argument has important practical implications. It suggests that unless structural inequality is also addressed, programs that focus purely on identifying and assisting 'high-risk' people, families and neighbourhoods may have limited impacts on the overall incidence of offending. In the worst-case scenario, such interventions merely result in a 'shuffling of deckchairs'. Program participants might be helped to climb the social ladder, but their advancement will be at the expense of others who experience similar disadvantage but have received no assistance. To improve their position, these new 'basement dwellers' now will be more likely to resort to violent or other crime.

Advocates of social prevention therefore should be wary that individual success stories such as the Perry Preschool not give rise to unrealistic expectations. Perry certainly demonstrated that early childhood interventions that reach out to the most disadvantaged and facilitate their inclusion in mainstream institutions can reduce subsequent dependence on welfare and adverse contacts with the criminal justice system. However, note that its highly publicised cost-benefits – like those of the

Elmira, Seattle and Montreal interventions – derived from comparing participants with equally disadvantaged youngsters who had not been included in a program. Architects of the Perry Preschool did not intend that, once the scheme had proven its worth, it should only be made available on a selective basis. They saw universal access to support at the preschool stage as a key to addressing structural disadvantage in the educational sphere.

Moving beyond the experimental phase and mainstreaming lessons from exemplary projects can be costly, and may run counter to broader government policies aimed at curtailing public expenditure in fields such as education, health and welfare. Social prevention premised on the idea of more targeted interventions – in effect intervening not with all individuals and families experiencing structural disadvantage, but only with those whose response is likely to be antisocial (e.g. to involve criminal behaviour) – is a far more attractive proposition for governments. However, experience in Australia and in other countries provides no reason to be confident that such targeting is possible.

Approaches to social prevention

Brantingham, Brantingham and Taylor (2005 [...] analogy between crime prevention and prevention in the health sphere [...] ealth, schemes are often classified on the basis of the stage at which inte [...] urs. Primary prevention refers to measures put in place early, and w [...] entire populations (e.g. by improving diet and sanitation). Secondary [...] generally occurs later, and focuses on individuals or groups assessed [...] e.g. smokers or people whose excess weight renders them more pro [...] es and other illnesses). Tertiary prevention aims to rehabilitate those [...] lready suffered a major crisis, such as a stroke. As noted in chapter 2, [...] ntion schemes can also be classified on this basis.

Because it targeted an at-risk population, [...] t argue that the Perry Preschool was secondary prevention. Howeve [...] nen governments learn from such initiatives, and try to ensure that prior to making the transition to formal education all infants are equipped with basic planning and problem-solving skills, they are engaging in primary prevention. This prevention also includes prenatal and family support programs that facilitate parent-child 'bonding'. The reasoning behind such schemes, empirically tested in the Elmira Project, is that children with attachment to parental figures who provide appropriate nurturing and support, and who apply discipline in consistent ways, are less likely to drift into serious or persistent delinquency (see Gottfredson & Hirschi 1990). Yet another way to deliver primary prevention is through education and publicity campaigns to change values that lead to or help justify problematic behaviour. Examples include campaigns in primary schools to reduce bullying and in workplaces to reduce sexual harassment, and national and regional advertising that targets male violence against women (e.g. the *Violence: Australia Says No!* campaign implemented by the Federal Government in 2006 and 2007).

Finally, primary prevention can include community development initiatives aimed at helping local neighbourhoods become more cohesive and capable of exercising effective social control. Criminologists have long theorised that 'social disorganisation' can render localities more vulnerable to offending, and empirical findings in the US and Australia lend some support to the view. On the basis of US data, Sampson (1997) has concluded that the most important correlates of violent crime are concentrated disadvantage, low residential stability and high immigrant concentrations. However, neighbourhoods that scored high on these factors but also were more close-knit and trusting, with inhabitants more prepared to intervene to control or correct young people's behaviour and to act together in the community interest, tend to experience lower than expected rates of violence. Similar findings on the buffering effects of social cohesiveness have emerged in Australia (Mazerolle, Wickes & McBroom 2010; Vinson 2004; Sargeant, Wickes & Mazerolle 2013; Wickes 2010).

Primary prevention reaches entire populations, many of whose members may not have broken the law even in the absence of relevant interventions. As noted earlier, secondary prevention, which focuses on 'at risk' individuals or groups, can appeal to governments as more cost-effective. Schools that incorporate risk-assessment theory and techniques include the so-called 'developmental' and 'pathways' approaches. Developmental prevention takes inspiration from studies that follow entire generations or cohorts from birth or even the prenatal stage through to adulthood, and try to identify factors common to the minority who accumulated serious criminal records as juveniles and adults (West 1973; Farrington 1995; Loeber et al. 2003). Some criminologists – for example, Farrington (2000) – are convinced that key problems (such as impulsivity, poor social and problem-solving skills, poverty, crime in the family and inadequate parental supervision) can be detected quite early in life, i.e. during the first five years. Interventions at this stage can help shift the developmental trajectory away from delinquency.

However, other researchers – for example, Sampson and Laub (2003) and Ross Homel (2005a) – reject the trajectory metaphor, with its assumption of 'one steady march towards adulthood whose direction becomes fixed after early childhood' (Homel 2005a, p. 81). Their preferred model is of a series of phases or transitions: for example, from home to a child-minding centre or preschool; from preschool to primary school; from primary to secondary education; from school to workforce, technical training or university, and so on. Each transition involves challenges, with one possible consequence of failure to meet these challenges successfully being a drift in the direction of anti-social behaviour. Transitions also can be points where individuals are more open to advice and support. Rather than concentrating purely on the early childhood phase, the 'pathways' (although perhaps it might better have been termed 'switchpoints') approach therefore advocates interventions at key stages throughout the life course. It also stresses the need to identify and strengthen relevant 'protective' factors at each stage (for a summary see Homel 2005a).

Other approaches that focus on intervening with at-risk groups include agency-based prevention and diversion schemes. Advocates of agency-based prevention argue that mainstream institutions (such as schools, businesses and recreational associations) often inadvertently help generate deviance and delinquency. For example, in schools where there is strong emphasis on assessing and ranking young people on the basis of scholastic, athletic and other achievement, less successful students can feel marginalised and devalued. As noted, some may then resort to less legitimate ways of achieving recognition and status (Merton 1938). This may involve linking up with anti-social subcultures or gangs, and committing crimes in order to generate income and inspire fear and respect (Polk 1997). France's so-called 'Bonnemaison' crime prevention program, implemented from the early to mid-1980s, involved key agencies in major towns or cities periodically assessing whether they might be helping marginalise sections of the population, and developing and implementing coordinated plans to try to be more inclusive (see also chapter 6).

Like some forms of developmental prevention, the diversion approach focuses on identifying individuals at risk of offending, and addressing factors likely to cause them to drift into delinquency. Such factors can include low self-esteem, lack of self-discipline, weak attachment to family or school and low social or vocational skills. However, rather than trying to work on these issues in everyday environments, diversion typically involves enrolling these young people in experiential learning programs. In the context of sports, wilderness adventure and other structured activities, program providers help participants identify and reflect on their problems, and rebuild self-confidence and coping skills. Diversion-based schemes tend to be more episodic than developmental prevention; consisting of one-off initiatives, albeit with some follow-up. Despite the fact that they can engender considerable enthusiasm among program participants and sponsors – and of course producers and directors of television documentary programs – evidence for the long-term effectiveness of such programs is not extensive (Castellano & Soderstrom 1992), and indeed there are some indications that they can be counterproductive. Learning in the context of camps and other activities can be as much from other high-risk youngsters as from program providers, and this informal learning can precipitate an escalation in deviance (Dishion, McCord & Poulin 1999 – see also discussion of the Cambridge-Somerville Program earlier in this chapter).

Tertiary prevention includes a wide range of schemes aimed at rehabilitating people who have already offended. Programs can be in prison or community-based. The restorative justice movement, pioneered by, among others, Australia's John Braithwaite (1989), has a strong emphasis on tertiary prevention – the key aim being to ensure that the act of sanctioning (or shaming) individuals who have transgressed social rules is followed by rehabilitative (or reintegrative) gestures.

From theory to policy

For some criminologists transition from research to practice should be straightforward. All initiatives – social prevention included – must be evidence-based. In deciding between the approaches outlined above, governments therefore should consider just one question: which works best in reducing offending?

As Freiberg (2001) points out, however, policy in relation to crime and social control always has been more complex. In fields such as sentencing, decisions need to 'work' at two levels: 'effective' and 'affective'. 'Effective' outcomes are instrumental – for example deterring and incapacitating offenders. 'Affective' results relate more to symbolic or expressive goals, such as reaffirming key social values. For sociologists such as Durkheim, the affective dimension of punishment always has been more important than the instrumental:

> [Punishment] does not serve, or else only serves quite secondarily, in correcting the culpable or in intimidating possible followers. From this point of view, its efficacy is justly doubtful and, in any case, mediocre. Its true function is to maintain social cohesion intact, while maintaining all its vitality in the common conscience. (Durkheim 1969 [1893], p. 23)

Academic advocates of prevention often overlook the need for strategies to succeed at the affective level. For those working in applied contexts, this dimension can never be ignored (Ekblom 2010; Sutton 1997). In democratic societies government ministers are regularly briefed on focus group and opinion poll findings, and are acutely aware that their policies must resonate with public perceptions and emotions. In practical terms, this means that social and other forms of prevention must be capable of conveying powerful symbolic messages. This helps explain why, despite the fact that criminologists have raised significant doubts about the diversion approach to offending, boot camps and wilderness adventure programs continue to receive support. Even if such projects do not 'work' instrumentally, they appeal to pervasive cultural narratives about the corrupting effects of sophisticated urban lifestyles, and the role that confronting physical challenges can play in helping young people 'build character'.

Similar factors may help explain the popularity of high-profile education and publicity campaigns, and ongoing resort to 'the community' for solutions to crime problems. Vast amounts of money have been expended on community-based crime prevention over recent decades; indeed this was a major theme in US policy during the 1970s and 1980s. Major initiatives include a $US30 million Community Anti-Crime Program and an Urban Crime Prevention scheme which provided funds to 85 voluntary associations in nine cities over a 17-month period.

As Skogan (1988) points out, despite numerous evaluations relatively few of these programs provided strong evidence that crime was reduced. A major problem was that while the word 'community' may bring to mind notions of consensus and harmony, grassroots dynamics tend to be different (Braga, Hureau & Winship 2008; Carson 2004a, 2004b; Miller 2008). Rather than uniting local residents and business people around a common objective, US experience was that the prospect of prevention funding became a catalyst for power struggles between interest groups with widely differing outlooks and philosophies. Skogan describes the voluntary associations that involved themselves with local programs as either 'preservationist' or 'insurgent'. Preservationists were conservatives, typically: 'long-term residents, home-owners, small business and local institutions with an interest in preserving the status quo' (1988, p. 43). Their approach to crime problems generally put stress on more intensive local policing and surveillance, and coordinated resistance to lower-cost housing, drug treatment centres and any other facilities likely to attract 'undesirables'. Insurgents, by contrast, represented more disadvantaged and marginalised elements, such as racial minorities and the unemployed or homeless. Their preference was to use prevention funds to address structural problems such as unemployment and racial discrimination, and difficulties of access to housing and health care (Skogan 1988, p. 56).

For both types of groups, attracting and controlling prevention funds was of major symbolic importance: a key way to express and validate their views. Neither approached crime prevention as a purely instrumental task. What they:

> prefer[red] to do about crime ... varie[d], but rarely resemble[d] the narrow, technical view favored by funding agencies, law enforcement agencies, and evaluators. (Skogan 1988, p. 69)

In light of the US experience, confirmed by more recent local controversies over the use of funds available under a federal government Weed and Seed program (Miller 2001), it might seem reasonable for contemporary administrations to be wary about relying on voluntary groups as a key source of ideas about crime prevention. Weed and Seed involved first using criminal justice interventions (e.g. zero tolerance policing, arrest and imprisonment) to 'weed' neighbourhoods of individuals identified as disruptive, then 'seeding' the neighbourhood with family support, community development and other social programs. Many neighbourhoods were polarised over whether, and to what extent, the 'weed' component should be applied, and some disadvantaged neighbourhoods successfully resisted this aspect.

One of Weed and Seed's key problems was that central government had strong reservations about the precise role local groups could and should play in crime prevention (Miller 2001). This is a problem that continues to this day (Miller 2008). Such decisions highlight the problems that occur when researchers and policy advisers gloss over the politics and symbolism of crime prevention. In our view, it is reasonable for politicians who have been prepared to defy law-and-order orthodoxy and invest resources on prevention to expect some acknowledgment and credit. This is why this book has maintained from the outset that crime prevention strategies and programs must be treated as more than technical and administrative exercises. The affective dimension of social prevention – its capacity to provide symbolic reaffirmation of the broader benefits of policies that address gross disadvantage in more inclusive, less coercive ways – should never be treated as 'mere rhetoric'. The challenge is to design and implement strategies and programs that can achieve symbolic goals without being rendered ineffectual or even counterproductive at the instrumental level.

Limits to social prevention

Later, in chapters 6 and 10, we discuss ways of achieving this. Before doing so, however, it is important to acknowledge the limits, as well as the potential benefits, of social prevention.

A common, but in our view mistaken, argument in criminology is that social prevention is the only viable way to reduce crime, because situational and other environmental approaches merely address symptoms. Because it fails to address 'root causes', it is argued situational prevention simply displaces offenders to other locations, times or types of crimes (Halsey 2001).

What such arguments tend to ignore is that the term 'crime' embraces a vast array of activities. Some – for example, major tax evasion or a large-scale armed robbery – will be carefully planned and executed. However, many others (such as shoplifting and other petty theft, minor vandalism, drink driving and even some instances of breaking and entering) are often casual and opportunistic. There is no evidence to suggest that individuals blocked from committing offences that are opportunistic and spur of the moment – or which, like drink driving, are more a product of carelessness than conscious intent – invariably search for other opportunities to break the law.

Nor are we convinced that crime displacement always should be viewed as a problem. Australian research indicates that a situational measure – the installation of electronic immobilisers in older vehicles – has significantly reduced the rate of car theft for 'joy-riding' by young males (National Motor Vehicle Theft Reduction Council 2005). It is possible, but by no means proven, that some of these individuals may have resorted to other forms of offending. However, given the dangers associated with teenage joy-riding, including the deaths and injuries that have occurred when stolen cars have become involved in high-speed pursuits and collisions, such displacement is still likely to be associated with net social benefits.

Advocates of social prevention should be wary of the utopian dream that every form of 'deviant' energy can and should be redirected into socially acceptable activity. The cultural and political climate generated by such relentless pressures to conform can be stifling. In Australia the criminalising of many behaviours – for example, smoking cannabis, writing graffiti, riding skateboards in public areas and playing music or dancing in the street without having first obtained a permit – is contested. Such contests can be healthy: an essential part of a dynamic, diverse society. Rather than striving to eliminate all symptoms of disorder and discord through social prevention, sometimes it may be more appropriate for governments to opt for less intrusive techniques (see chapters 7 and 8).

Graffiti writing is a good example. For many practitioners, a key attraction is that it provides opportunities for aesthetic and political expression in contexts that are not defined and controlled by mainstream institutions, such as public and private galleries, the critical establishment and the commercial art world (see Jacobson & Lindblad 2003; Gastman, Rowland & Sattler 2006). Even the best-intentioned initiatives aimed at helping writers find legitimate outlets for their work (e.g. legal murals or free zones for graffiti in towns and cities) can be perceived as 'repressive tolerance', whose end aim is to reincorporate writers into mainstream art worlds and associated forms of discipline. Situational prevention, which has the more limited aim of curtailing unauthorised graffiti in identified locations, may well be more consistent with – and perhaps even more respectful of – the forces that animate this culture.

The future

The Australian criminologist Ross Homel has argued there now exists 'persuasive scientific evidence' in favour of social prevention, in particular early intervention (see also Welsh 2012). What studies such as the Perry Preschool and the Elmira Prenatal and Early Infancy Project demonstrate is that:

> the systematic delivery to disadvantaged families with young children of basic services or resources that are taken for granted by middle-class populations in many countries eventually resulted in surprisingly large reductions in crime involvement among those targeted. Of equal or greater importance,

a variety of studies have found improved outcomes in terms of educational performance (mother and child), child maltreatment, maternal workforce participation, child and youth behaviour, income, substance abuse and similar measures ... So it seems that simple things that everybody believes in and can feel good about, like baby healthcare or preschool, if they are done 'right', might be an important component not only of successful crime policies but also of policies that promote many aspects of the health and well-being of disadvantaged populations. (Homel 2005a, p. 72)

These remarks presage a bright future, but they also exemplify a paradox. That is a key challenge in relation to social prevention has been to isolate its key working ingredients, then ensure that these are delivered to communities and populations that lack them. Homel's paragraph also acknowledges, however, that many Australians – indeed the majority – seem to be able to accomplish prevention outcomes routinely, without needing to rely on an expert intervention. When middle-class and upper-class people do all they can to ensure that their offspring cope with life's major challenges and transitions, they generally do not even perceive themselves as practising social prevention. They merely are doing 'simple things that everybody believes in', using 'basic services and resources that are taken for granted'. Only when the discourse relates to disadvantaged populations do we begin to portray social prevention as requiring 'something extra' whose addition to the mix requires research-based guidance and monitoring (see also Homel et al. 2006b).

We accept the view that social prevention often seems to 'come naturally' to more privileged groups. However, we have problems with the assumption that the disadvantaged somehow are different. In our view a better working hypothesis – one equally compatible with available evidence – is that all communities have capacity for social prevention, and that it always works best when deeply embedded in everyday routines and practices. Because social prevention needs to be thus embedded, expert attempts to isolate particular practices with high-prevention potential, and to use risk assessment and other targeting tools to introduce them to disadvantaged populations on a step-by-step basis, always have the potential to be counterproductive. As the Cambridge-Somerville experience showed, special support made available outside the context of normal life runs the grave risk of stigmatising recipients. As a number of commentators point out, moreover, using crime prevention as the rationale for rationing access to child and family support, educational, health and other relevant services runs contrary to all ideals of social justice and human rights, and can amount merely to 'the criminalizing of social policy' (Crawford 1994, p. 507).

None of this means we disagree with the view that we now have enough information and expertise to be confident that social prevention will succeed. Our starting point is to recognise that while individual demonstration projects and quasi-experiments are invaluable for confirming and quantifying the prevention value of inclusive institutions and practices, this does not mean that social prevention itself should take the form of discrete projects. Indeed we see it as essential that social prevention be *plan-based* rather than *project-based* (see also chapter 6). That is, rather than being a discrete one-off intervention, social prevention needs to be part of mainstream policy and practice. Supporting children's development needs to occur right across the life-course and through multiple intervention points, in particular through the school and family context. Lessons from one of the most successfully designed and evaluated social prevention programs in Australia - the Pathways to Prevention Project - highlight this very point (see Case study 3.1). Underpinned by developmental prevention, the key focus of the Pathways program has been on targeting transition points in young people's lives that involve changes in social identity and movement between social institutions (e.g. from home to school). These are points where things can go wrong for young people from disadvantaged backgrounds and can have a bearing on pathways into problematic behaviour, such as delinquency. Over a number of years this program has been refined and strengthened through close monitoring and evaluation and has been operating for 10 years in Australia. The Pathways program has been implemented in culturally and linguistically diverse communities, which include large numbers of Indigenous youth (Homel, Lamb & Freiberg 2006). Beginning as a demonstration project, the program has had an influence on federal and state policy on early intervention. A key lesson arising from the project is the need to adopt a holistic approach to early intervention that focuses on understanding how different contexts (institutional and social) impact on a child's development (France, Freiberg & Homel 2010; Freiberg & Homel 2011). This requires a plan-based approach to identify how key institutions and agencies can interact to enhance the developmental pathways of children. Putting this theory into action has been far from easy and moving from a demonstration project to a large-scale intervention has proven challenging (see Case study 3.1).

CASE STUDY 3.1   **PATHWAYS TO PREVENTION**

Pathways to Prevention is the most ambitious social crime prevention demonstration project ever implemented in Australia. A partnership between Griffith University and Mission Australia, it has been running since 2001 in one of the most disadvantaged urban areas in Brisbane. While the program has received ongoing support from state and federal governments, the main funding sources have been the Australian Research Council and corporate and philanthropic bodies. The following summary of the *Pathways* project is drawn principally from Homel et al. (2006a). Unless otherwise indicated, page references are to that source.

Pathways to Prevention aims to involve family, school and community in a broad set of planned interventions to reduce anti-social behaviour. Specific initiatives include a Community Insight Survey, a Family Independence Program and a Preschool Intervention Program.

The Community Insight Survey was conducted in 2001. Designed and implemented by local people with guidance from project staff, it involved 150 respondents of whom 60 per cent were parents and 40 per cent were 'cultural leaders'. The survey helped identify key community concerns, as well as perceptions and expectations of relevant institutions, such as preschools. From the survey it also became clear that there were 'subtle but important differences … between [Indigenous, Pacific Islander and Vietnamese] groups in terms of aspirations and perceived barriers' (p. 4).

Preschool Intervention Program objectives included enhancing children's communication and social skills in order to provide a basis for subsequent school success and helping them develop 'positive behaviours and interpersonal relationships' (p. 3). Activities took place during regular preschool sessions but involved 'specialist staff (visiting advisory teachers and psychologists) who provided enrichment activities and direct skills training for the children' (p. 3). Preschoolers were involved either in a program to improve their communication abilities or in a scheme aimed at enhancing their social skills. Participation was determined 'by a non-random assignment of preschools to intervention and non-intervention groups' (p. 3). Of the seven preschools in the intervention area, four received an intervention program while the remaining three were used as controls. Assessment of two cohorts indicates that the year-long language skills program resulted in significant improvements for all those who participated, while the social skills interventions generated measurable improvements in perceived behaviour among boys but not girls. Overall, the Preschool Interventions Program also helped improve the children's 'school readiness'.

The Family Independence Program (FIP) was more complex and multi-faceted. From 2001 through to 2003 it was available, on a voluntary basis, to all families with children aged 4 to 6 living in the area. Its broad goal was 'family empowerment and supporting families through adversity' (Freiberg, Homel & Lamb 2007, p. 226). Through the provision of 'culturally sensitive services' this program attempted to 'create a stimulating home environment that is harmonious and conducive to child development' (p. 3). Specific interventions included support and counselling for adults and children, behaviour management programs for parents, playgroups, family support group programs and schemes to link families with the school system. Assessment of effectiveness was hampered by the fact that families could not be 'assigned' to programs but had to choose to participate, and because in some instances relevant data on family circumstances and parenting styles and effectiveness was only provided after families had been in contact with the program for many months. Nonetheless, qualitative and other information did indicate that '[a]s a result of attending FIP, relationships between families and schools improved, as did relationships between parents and children who regularly attended' (p. 5). (For further examples of the Pathways Project see Branch, Freiberg & Homel 2010; Branch, Homel & Freiberg 2012; Freiberg & Homel 2011.)

Pathways to Prevention has been, and will continue to be, invaluable not just for confirming the effectiveness of family and preschool support and other forms of social prevention, but for also demonstrating *how* relevant support can be provided in universal, non-stigmatising and cost-effective ways. Architects like Homel (2005b) and Homel and Homel (2012) acknowledge, however, that finding ways to 'mainstream' these lessons (e.g. to ensure that they inform national, state and territory prevention policies) remains a major challenge (also see Freiberg & Homel 2011; Homel & McGee 2012). In this context, we see our arguments that policies should be plan-driven rather than project-driven as important. As Homel and colleagues acknowledge, moreover, local interventions such as those being tested in the *Pathways* project can only be fully effective if they are:

> simultaneously strengthened on a much wider scale through reform of social and economic environments within which family life is embedded. Efforts to bring such approaches to scale for the large numbers (14.7 percent) of Australian children who live in poverty will, in the end, depend on fundamental reassessment of national priorities and values. (Freiberg, Homel & Lamb 2007, p. 243)

Clearly, effective social prevention involves action at the structural and political as well as local levels.

For further information on the Queensland Pathways to Prevention program and its impact refer to www.griffith.edu.au/criminology-law/key-centre-ethics-law-justice-governance/publications/prevention-developmental-pathways

Conclusion

Our intention in this chapter has been to review the strengths, limitations and possibilities of social prevention. We have emphasised the importance of seeing social prevention as a holistic approach to crime prevention, one that does not need to be named 'crime prevention' at the grassroots for it to be effective. Indeed, such labelling tends to be counterproductive. In our view, social prevention ought to be as broad and inclusive as possible. In structural terms, social prevention frequently taps into issues surrounding societal distributions of community resources. We have also provided a working example of ways values such as social justice and social equity might be translated into prevention practice.

Throughout the chapter we have once again acknowledged the political processes and dynamics that intrinsically shape any foray into crime prevention at a policy, planning and project level. The accomplishments or otherwise of specific projects and programs have to be seen in the context of the wider social and economic environment.

The notion of 'special' intervention can, however, be problematic. This is so whether in relation to 'at risk' young people or to particular disadvantaged communities. For social prevention to be liberating rather than oppressive, empowering rather than stigmatising, a broad brush and consultative approach is essential. This takes considerable negotiation – and planning. In the end, for social prevention to 'work' it must resonate at both practical and symbolic (or affective) levels, and the closer it becomes ingrained as part of the everyday, the more likely it is to be effective.

CASE STUDY 3.2   HOW EARLY CAN YOU GET? THE CASE OF NURSE HOME VISITATION

A key feature of social prevention is its focus on early intervention and it often involves programs that, while not necessarily about crime prevention per se, do have an impact on offending and on the likelihood of young people becoming involved in crime. An example is nurse home visitation. There are many examples of nurse home visitation but the one we focus on here is the David Olds' model (Olds 2013). This US initiative is an early intervention program aimed at disadvantaged women bearing their first child. The program involves trained nurses visiting women in their homes during pregnancy and during the first two years of their child's life. Nurses focus on improving prenatal health and infant care, the mother's personal development, educational achievement and participation in the workforce. The initiative has been tested through randomised control trials (see chapter 5) and shown to improve mothers' mental and physical health, parenting skills, educational achievement and ability to secure employment. What is surprising is that nurse home visitation not only has positive benefits for women who experience such support, but also has positive outcomes for their children, such as reducing the child's likelihood of becoming involved in delinquency (Olds 2002; Olds, Hill & O'Brian, 2003). The Olds' model has been implemented in other countries (see Olds 2013) and is an example of how intervening early in a child's life (even before they are born) can have a beneficial impact by reducing the risk of youth becoming involved in offending.

QUESTIONS

Questions for further exploration

1. Is social prevention a viable approach to the control of crime or is it too broad and macro in its focus?

2. What key theories and approaches underpin developmental crime prevention? What evidence exists to support its effectiveness or any possible limitations?

3. How might the negative consequences of labelling children as 'at risk' be avoided in social crime prevention initiatives focused on early intervention?

EXTENSION TOPICS AND REFERENCES

1. Addressing risk and protective factors are an important component of social prevention, whether this is at the individual, family or community level. What is the difference between risk and protective factors? Are they useful concepts for understanding why young people become involved in crime and how can they help inform the design of prevention programs?

References

Farrington, D.P. (2000) 'Explaining and preventing crime: the globalization of knowledge – The American Society of Criminology 1999 Presidential Address', *Criminology*, vol. 38, no. 1, pp. 1–24.

France, A., Freiberg, K. & Homel, R. (2010) 'Beyond risk factors: towards a holistic prevention paradigm for children and young people', *British Journal of Social Work*, vol. 40, no. 4, pp. 1192–1210.

2. There is a large amount of research evidence in support of early intervention. Review this evidence and identify the types of programs that appear to be successful. Also in what contexts are these programs delivered and to which particular target groups?

References

Elliot, D.S (2013) 'Crime prevention and intervention over the life course', in C.L. Gibson & M.D. Krohn (eds), *Handbook of Life-Course Criminology: emerging trends and directions for future research.* New York: Springer, pp. 297–315.

Fagan, A.A. & Catalano, R.F. (2013) 'What works in youth violence prevention: a review of the literature', *Research on Social Work Practice*, vol. 23, no. 2, pp. 141–156.

Homel, R. (2005) 'Developmental crime prevention', in N. Tilley (ed.), *Handbook of crime prevention and community safety.* Devon: Willan Publishing, pp. 71–106.

3. Nurse Home Visitation programs have been shown to have an impact on levels of childhood neglect and family functioning, which can prevent children from becoming involved in crime. Should such programs be targeted at the most vulnerable and disadvantaged groups in society, or should they be universally available to all families regardless of their levels of disadvantage?

References

Farrington, D.P. & Welsh, B.C. (2007) *Saving children from a life of crime: early risk factors and effective interventions.* New York: Oxford University Press.

Olds, D. (2013) 'Moving toward evidence-based preventive interventions for children and families', in R.D. Krugman & J.E. Korbin (eds), *C. Henry Kempe: a 50 year legacy to the field of child abuse and neglect. Child maltreatment, vol. 1.* New York: Springer, pp. 165–173.

4

ENVIRONMENTAL PREVENTION

Introduction

This chapter will discuss the following topics:

- the theory and practice of situational crime prevention (SCP)
- crime prevention through environmental design (CPTED)
- CPTED theorists and concepts
- CPTED in practice
- SCP and CPTED as part of inclusive crime prevention.

Theorising relationships between crime and the physical environments in which it occurs has a long history (Taylor & Gottfredson 1986; Skogan 1990). In recent decades Wilson and Kelling's (1982) so-called 'broken windows' thesis has been particularly influential. Their argument is that people constantly monitor spaces they move through for signs that order is being preserved. Lack of order-maintenance (e.g. failure to replace broken windows, repair vandalism and remove graffiti) will be read as evidence of community breakdown, and increase the likelihood that people avoid these areas. Potential offenders, however, may see the same physical symptoms as indicators of a lack of guardianship and conclude that the location offers ample opportunities for crime. Research on 'crime hot spots' or 'crimes of place' also suggests that features of certain locations can make them, and those who frequent them, more vulnerable to crime (Eck & Weisburd 1995; Braga & Weisburd 2010; Weisburd, Groff & Yang 2012).

Environmental theory goes beyond the broken windows and hot-spot approaches, however. Theorists and practitioners can be grouped into two broad schools. The first is concerned with practice in fields such as urban planning and architectural design and maintenance, and has attracted the label 'crime prevention through environmental design' (generally shortened to CPTED). The second concentrates on more focused interventions in specific situations (and hence is termed 'situational crime prevention' or 'SCP'). There are overlaps between the two. Over recent decades a network of researchers has been systematically documenting theory and practice in both CPTED and SCP (see the International CPTED Association and the Jill Dando Institute of Crime Science).

We see it as critical that, in addition to trying to change social environments so that people have fewer motivations to offend, large-scale prevention programs and strategies pay attention to the physical contexts in which people interact and opportunities for crime arise. It is important though that practitioners do not treat environmental and social prevention as mutually exclusive and make a choice between the two. We do not perceive any inconsistency between understanding and employing environmental prevention techniques (whether CPTED or situational) and our argument that, in the Western democracies at least, crime prevention policy has been and should be about fashioning responses to crime that are more inclusive than 'law and order'. Some academic criminologists tend to dismiss situational and other forms of environmental prevention as based on mere physical exclusion (Farrell 2010; Halsey 2001). Such critiques fail to take account of the history of environmental prevention and the range of practices it encompasses.

Early pioneers of CPTED – such as the 'defensible space' theorist Oscar Newman (1972) and Jane Jacobs (1961), with her views on urban regeneration and 'natural surveillance' – were vitally concerned about the ways that modernist planners and architects – whose primary clients were big business and government – were producing built environments that ordinary people had difficulties relating to and managing, and which undermined their sense of safety and security. Contemporary advocates of environmental prevention, such as Marcus Felson, acknowledge their indebtedness to these writers and share their concerns. Urban planners and architects often apply CPTED and situational prevention techniques as much for their aesthetic appeal as for any proven capacity to reduce crime. It is not inappropriate to assume that environmental prevention amounts to little more than closed-circuit television, locks, bolts, bars and other forms of crude target hardening. We hope that by the end of this chapter readers will recognise that there is more to both schools than this.

This chapter will review CPTED and SCP and outline key concepts underpinning each. Our aim is not simply to catalogue technical components, but to analyse how they can provide insight into factors contributing to crime and ways it can be prevented. Developments in the situational field, in particular, suggest that projects that exploit its imaginative and flexible approach to analysing and solving problems can make important contributions to an innovative and inclusive prevention strategy.

SCP and CPTED

Is there a fundamental difference between situational prevention and crime prevention through environmental design? Both approaches are concerned with systematically modifying physical environments to reduce opportunities for crime. Both work on the assumption that in the vast majority of instances, committing an offence involves some type of choice, and that the calculus of this decision can be modified in ways that make breaking the law less attractive. CPTED and situational prevention often employ similar types of measures – for example, techniques to control access to particular locations or to improve natural or occupational (e.g. by employees or security staff) surveillance of possible targets. However, CPTED and situational prevention do need to be distinguished.

As Ron Clarke (1998b), the pioneer of situational prevention, notes, CPTED focuses on the design and maintenance of built environments, whereas situational prevention's concerns are broader, in terms of both the settings in which it intervenes and the techniques it employs. CPTED is also more preoccupied with public and semi-public space, and the human interactions occurring there, than is situational prevention. Specifically, it assesses and recommends the ways such spaces should be defined and managed, and tries to influence behaviour in and around locations. A recurrent theme in CPTED is that problems occur when planners, architects and place managers fail to plant visual and other cues that make the intended use of public spaces clear, because such failure heightens possibilities for conflicts between different types of users. In addition to avoiding 'designing problems in' to urban environments, CPTED also tries to ensure that the aesthetics of particular types of developments, such as public housing estates, do not inadvertently stigmatise their residents and other users.

Situational prevention and CPTED also differ in terms of proven capacity to reduce crime. Advocates of situational prevention now can cite an extensive inventory of case studies testifying to its successful application in a range of circumstances (Clarke 1997; Eck 2002a; Guerette 2009b). Many situational initiatives have been evaluated, and there have also been systematic attempts to take account of, and measure, possible unintended consequences, such as the displacement of offending from the intervention site to less protected targets – for example, of armed robberies from banks to convenience stores (for a review of the displacement issue see Guerette & Bowers 2009; Hamilton-Smith 2002). Evaluations of CPTED have been less favourable (Mayhew 1979; Shaftoe & Read 2005), although the evidence base in this field is improving (Ekblom 2011; Cozens, Saville & Hillier 2005; Minnery & Lim 2005; Poyner 2006; Reynald 2011; Wilson & Wileman 2005; Wortley & Mazerolle 2008; Wortley & McFarlane 2011). Finally, CPTED and situational prevention differ in the ways they have influenced policy and practice. As Hope and Sparks (2000) point out, situational prevention has had much greater impact in the UK than in other parts of Europe or in the US and Australia. For its part, despite the comparative lack of research support for claims of effectiveness, CPTED has had major influence in Australia (see Colquhoun 2004; Crime Prevention Victoria 2003; Schneider & Kitchen 2002; Queensland Government 2007; Western Australian Planning Commission 2006; Wilson & Wileman 2005), and has also found its way into policy in the UK and the Netherlands.

SCP: principles and approaches

The importance of opportunity

The starting point for situational prevention (SCP) is to view the world from the point of view of a potential offender. Specifically, SCP tries to understand how people perceive opportunities for crime, and to remove these opportunities or at least ensure that they are less easily recognised. Situational theorists point out that the term 'crime' embraces a very wide range of behaviours. Some, like shop theft and drink driving, can be impulsive and spur of the moment, while others are premeditated and planned (e.g. vehicle theft by organised criminals). They argue that in contemporary consumer societies even the most lavishly funded social programs are not likely to be able to ensure that all people will be able to resist the urge to commit every type of crime. However, certain threshold conditions can still have bearing on whether an offence occurs. These relate to the number and type of opportunities offered within specific contexts. For someone who is capable of, and not averse to, offending, the decision whether or not to commit a specific crime will be a function of both whether an opportunity presents itself and whether the likely rewards from exploiting that opportunity are sufficient to offset the perceived efforts and risks. Situational prevention revolves around identifying 'pinch points', or modifiable conditions that are susceptible to intervention and can reduce or pre-empt perceived opportunities for crime (Clarke 2005; Tilley 2005).

Situational theorists argue that dispositional or social structural conditions (e.g. poverty and disadvantage) should not be seen as the sole causes of crime. Opportunity should also be recognised as a necessary condition, or cause, which – unlike many other contributors – can often be addressed in cost-effective ways. While much of criminology has been concerned with understanding how and why criminality develops, the situational school's focus is on explaining the occurrence of crime itself (Clarke 2005). This does not mean that situational prevention is completely atheoretical. In fact, situational prevention is informed by – and helps reinforce – a range of macro-level, middle-range and micro-level theories that help explain how and why rates of crime vary in different eras and in different types of societies. Key elements of these theories are summarised in Table 4.1. Readers will note the relationship between situational crime prevention and routine activity theory, which was discussed in detail in chapter 2.

Table 4.1 suggests that situational prevention is about more than the psychology of individual decision-making. It sits within, and is informed by, broader frameworks that can help locate crime rates and trends in the context of large-scale economic

Table 4.1   Key theories underpinning SCP

Routine activity theory

(Macro-level theory)

Explains how changes in society create opportunities for crime

Opportunities for crime linked to the supply of suitable targets and availability of capable guardians

(See Clarke 2005; Felson 2002)

Crime pattern theory

(Middle-range theory)

Derived from environmental criminology

Explores how offender and victim interaction in particular environments produces more or less crime

Activity nodes and pathways generate crime by attracting criminals and providing pathways to offending locations

Activity nodes bring together motivated offenders and potential victims

Crime can occur along shared pathways (e.g. on train lines or public bikeways)

Ambiguous locations, where offenders cannot be distinguished from other users, generate crime opportunities

(See Felson 2006; Brantingham & Brantingham 1993)

Rational choice perspective

(Micro-level theory)

Focuses on offender decision-making

Offending purposive (e.g. aim is to benefit the offender materially or psychologically)

Decision to offend is the result of weighing up risks, efforts and rewards

Targets selected for different reasons

However, limits on offender's rationality

(See Clarke & Cornish 1986; Clarke & Felson 1993)

and other social developments. Advocates like Clarke also insist that their focus on opportunity reduction should not be taken as evidence that they are indifferent, or opposed, to programs whose aim is to reduce inequality and improve the life chances of disadvantaged classes and minorities. However, they contend that such initiatives should be supported for their own sake, rather than being justified by the promise that they might lead to some future reduction in crime.

These arguments are persuasive. Nonetheless, they are not sufficient to convince us that SCP can or should provide the sole basis for a national or regional strategy. Situational prevention may have the advantage of being able to be shown to 'work' cost-effectively in a range of circumstances: something that should not be discounted in an era when the expenditures on police, courts and prisons are escalating and governments are under pressure to restrain taxes and budget outlays. As noted in chapter 1, however, crime policies can never be legitimated purely on economic grounds. They also need to convey symbolic messages about political leaders' commitments to defending and maintaining social values and standards. Situational prevention, with its underlying assumption that given the right circumstances many, if not most, people will offend, and that society's best option is to try to minimise opportunities, is weak in this respect.

Key situational techniques

Having made this point we note that for practitioners at the grassroots, the capacity to demonstrate short-term and medium-term success in reducing offending will always be important for maintaining program credibility and guaranteeing continued funding. In this context, it is important that they are knowledgeable about, and be able to apply, situational prevention techniques. Current theory outlines five major approaches. Each addresses a specific aspect of the decision-making processes that can culminate in the commission of an offence. For any given crime, the five approaches involve:

• increasing the perceived efforts associated with its commission
• increasing perceived risks of detection
• reducing perceived rewards
• reducing provocations
• removing excuses.

Each broad approach has an associated range of techniques. Table 4.2 provides examples. This list is constantly expanding. As originally developed by Clarke (1980), situational prevention focused on increasing the perceived efforts and risks associated with offending, and reducing anticipated rewards. Subsequently it has been extended to address the ways people rationalise and excuse criminal behaviour (see Clarke & Homel 1997), and to incorporate research findings on factors that trigger violent confrontations. Problems to which these theories and techniques have been applied include organised crime, bushfire arson, border security, domestic violence, confrontations in correctional institutions, illegal smuggling of endangered species, poaching and terrorism (Christensen 2006; Freilich & Newman 2009; Guerette 2005; Hanmer, Griffiths & Jerwood 1999; Lemieux & Clarke 2009; Pires & Clarke 2012; van de Bunt & van de Schoot 2003; Wortley 2002). As noted, situational prevention also has been continuously evaluated. Box 4.1 lists techniques found effective in various contexts.

Table 4.2   Techniques of SCP

Broad approaches	Specific techniques
Increase the effort of crime:	Harden targets
	Control access to facilities
	Screen entries and exits
	Deflect offenders
	Control tools/weapons
Increase the risks:	Extend guardianship
	Facilitate natural surveillance
	Reduce anonymity
	Utilise place managers
	Strengthen formal surveillance
Reduce the rewards:	Conceal targets
	Remove targets
	Identify property
	Disrupt markets
	Deny benefits
Reduce provocations:	Reduce frustration and stress
	Avoid disputes
	Reduce emotional arousal
	Neutralise peer pressure
	Discourage imitation
Remove excuses:	Set rules
	Post instructions
	Alert conscience
	Assist compliance
	Control access to drugs, alcohol and other facilitators

(Source: Clarke & Eck 2003)

BOX 4.1:   SITUATIONAL PREVENTION TECHNIQUES APPLIED WITH SUCCESS

- Improved street lighting
- Substitution of glassware with plastic in pubs
- Street closures/alley gates
- Rapid removal/repair – graffiti and vandalism
- Restrictions on the sale of spray paints

- Use of screens, cameras and reduced handling of cash in banks to combat armed robbery
- Codes of practice and training of staff to reduce problems in and around pubs and nightclubs
- Caller ID to reduce obscene and annoying telephone calls
- Tagging and barcoding to combat shoplifting
- Provision of silent alarms and introduction of 'cocoon' neighbourhood watch to reduce repeat victimisation
- Introduction of phone entry systems to limit access to public housing
- Recruitment of public transport monitors
- Introduction of security personnel/police on bikes in specific environments (e.g. parking lots)

(Source: Eck 2002a)

Readers should never be overconfident, however, about transferring these techniques to new locations. Each was developed and applied after close and systematic analysis of specific problems occurring in particular contexts (e.g. brawls involving the resort to glasses and bottles in specific pubs at specific times). Only after they had been shown to work in these situations were attempts made to extend their use to places deemed similar (e.g. to other pubs with a similar clientele). Situational prevention always allows for the possibility that an approach that has proven successful in one location may not work in another, because the characteristics of the new site and its problems differ in subtle but important ways from those where the technique was developed. For example, while 'improved lighting' may well help reduce assaults and other victimisation in streets that provide ample opportunities for natural and professional surveillance, it may not have the same effect in thoroughfares that lack these features. In these latter locations better lighting may, in fact, simply make it easier for potential offenders to identify possible targets. As Eck (2002b) points out, the most transferable aspect of SCP is its capacity for in-depth problem analysis, not the various techniques that have emerged in the course of its application.

Critiques of SCP

As noted, SCP has been the subject of vigorous critiques (see also Farrell 2010; Gabor 1990; Hughes 1998). Its advocates claim this is simply because they are out of step with traditional criminology, where the preoccupation is with trying to understand and change social background factors that predispose some individuals, and members of some groups, to offend (Clarke 2005). While this may be true, we think there are deeper reasons for reservations about SCP. They reflect what Max Weber (1991) saw as the tendency for knowledge professionals to become increasingly specialised, and to lose capacity to understand and communicate with those working outside their particular spheres of expertise.

In the case of situational prevention, specialisation has involved adhering to a 'crime science' paradigm which maintains that government policy should be dictated purely by experimental evidence on 'what works'. Situational theorists seem reluctant to contemplate the possibility that broader economic and political forces will result in their approaches and findings being implemented selectively, in ways that exacerbate social division and social exclusion. This is the concern for a wide range of criminologists (von Hirsch et al. 2000). Many are prepared to concede that SCP is technically neutral and targets places rather than specific types or categories of people. Nonetheless they argue that the very fact that it costs money to implement will ensure that in market-based economies it deflects crime away from the affluent, who can pay for relevant measures, towards groups who cannot afford its protection. In the long term, therefore, reliance on situational prevention is consistent with the emergence of gated estates, the proliferation of CCTV (see Box 4.2) and the advent of the fortress and surveillance society (Davis 1990).

BOX 4.2:   OPEN-STREET CLOSED-CIRCUIT TELEVISION

It is not unusual for politicians, business interests and members of the general public to assume that crime and disorder in town centres and malls can be reduced by installing a closed-circuit television (CCTV) system. For example, of the £400 million budgeted for the UK's three-year (1999–2002) Crime Reduction Programme, £150 million was set aside solely for the installation of CCTV. In 2006, the Australian Government announced it would be encouraging local authorities and traders' associations to apply for funds from a $6 million 'security related infrastructure' grant scheme to install CCTV in shopping malls and town centres (see chapter 6).

Why is CCTV so popular and what evidence is there that it is effective? Welsh and Farrington's review (2006) found that of the many hundreds of open-street CCTV systems put in place in the UK and the US since the early 1990s, just 19 had been the subject of rigorous evaluation. While these studies found an average 8 per cent decrease in crime in areas that had installed CCTV compared with a 9 per cent increase in control areas, not all interventions had been equally successful. CCTV worked better to reduce offending in car parks and other closed or semi-closed environments than in more open settings, such as city centres and housing estates. There is little evidence that CCTV deters violent crime or offending that is alcohol-related. Successful camera systems tend to be part of a package of initiatives that also include measures such as improved lighting and the introduction of security guards.

Open-street CCTV is popular with police because it can help them rationalise their use of resources. Rather than allocating large numbers of officers to routine street patrols, appropriately trained local government personnel can use the cameras to surveil relevant areas, and help direct police attention to places where trouble seems to be brewing. Camera footage can also provide evidence of, and can be used in investigating, offences after they have occurred (Wilson & Sutton 2003).

Local business interests often see installation of a camera system as a powerful statement that their region is 'progressive' and dedicated to ensuring the safety and wellbeing of shoppers and other clients. CCTV's capacity to be used to quickly identify people whose behaviour or appearance fails to conform with local standards can also be reassuring for 'preservationist' interests who are convinced that maintaining the status quo and keeping more disadvantaged individuals and groups away from their community is the key to keeping crime rates low (see Sutton & Wilson 2004; see also chapter 3 of this book).

Simply assuming that CCTV is the most effective way to address crime problems affecting a particular area is inconsistent with situational prevention's emphasis on systematically analysing patterns of offending before proceeding to implement countermeasures. CCTV alone is not likely to eliminate crime and disorder, and is only effective against certain types of offences in certain types of locations.

Faced with such concerns, defenders of situational prevention tend to argue that many – if not most – of their techniques are subtle, unobtrusive and non-stigmatising, and that gated communities are not necessarily as socially divisive as their opponents portray (Clarke 2005). It certainly is true that graffiti removal and the use of graffiti-resistant surfaces, better surveillance and access control at automatic teller machines, time locks in safes, cameras in taxis and enhanced street lighting hardly present as intimidating or oppressive. However, such observations alone are not sufficient to dispel the criticism that SCP lacks a core ethical framework that would enable it to confront important social and political questions about who benefits from its measures, who will be left unprotected, and why (Hope & Sparks 2000; Shapland 2000).

To defend situational prevention from this type of criticism it is necessary to move beyond the 'crime science' paradigm. Readers will be aware that for the current authors, commitment to prevention stems from a belief that it can and should provide the basis for a distinct policy alternative to 'law and order', punishment-based responses (chapter 1). From this value position, what might be the advantages of including situational as well as social prevention in strategies and programs?

The first and most obvious one is pragmatic. As noted, including some opportunity reduction schemes in a local or regional crime prevention plan will significantly enhance the possibility that it can generate short-term and medium-term 'success stories'. Capacity to present evidence of such successes to government ministers and other funding sources can, in turn, be critical when it comes to buying the time required for longer-term developmental and other social interventions to be implemented and take effect.

A second, perhaps even more powerful, reason for recognising and trying to make use of SCP is that given its capacity to be sold as a commodity (e.g. in the form of private security and surveillance systems), practitioners who shun it may simply be helping ensure that their pessimistic predictions about unequal access to protection are vindicated. In policy fields such as health, education and housing, the need to work with markets has long been recognised. In these spheres it would be absurd to treat a benefit or service as 'taboo' simply because it was capable of being offered by private providers. Policy makers concerned about equity and social justice in health, education and housing use subsidies and direct state provision to supplement and rectify biased market outcomes. There is no reason to believe that governments could not play a similar role in ensuring more equitable distribution of situational prevention and its benefits. This is one of the reasons why Hill and Pease (2002) argue that state programs should give priority to the prevention of repeat victimisation. Statistical data consistently confirm that economically and socially disadvantaged individuals and householders are more likely to be affected by crime on repeated occasions. Situational programs that focus on people and places already victimised, with the aim of avoiding repeat attacks, can therefore help achieve redistributive goals.

It should now be clear that we do not agree with commentators like David Garland, who see situational prevention as part of a 'new criminology of everyday life' that 'blames the offender, silences excuses, ignores root causes, and sees the punishment of wrongdoers as the proper response' (2001, p. 131). On the contrary, we see situational prevention as compatible with a longstanding conviction among criminologists that much offending (e.g. most crimes by juveniles) is symptomatic of temporary weaknesses such as poor impulse-control rather than of deep-seated malfunctions that require heavy-handed 'correctional' interventions (Moffitt 1993). The fact that situational prevention does not see everyone who breaks a law as damaged or deviant should not necessarily be held against it.

While many crimes (e.g. sexual assault and family violence) are symptomatic of social and individual problems that must be addressed, in other instances situational prevention's less judgmental approach may be appropriate. When it comes to graffiti, for example, we see nothing inherently wrong in its exponents' views (Jacobson & Lindblad 2003) that there should be places in a healthy society for spontaneous public displays of creativity and social comment. However, we also accept that some graffiti can be so unsightly, racist or otherwise disturbing that if left unaddressed it can detract from the public amenity. Situational prevention, which works on the basis that even when a behaviour is unacceptable this does not necessarily mean that the person responsible must be changed in fundamental ways, can therefore be the best option for graffiti management (see also chapter 7). It provides mechanisms for containing problems caused by, or associated with, graffiti without seeing any need to force or encourage writers to compromise their freedoms and submit to the strictures and constraints of the commercial or high-art worlds.

This brings us back to another criticism of SCP: one that Crawford (1998) sees as exposing its 'Achilles heel'. This is, that its single-minded focus on opportunity, and apparently wilful neglect of underlying social factors known to be associated with criminality (see chapter 3), means that its most likely outcome will be to displace crime rather than eliminate it altogether. When individuals damaged and rendered 'deviant' by social dislocation and disadvantage find specific opportunities blocked they will simply adapt by committing a new crime or selecting a different, less well-protected target.

Advocates of SCP respond by citing empirical evidence that shows that for many if not most offences, displacement is less than total (Guerette & Bowers 2009; Guerette 2009a; Hesseling 1994) and that in some circumstances – for example, when it leads to a less serious crime being committed – it may even be benign. They also point to studies indicating that when applied to vulnerable targets in high-crime areas situational prevention in fact can have effects beyond these specific locations ('diffusion of benefits'), and that on some occasions crime reductions can be achieved even before relevant situational measures have been implemented ('anticipatory benefits') (Barr & Pease 1990; Clarke 2005; Clarke & Weisburd 1994; Guerette & Bowers 2009; Guerette 2009a). With a comparatively 'minor' offence like graffiti it should also be noted that even if displacement is total, net social benefits may still occur. Writers prevented from 'tagging' heritage buildings and other high-profile public locations may have been displaced to sites or suburbs where residents or passers-by find graffiti less of a concern (e.g. to gentrified inner-city suburbs, where some residents see graffiti as enhancing the local ambience).

Situational analysis: being creative

We hope that this chapter has convinced readers that in some circumstances at least, SCP can make useful contributions to local crime prevention plans. The adoption of situational analysis, within the context of the problem-solving methodology outlined in chapter 2, can be integral to the development of context-relevant strategies and help identify interventions that usefully supplement socially-oriented forms of prevention. Adoption of the core principles of SCP can also help promote innovative thinking about ways to prevent crime. For example, analyses of the specific factors rendering some situations more crime-prone has helped generate a knowledge base around why crimes can tend to be clustered in specific locations and regions (Braga & Weisburd 2010; Clarke 1999; Eck & Weisburd 1995). Routine activity theory, crime pattern theory and rational choice all provide insight into the reasons some products or places are more often victimised. The core message of these approaches is that opportunity reduction needs to be focused, systemic and tailored to the nature of the crime problem in question.

For example, it is no surprise that cash, VCRs, CDs, MP3 players and mobile phones are the most commonly stolen goods: as Clarke (1999) points out, they are CRAVED: concealable/removable/available/valuable/enjoyable/disposable. Characteristics 'designed into' these products (i.e. the very qualities that make them desirable consumer goods) mean they are more likely to be stolen, with different techniques of SCP aiming to alter these qualities in subtle ways in order to render them less accessible targets for motivated offenders. Understanding the key characteristics of stolen products, and how such characteristics can place them at risk, can help in the development of relevant precautions and the design of anti-theft measures.

Analysis of crime hot spots also illustrates how detailed understanding of specific situations where crime is occurring can assist prevention planning. Crime is often concentrated not only among certain victims but also in particular locations and facilities (Braga & Weisburd 2010; Eck & Weisburd 1995; Eck, Clarke & Guerette 2007). Brantingham and Brantingham (1995), drawing on routine activity and crime pattern theory, argue that specific features of some locations can make them more likely to become hot spots, with such places being:

- crime generators – places that attract larger numbers of people as a result of routine activities (unrelated to crime) but provide opportunities by bringing potential offenders and targets together (e.g. entertainment festivals and shopping centres); or
- crime attractors – places affording criminal opportunities that are well-known to offenders (e.g. drug dealing locations); or
- crime enablers – places where there is little regulation of behaviour or where guardianship and place management have been eroded (e.g. poorly managed public housing).

Understanding why locations have become hot spots can help identify paths to possible solutions. Crime generators arise due to many unprotected targets being available, with problem analysis and responses concerned with understanding the precise factors that are exposing targets to risk and what might help improve protection. Crime attractors need to be analysed to understand what features are attracting offenders and what modifications will discourage them. Places become crime enablers due to the erosion of either formal or informal social controls. Responses need to restore guardianship, strengthen handlers or improve place management (Brage & Weisburd 2010; Brantingham & Brantingham 1995; Clarke &

Eck 2003). In-depth situational analysis of location characteristics should be a required part of crime prevention planning, and can help ensure that responses are tailored to the nature of the problems in question.

Guardianship is a core SCP concept. As outlined in chapter 2, it can entail both hardware (e.g. CCTV) and people. A key theoretical aim of SCP has been to understanding how changes in society can undermine effective guardianship (Felson 2002). Innovative thinking about ways to strengthen the guardianship function can generate responses that extend SCP beyond a simple focus on crime opportunities towards helping achieve more widespread social and cultural benefits. For example, a Dutch strategy that aimed to improve formal guardianship on public transport and in other public space involved recruiting and training unemployed people as safety, information and surveillance officers and as city wardens (Crawford 1998). Not only was this strategy effective in reducing crime and fear of crime (van Andel 1992; Willemse 1994), it generated social benefits beyond crime control by providing meaningful work for people who previously had been unemployed.

The implementation of community patrols in remote Australian communities also illustrates how situational prevention can be fashioned in culturally appropriate ways to help achieve broader social benefits. Operated by Indigenous groups, the core aim of community patrols is to restore social regulation by strengthening guardianship within communities through helping local residents carry out a self-policing function (Blagg & Valuri 2004a, 2004b). Often staffed by women or elders, patrols can help defuse violent situations and divert intoxicated people away from contact with the criminal justice system. Hence intervening in the situations that typically create problematic outcomes for Indigenous people is a key objective. This restoration of local Indigenous guardianship can also operate as a catalyst for developing socially-oriented responses, such as referring Indigenous people intercepted by patrols into treatment programs. Thus, sensitivity to what may or may not be acceptable guardianship in specific social contexts can be the basis for culturally-relevant situational responses that help empower communities.

Yet another example of situational techniques used successfully to address problems in Indigenous communities relates to petrol sniffing (see Box 4.3). These and other examples show how innovative responses to crime can be generated from the application of SCP theory and concepts. Understanding the factors that contribute to crimes occurring in specific situations, and thinking about ways these situations can be addressed – for example, by the restoration of guardianship – shows how SCP can be applied in ways that fit in with this book's understanding of crime prevention. Properly applied, situational prevention need not exacerbate inequalities. Rather, it can help counteract them by reducing concentrations of crime among disadvantaged people and locations and enhancing systems of social control in contexts where controls have been eroded.

BOX 4.3: ADDRESSING PETROL SNIFFING

Replacement of conventional leaded and unleaded petrol with fuels such as AVGAS and OPAL, which contain extremely low levels of the dangerous chemicals (i.e. sulphur, benzene and aromatic chemicals like toluene and xylene) that give petrol sniffers a high, has been credited with significantly reducing the extent and effects of petrol sniffing in Indigenous communities throughout Australia (see *Weekend Australian* 17–18 March 2007). Research supports this observation (see Gray et al. 2006; Shaw et al. 2004). Such a strategy is based on situational crime prevention: reducing rewards through target removal and denial of benefits. Such strategies not only lead to improved individual and community health outcomes but also provide the catalyst to divert former petrol sniffers into social and community support programs.

CPTED: impact and use of the physical environment

CPTED, which is concerned with broad-based urban planning and architectural design issues, draws on aspects of SCP theory and practice. Its key aim is to influence people's perceptions of the built environment and the ways public space is defined and used. How the use of space is defined by its physical appearance and the ways it influences behaviour are core themes of CPTED. The aim is to understand how 'non-problematic' uses of space can be generated by providing environments that are both objectively and subjectively safe, and how uses of space that are not desired (e.g. crime and disorderly behaviour) can be discouraged through physical and symbolic barriers and modifications that help generate effective systems of social control and surveillance. Definition of space is, of course, a social process. Such definitions can exclude groups perceived as undesirable (e.g. young people from public spaces such as shopping malls). However, as chapters 7 to 9 show, this need not be the case. Again, the problem is not so much with the theory and concepts of CPTED but with the ways it is implemented. Capacity to reflect on this issue is an important part of crime prevention planning and evaluation, and will be covered in later chapters.

CPTED pioneers

We cannot begin a discussion of CPTED without canvassing the work of Jane Jacobs and Oscar Newman, two of its pioneers. In 1961, Jacobs published *The death and life of great American cities.* In it she argued that unrestrained commercial and industrial development were the primary reasons US cities were becoming desolate zones, characterised by high rates of crime and other social problems. Jacobs argued that by allowing land use to be fragmented into specifically concentrated zones (e.g. commercial and residential), urban planners of her time inadvertently were helping ensure that cities became 'custom built' for crime. Lack of residences in the inner city meant that people fled to the suburbs at night, leaving these areas desolate. This in turn would attract people who did not want their activities observed by the general public (e.g. drug dealers and users; prostitutes and their clients), while during the day residential neighbourhoods would be largely devoid of any form of guardianship due to people being at work or school. This in turn would afford opportunities for crime and other forms of disorder (e.g. household burglaries and vandalism).

Jacobs' proposed solutions were to enhance natural surveillance through planning (i.e. providing opportunities for people to exert social control in the course of their normal routine activities), and to ensure that the design features of city buildings would facilitate this process. Jacobs believed that improving an environment's capacity for natural surveillance acted as a means of deterring offenders and increasing their risk of apprehension. A key solution proposed by Jacobs was to draw people back to city centres through the establishment of mixed land uses and the provision of amenities (e.g. shops, pubs, restaurants and parks) and activities that would draw people out of their homes and onto the streets both during the day and at night. Natural surveillance is all about having 'more eyes on the street' and has become a key element of the CPTED lexicon.

Oscar Newman's work focused on architectural solutions to crime problems in and around public housing. It arose from observations and analyses that Newman carried out during the 1970s on some of the most crime-prone and stigmatised public housing estates in the US (Newman 1972, 1975, 1996). Newman was critical of modernist public housing design, with its obsession with economies of scale (i.e. the emphasis placed on cramming large numbers of people into high-rise housing). This made it difficult for residents to assert functional control over their lived environments. There were too many anonymous areas, no clear distinctions between public and private space, inadequate amenities, poor natural surveillance and lighting, numerous access routes, unrestricted pedestrian movements, dead-ends, cavernous corridors and poorly-maintained facilities (e.g. lifts always out of order and covered in graffiti). Such physical features led to a 'spiral of decline' into crime and disorder – increasing fear of crime among residents, which caused them to retreat indoors – and the likelihood that people would avoid areas populated by public housing. These factors in turn led to the stigmatising of public housing estates.

Newman contended that crime in and around public housing could be reduced by dividing relevant territory into smaller lots. The aim was to ensure that the physical environment was manageable on a human scale. Newman argued that such architectural solutions would allow residents to exert functional control by engendering a sense of territoriality and community among residents (i.e. a desire to defends one's space and feelings of belonging) and facilitate responsibility for preserving a safe and well-maintained living environment. This would generate what Newman termed 'defensible space':

> [a] model of residential environments which inhibits crime by creating the physical expression of a social fabric that defends itself ... 'Defensible space' is a surrogate term for a range of mechanisms – real and symbolic barriers, strongly defined areas of influence, and improved opportunities for surveillance – that combine to bring an environment under the control of all its residents. (Newman 1972, p. 3)

Newman's work has been criticised for ignoring important social factors that can affect crime rates; for example, the fact that public housing tends to have higher concentrations of poor, unemployed, single-parent families and people from minority group backgrounds (Bottoms 1974; Mawby 1977; Merry 1981). Despite these criticisms, Newman's theories on design solutions to crime have been extended to a range of contexts, such as car parks, office spaces, schools, parks and residential streets (Crowe 2000; Feins, Epstein & Widom 1997; Poyner 1983, 2006; Smith 1996). In particular Newman's theory of defensible space provides the foundation on which many modern CPTED techniques have been based.

Core CPTED techniques

Contemporary CPTED practice boasts a number of experts, each of whom describes their approach somewhat differently (e.g. see Cozens, Hillier & Prescott 2001b; Cozens, Saville & Hillier 2005; Crowe 2000; Poyner 1983). The core theories, however, are similar. CPTED relies on four basic techniques: territorial reinforcement, surveillance, access control, and activity support and image management. None of these approaches should be seen as stand-alone. Rather, they are used in concert to subtly influence human interactions in ways that will discourage and reduce anti-social behaviour.

> **Territorial reinforcement**: This is a key 'defensible space' concept and involves generating and confirming a sense of proprietorship and owner-ship among the approved users of particular spaces, and discouraging illegitimate users. Territorial reinforcement requires creating and maintaining spatial hierarchies and ensuring clear, well-recognised boundaries between public and private areas. Through the use of physical and symbolic barriers, space can be divided into four distinct categories:

public, semi-public, semi-private (gardens) and private. Barriers can include hedges and walls between public and private areas, signboards (e.g. notices stating 'you are entering private property'), vegetation or changes in surfaces to create 'zones of transition' that give people cues that they are moving from public to private space. Zones of transition make it easier for residents and other authorised people to keep an eye on an area, and make it more legitimate for them to challenge individuals who seem to be intruding (Cozens, Saville & Hillier 2005; Colquhoun 2004; Feins, Epstein & Widom 1997; Newman 1996; Crowe 2000).

Surveillance: This can be both formal and informal. The key principle is to increase the perceived risks associated with offending by increasing the likelihood that behaviour within a particular area will be observed. Surveillance aims to increase the potential for intervention, apprehension and prosecution. Informal systems incorporate natural surveillance, which can be applied to both internal areas (e.g. offices, stores, supermarkets and undercover car parks) and external areas (e.g. streets, parks, car parks, bus shelters and train stations). It involves ensuring there are clear visible sight lines so individuals can observe and be observed as they go about their routine activities, positioning paths, shops and houses so they can be seen by adjoining users, creating well-lit areas and having activity generators and facilities that increase the outdoor use of a space (e.g. balconies, yards, and pedestrian and bike pathways) and attract people who can act as watchers or gatekeepers. Formal or organised systems of surveillance aim to increase guardianship and place management by assigning responsibility for surveillance to a designated third party. Such responsibility can form part of a third party's routine activities (e.g. a concierge, bar staff, private security personnel, attendants or store persons) (Cozens, Saville & Hillier 2005; Crowe 2000; Eck 2003; Smith 1996). Mechanical surveillance like CCTV is generally associated with situational crime prevention rather than CPTED.

Access control: Strategies of access control encourage, restrict and channel activities and aim to deny access to a potential crime target. Access control can involve informal, formal and mechanical strategies. Informal strategies incorporate natural features that change the spatial definition of locations (e.g. changes in land elevation, garden beds, road closures, and 'celebrated' entries that signify movement from public to private space and channel pedestrian movement along designated paths). Formal access control is more purposeful and organised and, like formal surveillance, is carried out by third parties who in their normal functions can deny people access to specific areas (e.g. security guard, receptionist,

concierge, secretary and ticket collector). Mechanical access control involves the use of gates and barriers (e.g. entry phones, alley gates and
bollards) (Crowe 2000; Poyner 2006; Queensland Police Service 2006).

Activity support and image management: Activity support involves placing facilities and amenities in safe locations that afford, for example, improved natural surveillance. Likewise, certain activities and features can
be incorporated into locations so they can serve as magnets for 'ordinary'
people who, through their very presence, will discourage crime. Typically, this involves having mixed land usages that integrate residential,
recreational, entertainment and restaurant precincts. The aim is to generate activity throughout the day and night and ensure that areas are not
abandoned. Giving various resident groups (e.g. parents and infants, the
elderly and teenagers) their own dedicated spaces, and reinforcing the
intended usage through appropriate design and management rather than
leaving it to these groups to 'sort it out themselves', can reduce conflicts
over space, which, if unattended, can escalate into harassment and even
crime. This helps prevent areas being abandoned by the very people
who can do most to prevent offending. Appropriate activity support can
improve the image of an area by attracting legitimate users. Image management also relates to tackling incivilities and removing signs of crime
(e.g. vandalism, graffiti, abandoned vehicles and rubbish), which can undermine perceptions of safety, and instead transmit the positive message
that this area is under control. Such functions can be carried out by a designated third party, such as a groundsman or a property manager (Feins,
Epstein & Widom 1997; Newman 1972, 1996; Crowe 2000).

Influence on policy and practice

In Australia, CPTED has become very popular among police, state and territory
crime prevention units and local government authorities. A number of CPTED
policies or guideline systems have been formulated. For example, in Victoria,
Queensland and Western Australia CPTED has been developed as a distinct priority,
with central government units working with relevant state government departments
to integrate CPTED guidelines into planning advice (see Crime Prevention Victoria
2003; Queensland Government 2007; Western Australian Planning Commission
2006). The WA Office of Crime Prevention has an extensive Designing Out Crime
initiative that provides funds for local governments to conduct CPTED projects
(see the Australian Institute of Criminology website). Police in New South Wales
and Queensland have developed CPTED guidelines and use these as a basis for
training community groups and state and local government authorities (Clancey,

Lee & Fisher 2012; Queensland Police Service 2006; NSW Police Service 2001, Safer by Design program). The aim of all these schemes is not just to assist in the development of local initiatives, but to influence planning decisions by state and local authorities and ensure that CPTED becomes part of mainstream planning processes (see Clancey, Lee & Fisher 2012).

A number of overseas programs have also endeavoured to make CPTED a part of mainstream urban design practice. Both the British Secured by Design (SBD) strategy and the Dutch Labelling Secured Housing scheme aim to give developers and builders incentives to incorporate CPTED principles into the design of residential and commercial complexes (Ekblom 2011; Stummvoll 2012). Developments that satisfy these standards are accorded official recognition, and developers can mention this in advertising and other marketing. SBD is a UK police initiative. The primary aim is to encourage the building industry to adopt recommended crime prevention guidelines in the design and construction of public and private housing (Colquhoun 2004). Designated Police Architectural Liaison Officers promote and implement the program. Developers who abide by SBD guidelines are officially recognised and companies can receive an SBD licence for the manufacture of products designed as police tested and preferred (Cozens, Pascoe & Hillier 2004). SBD guidelines emphasise effectively managing sites, controlling access, and ensuring that private space is well-defined and that natural surveillance is encouraged in public spaces and access routes (Colquhoun 2004; Ekblom 2011; Kitchen 2002; Schneider & Kitchen 2002).

The Dutch strategy is also operated by the police and focuses more broadly on urban development issues. It, too, awards certificates for dwelling, building and neighbourhood design, and sets security standards for doors, windows and frames, hinges and locks. Guidelines developed under the Labelling Secured Housing scheme focus on mixed land uses; housing variety and height; access routes; recreational facilities; site management; graffiti-resistant surfaces; limited access to dwellings; demarcations between public and private space; site lines and fencing; and the positioning of housing, shops, storerooms and garages to facilitate natural surveillance (Stummvoll 2012). Evaluations of the British and Dutch schemes indicate reduced crime and fear of crime in locations that adopted the programs (Armitage 2000; Colquhoun 2004). Both programs allow businesses to be accorded recognition and to receive awards to publicise their achievements. This may give them a competitive advantage with security-conscious customers. Thus, both the British and the Dutch schemes work with market systems, and exploit the fact that CPTED can be commodified, to try to make it more attractive for producers and consumers (see Farrell and Roman 2006 for further ways crime prevention can be 'incentivised').

While popular, CPTED is not without flaws (Ekblom 2011). For example, attempts to enhance territoriality (i.e. attitudes among legitimate residents and users that promote ownership of space, and encourages them to assert control over it) may only be effective in neighbourhoods that are characterised by high levels of home ownership. The requisite sense of proprietorship may not exist in areas characterised by different demographics (e.g. high levels of people renting, or high levels of transient populations) and hence CPTED approaches may not be effective there (Cherney 2006a). Merry (1981) discusses the ways factors at the cultural, neighbourhood and individual levels can affect territoriality. Note also that the effectiveness of natural surveillance is highly reliant on people's willingness to intervene when they see a crime occurring, and to challenge disorderly behaviour – or at the very least to report crime when it is observed. However, most complex societies are characterised by a waning capacity and inclination for onlookers to intervene in these circumstances, and reporting rates to police are relatively low.

Mayhew (1979) has discussed the way various social variables can affect whether and how CPTED techniques are effective. Criminologists also have expressed doubt about whether highly motivated offenders will be deterred by environmental features, such as changes in footpath textures (indicating a transition from public to private space), or will take note of environmental modifications that enhance natural surveillance. This argument is very similar to the displacement critique levelled at situational prevention. In response, it is worth noting again that not all potential offenders are similarly determined. Research has confirmed that many do, in fact, take note of environmental cues and that this influences their perceptions of risk and reward (Cozens, Hillier & Prescott 2001b; Cromwell & Olson 2004).

One recurrent criticism of CPTED relates to its tendency to ignore the ways social processes interact with physical environments to influence both how such environments are defined and how they are used (Merry 1981). This can vary by gender, age, ethnicity or socio-economic status, and be determined by both the perceived and actual levels of crime in an area. Concern about such social factors has led to the development of so-called 'second generation' CPTED, which places emphasis on risk assessments (e.g. surveys of real and perceived crime levels), socio-economic and demographic profiling and processes of community consultation and participation (Cozens, Saville & Hillier 2005; Saville & Cleveland 2003a, 2003b). While drawing on all the core concepts of CPTED outlined above, second generation CPTED maintains it is essential for practitioners also to understand the social characteristics of neighbourhoods (e.g. whether residents participate in a neighbourhood's social life), and argues that CPTED should be integrated in broader community development (Clancey, Lee & Fisher 2012; Ekblom 2011; Reynald 2011; Saville & Cleveland 1997).

This chapter has highlighted the need for policy makers and practitioners to think through the ways social context can affect the implementation and effectiveness of

CPTED strategies. For example, physically redesigning residential areas to promote territoriality and natural surveillance will achieve little if residents do not know one another and are distrustful of their neighbours, and for these reasons are fearful of walking the streets during the day or night. This is why second generation CPTED puts emphasis on community consultation and participation. The aim is to foster the social processes that help determine whether physical design changes will be effective.

Applying CPTED

Like situational prevention, CPTED needs to be informed by in-depth problem analysis. Site survey or safety audit methodologies have been developed to assist with this task. Such preliminary work is essential. One of the key aims of a CPTED site survey is to generate a detailed understanding of types of problems affecting a location. Without such understanding it will not be possible to fashion and implement an effective CPTED program. Surveys are also essential for helping users and owners of relevant space to identify what needs to be done to improve their feelings of safety and their perceptions of the physical environment.

Various methodologies have been developed to guide site surveys and CPTED safety audits. Some involve the application of a simple CPTED checklist that requires assessment and documentation of sightlines, lighting levels, numbers of pedestrian access routes, entrapment points and levels of natural surveillance (Crowe 2000; New Zealand Ministry of Justice 2005). Others methodologies are more complex. For example, a site survey developed by the NSW Police Service requires users to score both social (i.e. levels of crime and the socio-economic status of an area) and physical characteristics of the environment. These are then added together to generate an overall 'risk index', which in turn is used to suggest particular CPTED interventions (NSW Police Service 2001). A key problem with all types of CPTED site surveys, however, is that their application can be affected by users' subjective interpretations of particular environmental features (McCamley 2002). Risk assessment of a specific site can vary widely according to gender perspectives and personal experience. This can have implications for the general validity of survey findings.

Two key questions that need to be considered in any CPTED site survey are:

1. Do the physical features of the environment negatively impact on, or undermine, the location's CPTED potential (e.g. is there a poor demarcation between public and private space that undermines potential territorially)?

2. Are there environmental features that actually enhance CPTED and thus can be strengthened (e.g. is there existing infrastructure that would support improved amenities and enhance the location's milieu)?

The reason for outlining these two principles is that implementation of a CPTED-based program need not necessarily involve the wholesale redesign of an area. CPTED can be used both in the pre-planning stage and as a method of 'retrofitting' when problems do emerge. Prevention practitioners should be aware that the CPTED approach builds upon, and incorporates, principles that urban designers and architects often adhere to for aesthetic, rather than crime prevention, reasons. There are many examples of buildings and urban layouts that seem to be informed by CPTED theory, but which were not designed with crime prevention in mind. The fact that CPTED resonates with much contemporary urban design and architectural practice means that while it is preferable that CPTED rules be adhered to in the planning and design phase, it often can be possible to make corrections retrospectively if and when crime problems arise.

CPTED can be popular with local crime prevention and community safety officers because it endows them with authority in the planning and development process. The fact that it promises to reduce crime by modifying physical environments rather than requiring expensive social interventions can also make it attractive to public and private sector organisations (e.g. police and local business). Despite these attractions, CPTED has its own implementation challenges. A requirement that mainstream planning processes provide evidence that they have taken account of CPTED principles would impose significant additional costs on the development of infrastructure at the state and local levels. Business and commercial interests are likely to resist such an impost. State and local governments, under pressure not to impede investment by imposing additional burdens on the private sector, therefore are likely also to be reluctant to require CPTED assessment as a routine part of the development approval process.

The net result is, according to Wilson and Wileman, that 'CPTED can often seem like motherhood, something everyone respects but often does not support by way of action' (2005, p. 326). There is little doubt, however, that if knowledge about 'defensible space' had been built into the planning stages of physical infrastructure many of the crime and disorder problems associated with some of Australia's worst residential, commercial and public housing areas could have been mitigated. This point made, it is important that grassroots prevention practitioners guard against becoming CPTED zealots, and remain aware of its pitfalls and limitations.

Conclusion

There are sound ethical and practical reasons for ensuring that large-scale crime prevention schemes include environmental approaches. From an ethical point of view, situational prevention and CPTED can be far less judgmental than social prevention. They smack less of 'social engineering', with all its possible untoward consequences.

Situational prevention's emphasis on 'stopping people doing harmful things' (e.g. shoplifting, graffitiing, stealing a car on impulse) rather than on 'changing' them in fundamental ways *can* be consistent with ideals of a liberal, tolerant society. It works on the basis that while the specific *behaviour* may be unacceptable, the *person responsible* does not necessarily need to be the subject of intensive 'correctional' intervention. CPTED's emphasis on creating orderly and amenable spaces is about generating user-friendly environments that have crime prevention potential. Properly applied, CPTED interventions can provide what Giddens (1991) has termed 'ontological security' or confidence and trust in the environment around us.

From a practical point of view environmental prevention provides options that are within the capacities of agencies to implement (e.g. the police, private sector, communities and individual citizens). Like social prevention, it can and should involve empowering communities by providing them with the knowledge and capacity to assert control over factors making them insecure (Cherney 2006a). Prevention programs and strategies based on the idea that only 'root causes' (such as poverty, social dislocation and disadvantage) should be addressed can in fact be disempowering for local communities, because such communities lack the resources needed to make inroads against these types of problems. By contrast, environmental prevention – with its emphasis on opportunity reduction – can provide the basis for a program that agencies and people at the local level can influence directly.

Rather than viewing environmental prevention as 'taboo', the aim should be to ensure that it is used in ways that are inclusive and equitable (e.g. it does not simply deflect problems from rich to poor areas). There is little doubt that in some contexts environmental prevention needs to be augmented by social prevention. This is a recognised best-practice principle. The aim should be to achieve an appropriate balance.

CASE STUDY 4.1 A POSITIVE EXAMPLE OF DISPLACEMENT

As mentioned, the possibility of displacement is a key criticism of situational crime prevention. Advocates of situational crime prevention argue that displacement does not always occur and that in some circumstances positive forms of displacement can result, such as the diffusion of benefits or anticipatory benefits. For example, a UK evaluation of CCTV in a university car park found that not only did incidents of theft and vandalism decline in the parking lots covered by the CCTV, they also declined in parking areas that were not monitored by the CCTV (see Poyner 1997). A key argument made is that the benefits of CCTV diffused beyond the area monitored by the CCTV through communicating a credible risk of apprehension to offenders. The diffusion of benefits has also been found in the area of hotspot policing (see Weisburd et al. 2006 – see chapter 9). Other interesting outcomes of situation crime prevention are anticipatory benefits. For example, evaluations in the UK of situational crime prevention schemes aimed at reducing burglary found that when they also involve publicity campaigns, reductions in burglary can occur before the schemes have been implemented (see Johnson & Bowers 2003). Hence the risk of apprehension is communicated via the publicity campaign, which increases the anticipation among offenders that the risk of apprehension has increased.

Questions

Questions for further exploration

1. What physical features/characteristics of particular locations help to generate crime?

2. In conducting a situational analysis of a crime problem what key questions would you ask to inform the development and design of a situational crime prevention strategy?

3. Do you think situational crime prevention is a viable method of crime reduction?

4. What is meant by the term 'natural surveillance'?

5. Walk around your local neighbourhood and identify any physical features that would be regarded as crime generating according to the theory of crime prevention through environmental design.

EXTENSION TOPICS AND REFERENCES

1. Displacement is regarded as a key weakness of situational crime prevention. When it comes to the causes of crime, what assumptions about criminal motivations underpin arguments about displacement? Is the criticism that situational crime prevention simply displaces crime valid?

References

Guerette, R.T. (2009) *Analyzing crime displacement and diffusion.* US Department of Justice, Office of Community Oriented Policing Services, at www.popcenter.org/tools/displacement

Guerette, R.T. & Bowers, K.J. (2009) 'Assessing the extent of crime displacement and diffusion of benefits: a review of situational crime prevention evaluations', *Criminology*, vol. 47, no. 4, pp. 1331–1368.

2. Both situational prevention and CPTED regard crime as resulting from proximate causes (e.g. the immediate environment), while social prevention regards crime as the result of distal causes (background or social factors). Given these different perspectives are social and environmental crime prevention incompatible? How might situational crime prevention and CPTED complement forms of social prevention?

References

Clarke, R.V. (2005) 'Seven misconceptions of situational crime prevention' in N. Tilley (ed.), *Handbook of crime prevention and community safety.* Devon: Willan Publishing, pp. 39–70.

Welsh, B.C. & Farrington, D.P. (1998) 'Assessing the effectiveness and economic benefits of an integrated developmental and situational crime prevention programme', *Psychology, Crime and Law*, vol. 4, no. 4, pp. 281–308.

3. For useful summaries of key CPTED techniques and their application in practice, see the following resources:

Clancey, G. (n.d.) *Natural surveillance*, at http://garnerclancey.com/case_studies.php.

Clancey, G. (n.d.) *Promoting natural surveillance: balconies and patios*, at http://garnerclancey.com/case_studies.php.

Clancey, G. (n.d.) *Access control and territorial reinforcement*, at http://garnerclancey.com/case_studies.php.

5

IMPLEMENTATION
AND EVALUATION

Introduction

This chapter will discuss the following topics:

- an evidence-based approach to crime prevention policy and practice
- the challenges of implementing crime prevention strategies
- key knowledge and skills to 'do' crime prevention work
- factors essential to successful strategy implementation
- various evaluation methodologies
- capturing context-relevant factors within crime prevention evaluation, including the political
- building capacity for implementation and evaluation.

Implementation

Implementation failure has been identified as a key problem plaguing crime prevention programs both in Australia and abroad (Bullock, Erol & Tilley 2006; Ekblom 2010; Homel 2009b; Homel & Homel 2012; Hough 2004, 2006 – see chapter 6). There are numerous reasons for this, including a lack of ongoing funding, poor strategy design, ineffective systems to govern implementation, incompatible priorities between central and local government, inadequate political leadership and support among stakeholders, rivalry and an unwillingness to share data between agencies, and insufficient capacity at the local level to facilitate and coordinate program delivery. One factor that confounds the process of implementation is that often it relies upon partnership approaches, with it becoming more challenging to coordinate and achieve strategy outcomes when there are multiple partners participating in a crime prevention program. While partnerships have become a unifying feature of modern crime prevention initiatives they are not without their problems and require significant effort and support. In this section on implementation, partnerships will be discussed at length. Successful partnerships also require support by a dedicated coordinator and in agencies such as the police and local government, distinct roles have emerged (e.g. crime prevention officers or community safety officers) to support the implementation of crime prevention initiatives. This is a challenging task and requires a number of skills and knowledge bases, which will be discussed in this chapter. While implementation is rarely a linear, straightforward process, there are a number of factors that help maximise its success. One key argument we make is that maximising successful implementation not only requires resources and technical assistance, but also political support.

Crime prevention partnerships

As mentioned, partnerships have become a distinctive feature of crime prevention policy and practice worldwide. One of the key justifications for agencies to work in partnership is that crime is a complex problem that is beyond the capacity of any single agency to address. Hence by working together a more holistic response to crime is possible, whereby agencies such as the police, schools, local government and businesses can pool resources, expertise and information and coordinate their efforts to address crime problems. There are different types of partnership models, but the size of a crime prevention partnership will vary by the crime problem being addressed. For instance, for the problem of graffiti at a railway station all that may be required is for police and public transport officials to work together to rapidly remove graffiti and undertake targeted patrolling. However, for the problem of truancy more agencies may need to be involved, including the police, schools, families and service providers. Such decisions need to be guided by in-depth planning that is underpinned by the problem-oriented framework outlined in chapter 2. However, crime prevention partnerships are not without their problems, and studies highlight that they can be problematic and become dysfunctional, to the extent that they undermine strategy implementation and the achievement of program outcomes (Bullock, Erol & Tilley 2006). This is often the result of conflicting agendas and priorities amongst agencies participating on a partnership. There are, though, some key features that underpin effective crime prevention partnerships.

Effective partnerships are underpinned by clear priorities that provide a sense of focus for all members. The objectives of a crime prevention partnership should be compatible with the organisational plans of agencies participating in the partnership, which provides further impetus for agencies to follow through on their commitments and responsibilities. Strategies underpinning crime prevention partnerships should clarify the inputs and responsibilities of agencies, so each clearly understands why they are involved and what needs to be achieved. Members of a partnership should be drawn from senior levels, which can help ensure the partnership has authority to influence the decisions of agencies on the partnership, as well as external stakeholders. It is important that any disagreement among members of a crime prevention partnership is addressed in an open and constructive manner so that participants feel they can voice their opinion. Partnerships will not be sustained on their own and require support from a dedicated coordinator who can monitor progress and ensure each member's participation is maintained. In order for crime prevention partnerships to develop and implement plans of action they need access to good-quality data on crime and community safety, and also training in crime prevention theory and practice. This helps ensure partnerships are problem-oriented (see chapter 2 on the problem-solving method) and systematic in the process of strategy design. Crime prevention partnerships need 'quick wins' so that members can see they are achieving results, which can help sustain commitment to more long-term outcomes by indicating that the partnerships are effective (Cherney 2004b; Crawford 1997, 1998; Crawford & Jones 1995; Gilling 1997; Homel 2006, 2009b).

Essential crime prevention knowledge and skills

To be competent in the field of crime prevention requires a range of skills and knowledge that span effective problem solving and analysis, understanding about techniques of crime reduction, the ability to manage partnerships and also the capacity to evaluate processes and outcomes (see the section below on outcome and process evaluation). In actual fact within the police and also agencies such as local government, there exist personnel (e.g. crime prevention or community safety officers) whose role is to implement crime prevention programs (Cherney 2004a; Clancey, Lee & Crofts 2012; Gilling & Hughes 2002; Hughes & Gilling 2004). Studies indicate that crime prevention/community safety officers are less involved in actually implementing specific techniques of crime reduction, and are often required to identify and motivate third parties to act against crime problems and coordinate partnerships (Cherney 2004a; Clancey, Lee & Crofts 2012). This necessitates a mix of the skills and knowledge bases that are outlined in Box 5.1.

BOX 5.1: KEY KNOWLEDGE AND SKILLS IN CRIME PREVENTION

- 'Know about' knowledge: this relates to knowledge about crime patterns, offender modus operandi, risk and protective factors and theories of crime.
- 'Know what works' knowledge: this includes knowing what causes of a crime problem can be manipulated and understanding how particular prevention methods:
  - reduce a particular crime problem (e.g. by decreasing opportunities)
  - work effectively in particular contexts (e.g. public verses private housing)
  - produce any negative side effects (e.g. displacement)
  - carry certain costs and benefits (e.g. resource implications).
- 'Know how' knowledge: this relates to knowledge and skills about formulating plans of action and getting them implemented. It can encompass:

- understanding of organisational practices within partnership agencies that may impact on commitments to a crime prevention plan
- negotiating roles and responsibilities of agencies identified as responsible for strategy implementation
- forming and sustaining partnerships and generating ownership of a program among participants
- motivating agencies to implement relevant components of an initiative.

• 'Know who' knowledge: this includes not only knowing who are the most relevant agencies to include in a crime prevention partnership, but also being aware of contacts (e.g. senior decision-makers and managers) who can help ensure agencies participating in a strategy fulfil their responsibilities, and who can provide access to resources, data and funds to assist with implementation.

• 'Know why' knowledge: not only do crime prevention practitioners need to have an understanding of the technical qualities of 'doing' crime prevention, they also need to take account of its symbolic, emotional, ethical, cultural and political dimensions. This can relate to understanding why some groups may or may not support a particular crime prevention approach due its cultural applicability, or the ethics of delivering a program in a particular context (e.g. the family environment).

What is important to note is that these competencies are not simply concerned with technical skills relating to knowledge about methods of crime prevention, but also relate to expertise in engagement and negotiation. This is because crime prevention/community safety officers need to deal with agencies or groups (e.g. commercial businesses, government departments or home owners) whose activities are potentially generating opportunities for crime, and who need to be convinced that crime prevention is an important responsibility. Convincing third parties this is so can be a difficult task.

Evaluation

It is clear from preceding chapters that evaluation and accountability are an important part of crime prevention. If a key component of crime prevention is to enable governments to win support for a shift away from 'law and order' and to support local initiatives that do so, it is essential that strategies and programs are able to demonstrate that their 'alternative' crime prevention investments are 'producing results'. Evaluation also provides the basis for an evidence-based approach that can help inform future policy developments. However, just like implementation, evaluation is a challenging task. There are divergent opinions on how evaluation ought to inform crime prevention planning and the types of evaluation methodologies that should underpin an evidence-based approach (Pawson 2006; Welsh & Farrington 2011; Sherman et al. 2002, 2006).

As noted, some forms of crime prevention (particularly social) work best when 'embedded' in other programs (e.g. education, family support or employment creation) whose ostensible purpose is not preventing crime. This can make evaluation difficult because the demonstration of clear results may be evident in other ways (e.g. reduced truancy rates, less family breakdown and stressful family environments, improved feelings of community connectedness and reversal of educational deficits) rather than via immediate reductions in crime.

The authors agree that crime prevention should be evidence-based and that efforts need to be made to expand knowledge about 'what works'. However, an evidence-based approach also requires a clear understanding of what crime prevention is trying to achieve; that is, it is not just about preventing crime, but also about changing perceptions and attitudes towards social control.

This section outlines various approaches to evaluation, giving particular attention to *impact* and *process* evaluation. A key argument is that context matters, and that no one method of evaluation will necessarily be appropriate in all circumstances. Understanding the strengths and weaknesses of various evaluation methods is important to building a repertoire of evaluation designs and evidence that can inform the development, implementation and assessment of crime prevention plans. Much can be learnt from both strong and weak evaluations. Such knowledge can provide the basis for proving that alternatives to 'law and order' do work.

In the context of achieving a sustained approach to crime prevention policy development, evaluation should also aim to measure whether crime prevention plans are resulting in more widespread recognition and acceptance that 'embedded' social and environmental initiatives in fact help reduce crime and improve security. In this context, it is essential not just to measure whether crime and fear of crime have been reduced, but also to assess whether prevention measures are recognised and supported among key constituencies and the broader public. Such support is essential to the political sustainability of crime prevention.

Different methods of evaluation

A key criticism of crime prevention policy both in Australia and abroad is the lack of investment in program evaluation (Homel 2009b; Welsh & Farrington 2011, 2012a). Rarely is evaluation a systematic part of project planning, which has key implications for lesson learning. Often the pressure on practitioners and policy makers is to get 'quick wins'; that is, to get projects 'up and running', which leads to evaluation being an after-thought, left until a project has run its course (Cherney

2004a; Wikstrom 2007). However, an important best-practice principle of program evaluation is for evaluation to be ongoing and part of the early design of a crime prevention strategy.

It needs to be recognised that evaluation is a difficult task. It takes planning to ensure that the appropriate data is collected. Often accessing data can be difficult with different agencies protective about data, and reluctant to provide it to external agencies or independent third parties. This is why in some jurisdictions, such as the UK, data-sharing protocols have been a key focus of crime prevention policy development (Moss & Pease 2004). Compounding this, even when access is granted, transferring the data can take time, and the form in which it is received may require large amounts of data clearing and manipulation to ensure it is in a usable format. If primary data is collected, conducting surveys and interviews also requires time and can be resource-intensive.

The above activities can be time consuming and distracting from the tasks of actually implementing a strategy. Hence evaluation can only add to the costs of designing and implementing a crime prevention strategy: money that, at times, may be seen as better spent on the intervention itself. Evaluation can also require skills and knowledge that practitioners may lack and require procedures and processes (e.g. time series analyses and selection of sample sizes or experimental and control groups) that may seem daunting to the non-technically trained. Finally, practitioners and policy makers can regard evaluation as threatening, particularly if they have invested large amounts of time and resources (or banked their reputations on) a program. It can indicate that a scheme has been a failure and a waste of resources.

It is little wonder that evaluation is neglected, given the challenges it presents. Despite this, evaluation is essential to creating a culture of learning by spreading knowledge about the successes and failures experienced when attempts are made to implement different crime prevention approaches. Such learning cultures should not shun the use of complex and rigorous evaluation designs. Indeed, the idea of having crime prevention plans, as outlined in preceding chapters, provides scope for various evaluation methods to be incorporated as a systematic part of crime prevention policy design. These different methods of evaluation will now be outlined.

Outcome evaluation

Outcome evaluation is concerned with examining the impact of the intervention; that is, answering the question 'Did it work?' This relates to identifying whether an intervention actually led to a reduction in crime or perhaps fear of crime. Identifying the substantive impact of an intervention is perhaps the raison d'être of most program evaluation. However, identifying whether any measured reduction in crime was the direct result of a particular initiative can be challenging. Many other intervening variables can influence the outcomes of a crime prevention strategy. For example, it has been shown that there is a maturation effect relating to young offenders desisting from crime (e.g. see Bushway & Paternoster 2013). Hence, attributing a young person's desistance to a particular intervention may be misleading, because it could be more a result of their transition to a mature adult and the life changes this brings (e.g. marriage, changes in friendship networks and full-time employment) than the direct result of the intervention itself. Also, crime levels can be subject to fluctuations and any reductions in crime could just be the result of seasonal or random downward trends.

Target groups also may not cooperate in a particular intervention, thus influencing its effectiveness. As outlined in the previous section on implementation, often crime prevention strategies employ partnership approaches and the more partners there are the higher the levels of coordination required. If one partner fails to undertake tasks agreed to and required under a particular scheme, then failure to do so means a particular strategy component is not being delivered, which can negatively affect program outcomes. Hence the initiative itself may be underpinned by a coherent theory, be based on evidence and be shown to have worked in other jurisdictions, but nonetheless fail to have an impact due to the action (or inaction) of one particular partner agency. Therefore, evaluation requires a lot of planning, with different methods of evaluation aiming to control and account for factors that influence whether a crime prevention intervention is effective.

Experimental method

One method of evaluation – held up as the gold standard of evaluation methodologies in the crime prevention field – is the experimental model, especially the use of randomised control trials (Welsh & Farrington 2011, 2012a, 2012b). Experimental methods involve the random allocation of people (i.e. members of the target population) to treatment and control groups, and comparing the two in relation to program outcomes pre and post the intervention period (Welsh & Farrington 2001). The treatment group receives the intervention, while the control group does not, and due to the two groups being formed randomly it reduces threats to what is termed internal validity (e.g. groups have not self-selected into the treatment or control group and both groups represent the same population, do not differ greatly and receive the same amount of testing). Thus, any substantive difference between the treatment and control groups can confidently be attached to the specific intervention, since this is the only thing that has changed between the two groups (Pawson 2006; Welsh & Farrington 2001). An example of an experimental evaluation to examine the impact of the Big Brothers, Big Sisters program in the US is described in Case study 5.1.

CASE STUDY 5.1   EXAMPLE OF AN EXPERIMENTAL EVALUATION

- Big Brothers, Big Sisters (BBBS) is a mentoring program provided to young people from disadvantaged, single-parent homes. It aims to influence the behaviour and attitudes of children regarded as 'at risk' of delinquency through exposure to pro-social role models (i.e. BBBS volunteers).
- Youth were randomly assigned to either a treatment or control group. Those youth included in the program were aged 10–16. Eight agencies were involved in the evaluation. The control group was placed on a waiting list for the duration of the study. Over a 17-month period 1138 youths from eight agencies were enrolled in the study. Information was collected from youths, parents and case managers at three points in time: at the time of random assignment, at the time youths were matched with a volunteer and during a follow-up period. Comparisons were then made between the control group and those who participated in the BBBS program.

(Source: from Tierney, Grossman & Resch 1995)

The experimental method is based on the medical model with its emphasis on treatment and control groups (in medical research, control groups would receive the placebo). Such methods of evaluation can be difficult (but not impossible) to employ in crime prevention contexts, given this involves dealing with human behaviour, which, outside a laboratory setting, can be highly unpredictable and difficult to control. Also, random allocation raises ethical dilemmas and objections, especially when a group of people is placed at a disadvantage because they are not receiving assistance arising from the intervention (Posavac & Carey 1997). Eck (2002b) argues that while experimental methods may be appropriate for social prevention programs when the focus is a particular population, random allocation of control and comparison groups is more difficult to employ when programs focus on specific settings or physical locations, such as situational crime prevention (SCP) and CPTED. Similar arguments have been presented in relation to the adoption of randomised control trials in the area of problem-oriented policing, which also tends to be place-based (Eck 2002b; Knutsson 2009; Tilley 2010). However, other scholars have argued the use of experimental methods should be a mandatory component of any crime policy, being used to improve the standard of evaluation research in the field of crime prevention (Braga 2010; Welsh & Farrington 2012a, 2012b). It needs to be recognised, though, that in some contexts such methods may be difficult to adopt because of insufficient cases being available for random assignment or because resources may be lacking to fund an experimental design (Eck 2002b, 2005; Nagin 2001). Hence, other evaluation designs may have to be adopted.

Quasi-experimental designs

Similar to experimental designs, quasi-experimental evaluations utilise treatment and comparison groups. However, the selection of these groups is not done randomly; rather treatment and control groups are chosen that match each other on the basis of similar characteristics. For example, the evaluation of improved street lighting outlined in Case study 5.2 used a quasi-experimental design that involved two similar geographical locations – one in which street lighting was implemented in a public housing estate, the other in which no street lighting was installed – and outcomes compared in relation to crime and fear of crime. These two areas were not chosen randomly but simply selected because they had similar characteristics. Hence, there is always the possibility that differences can exist between the control and intervention groups. This can call into question whether program outcomes resulted from the intervention or occurred because of treatment and control group variations (e.g. in age, socio-economic status or family support). Such possibilities threaten the validity of results arising from a quasi-experimental design. It is recommended that efforts should be made to match as closely as possible the control and intervention groups to minimise

CASE STUDY 5.2   EXAMPLE OF A QUASI-EXPERIMENTAL EVALUATION

- The aim of this evaluation was to assess the impact of improved street lighting on crime and fear of crime.
- Two adjacent public housing estates were used as treatment and control areas.
- The evaluation assessed before and after measures of crime and fear of crime in the public housing estate that received improved street lighting (treatment area), and the public housing estate that was not subject to improvements (control area).

(Source: Painter & Farrington 1997)

such problems and that outcome measures (e.g. rates of offending, truancy and vandalism) should be taken well before the intervention occurs and for some time after (Posavac & Carey 1997).

When it comes to highly location-specific interventions, quasi-experimental methods may be more appropriate because it can be far easier to match geographical locations and divide them into treatment and control groups compared to when an intervention involves a particular population or at-risk group (e.g. young people). Also, quasi-experimental designs are far less unobtrusive than experimental designs and can rely on data routinely collected by agencies (Eck 2005). Furthermore, they can be more easily integrated into mainstream evaluation procedures because, unlike experimental methods (which necessitate close monitoring to maintain high levels of internal validity), they do not require extreme levels of administrative oversight and control.

Non-experimental method

Unlike experimental and quasi-experimental methodologies, a non-experimental design does not use random allocation or comparison groups. It is the simplest form of evaluation and involves taking pre-test and post-test measures of program objectives, such as assessing if crime was reduced following the intervention, or if the behaviour or life circumstances of the target group was improved while being served by the program. Such methods of evaluation are regarded as quite weak, because one cannot be certain any recorded change was the direct result of the intervention. This is because comparison data from a similar group or area is not relied on to identify that any observed change only occurred in the problem location or target group, and hence can be attributed simply to the intervention.

This does not mean that non-experimental methods are not without merit. While they lack strong internal validity they can still have strong external validity, an issue discussed further below. They are easy to employ and offer a quick and straightforward method of evaluation, which can be an advantage for local practitioners who are time-poor and have many competing priorities. When it comes to comprehensive community-based initiatives implemented nationwide, before and after measures may be the most realistic strategy, particularly when it comes to assessing the long-term impact of a policy through longitudinal data (Connell et al. 1995; Eck 2005; Posavac & Carey 1997). While not as rigorous as the evaluation methodologies outlined above, non-experimental methods are better to conduct than no evaluation at all. Case study 5.3 describes a non-experimental evaluation of a bully prevention campaign in Norway.

CASE STUDY 5.3   EXAMPLE OF A NON-EXPERIMENTAL EVALUATION

NORWEGIAN BULLYING PREVENTION PROGRAM: NATIONWIDE CAMPAIGN

- Four cohorts of students were followed over two-and-a-half years (500 and 700 students in each cohort).
- Data was collected on the frequency that students were bullied or bullied other students, student attitudes towards bullying and teacher responses to bullying incidents, levels of bullying problems in schools, and teacher ratings on the extent of bullying behaviour in class.
- This data was collected four months prior to the program, twice during its implementation and twice after schools had completed the program.

(Source: Olweus 1993)

Systematic reviews

Systematic reviews are a form of outcome evaluation; however, they do not involve researchers or academics immersing themselves in a primary (real time) evaluation that requires coordination and management of an evaluation plan. Rather, they are a form of secondary analysis of existing evaluation studies and involve two key methods: *meta-analysis* and *narrative reviews*.

Meta-analysis has become quite popular in the crime prevention field through the work of the Campbell Collaboration Crime and Justice group and many of its high-profile proponents (Farrington, Weisburd & Gill 2011). As Pawson states, these forms of systematic reviews:

> focus on the 'does it work question' ... about a particular class of interventions, collecting data only from reputable primary studies on their effects, and then reaching a statistical verdict on whether, on balance, they indeed work. (Pawson 2006, p. 39)

Meta-analysis examines a particular program family (e.g. this could be hot-spot policing, place-based crime prevention, juvenile awareness schemes or street-level drug law enforcement). It synthesises existing evaluation findings of the tactics that constitute these particular approaches to crime prevention (e.g. police crackdowns, SCP, offender treatment programs or police problem-oriented projects) and calculates the relative impact of each particular technique (e.g. see Bennett, Holloway & Farrington 2006; Weisburd, Groff & Yang 2012; Mazerolle, Soole & Rombouts 2006; Petrosino, Petrosino & Buehler 2003; Koehler et al. 2013). By comparing the mean effects achieved by each subtype within an overall program family, the most effective techniques can be identified. Meta-analysis therefore is seen as providing a straightforward indication of the 'best buy in' for policy makers and practitioners (Pawson 2006). A key part of meta-analysis involves the utilisation of particular statistical techniques that allow one to compare studies that employ different sample sizes, so meaningful conclusions can be drawn (Wilson 2001).

Meta-analysis is only as good as the primary evaluations utilised in the review; hence particular criteria have been formulated to outline the types of evaluation designs that should be included in a systematic review of this kind. The well-known Sherman report (see Sherman et al. 2006) utilised a scientific rating score to stipulate the rigour of the evaluation studies used in that particular systematic review. Those rated as 'gold standard' used random allocation to treatment and control groups. Welsh and Farrington (2012a, 2012b) state that, at a minimum, only studies that involve before and after measures of crime in treatment and control areas should be included in systematic reviews. Studies completed by the Campbell Collaboration have a strict exclusion criterion to eliminate weak studies that rely on, for example, non-experimental methods. Hence experimental designs are typically seen as the most valid studies to include in a meta-analysis (Welsh & Farrington 2001). Case study 5.4 describes meta-analysis carried out on Scared Straight and juvenile awareness strategies (Petrosino, Petrosino & Buehler 2003). The implications of the study's findings are elaborated on in the next section.

CASE STUDY 5.4   META-ANALYSIS OF SCARED STRAIGHT

- Scared Straight and juvenile awareness programs involve identifying children regarded as at risk of future offending and taking these children on organised visits to correctional institutions. This provides firsthand observations of prison life and in some contexts firsthand accounts from prisoners. The assumption is that by exposing children to such realistic experience, it will deter them from future offending behaviour by providing them with a key motivational reason to change current and future delinquent behaviour, because it shows 'what could happen to them'.

- Only studies that involved juveniles (17 years of age or younger) or overlapping samples of juveniles and young adults (13–21), had prison visits as their main component, included outcomes of subsequent offending, had some level of random assignment and had a no-treatment control group, were included in this review.
- The overall conclusion was that Scared Straight programs fail to deter crime and can actually lead to more offending behaviour.

The overall objective of narrative reviews is similar to that of meta-analysis. However, they differ in relation to the type of data extracted from the primary studies, the 'quality' of studies drawn on and the comparisons made between the different types of interventions (Pawson 2002). Narrative reviews are more descriptive and can form part of a meta-analysis, especially if there are few rigorous evaluation studies to include in the final meta review. They aim to describe program aims, components and processes (e.g. strategy implementation) and the full gamut of outcomes achieved. However, they do not employ the statistical methods adopted in a meta-analysis. Narrative reviews can offer a good overview of particular crime prevention approaches and indicate what may constitute exemplary programs. Also, given they focus on program processes and describe the components that constitute a strategy, narrative reviews can provide insight into the relative effectiveness of a particular program configuration. However, they can be criticised as overly descriptive and lacking in rigour (Welsh & Farrington 2001).

As they are concerned with program descriptions, recommendations arising from narrative reviews about exemplary programs can oversimplify the complexity of particular program processes by failing to highlight problems associated with schemes replicating in another context. For narrative reviews to be useful they need to stipulate program theory, which is important in helping to establish a theory of generalisation. This can help inform policy decisions by providing insight into the preventative mechanisms that a particular crime prevention strategy or approach aims to trigger. This not only helps policy makers understand how a particular crime problem can be reduced (i.e. the tactics involved in reducing the problem) but also why a particular intervention will reduce the problem. When this information is coupled with empirical evidence about program effectiveness, then policy makers are in a far better position to make grounded decisions about the viability of adopting a particular crime prevention approach.

Cost-benefit analysis

As outlined in chapter 3 on social prevention, one of the great successes of the Perry Preschool Project has been to persuasively show that the program achieved monetary savings in relation to criminal justice and welfare expenditures (see Manning, Homel and Smith 2006 as these issues relate to the Pathways to Prevention program in Australia). Examining the outcomes of crime prevention programs in relation to their monetary costs and benefits has generated increasing attention among academics and governments in Australia and abroad (Australian Institute of Criminology 2003; Dhiri and Brand 1999; Farrell, Bowers & Johnson 2005; Manning, Homel & Smith 2006; Welsh, Farrington & Sherman 2001).

There are different ways of assessing the cost and benefits of crime prevention programs (see Australian Institute of Criminology 2003; Welsh & Farrington 2000) with a key aim to measure the savings (either in monetary values or harms reduced) accrued from the implementation of a particular crime prevention approach. Cost-benefit analysis examines whether the effects produced by a crime prevention program (e.g. reductions in crime) exceed the resources spent on the program (Welsh & Farrington 2000); that is, whether savings incurred by an intervention outweighed the actual costs of program inputs.

For example, assume that police want to know whether the financial benefits of a burglary prevention project involving 'target hardening' outweighed the costs of its implementation. They might estimate that the average financial impact of burglary is $400 per 100 households. This takes into account the average value of goods stolen and police personnel costs relating to investigating the burglaries. However, it may cost $800 per 100 households to target harden houses (i.e. to install window locks, security doors, grilles and alarms). So, for every dollar spent on implementing the intervention the police are losing $2, which is a 100 per cent loss. It costs double to implement the program compared to any savings that might be achieved if burglary was prevented. Hence the cost-benefit achieved from this program would be poor.

This is a hypothetical example used for illustrative purposes. In fact it is unlikely that the financial impact of burglary would be only $400 per 100 households. Many studies have shown significant cost-benefits from situation and social approaches, such as early intervention and target-hardening (Manning, Homel & Smith 2006; Welsh & Farrington 1999; Welsh 2012). Nevertheless this example illustrates a key dilemma associated with measuring the benefits of crime prevention; that is, that while there may seem to be an obvious need for a particular intervention, and it may appear far more rational than criminal justice reactions, it may not be cost-efficient. As discussed below, conclusions about the cost-benefit of crime prevention can be strongly influenced by the narrowness or broadness of the parameters set for a cost-benefit analysis.

One key criticism of cost-benefit analysis is that despite its claims to be an objective assessment of crime prevention programs, such claims are highly suspect because assigning a monetary value to costs and benefits can be an inherently subjective undertaking. Haggerty's (2007, p. 86) criticism of the 'crime science' movement, which includes cost-benefit analysis as a key component, argues that any decision about the costs of anti-crime measures is inherently 'contingent on a host of ultimately contestable decisions about what costs should be included and how those items should be valued'. This in particular relates to estimating more intangible costs, such as the value placed on a victim's pain and suffering, or costs associated with the vicarious impact of crime through increased fear of crime.

While attempts have been made to prescribe formulas by which to estimate costs and benefits (see Farrell, Bowers & Johnson 2005), the significance of the parameters chosen to measure costs and benefits should not be underestimated. Nagin (2001) makes the point that the unit of analysis (i.e. individuals, society or government) adopted by a cost-benefit or cost-effective analysis of early intervention programs will have an impact on the results. Awareness of this is particularly important if supporters of early intervention wish to support its attractiveness over criminal sanctions. Nagin (2001) states that when early intervention is compared to criminal sanctions, some developmental programs are not seen as cost-effective alternatives. However, given that developmental prevention aims to achieve wide-ranging effects, its benefits should not be framed in narrow terms relating to reducing criminality. Nor do its benefits relate only to fiscal impacts.

Nagin (2001) suggests that in measuring the benefits of developmental prevention, assessments should include whether programs have influenced the decisions parents make about raising their children and their preferences to make investments in their own and other children. The same could apply to measuring the benefits of situational measures in relation to influencing people's willingness to invest in opportunity reduction. Evaluating the effectiveness of crime prevention needs to involve assessments of whether people recognise and accept that 'embedded' social and environmental initiatives have utility. This can be reflected in the preferences they make about such interventions, and if they should be supported either in the context of their own choices and actions or those of governments. These are broader benefits that have worth beyond any monetary value.

Caution needs to be adopted in making decisions about criteria for a cost-benefit analysis, because the potential danger is that by increasing the number of benefits accrued by a program, the more likely the chance that it will be shown to produce a return than a loss (Welsh & Farrington 2001). While this might be regarded as a good outcome and a sensible strategic decision to persuade political sponsors of the benefits of crime prevention, it can oversell a particular approach or exaggerate its effectiveness.

It is important that any attempt to measure the costs and benefits of crime prevention should be guided by an explicit framework. We would argue that such frameworks cannot be based solely on economic objectives, but also criteria about the social desirability of crime prevention and normative perspectives on what crime prevention achieves politically.

Process evaluation

As indicated, the process of implementation is central to achieving program outcomes and dictates whether a strategy will succeed or fail. Hence when it comes to evaluating crime prevention programs we cannot simply be concerned with measuring whether an initiative reduced crime, but also how it was implemented in order to understand why it did or did not work. The task of process evaluation is concerned with examining strategy implementation. Rather than focusing on outcomes, a process evaluation looks at the underlying mechanisms that drove the implementation of a strategy and assesses whether they hindered or facilitated its delivery. A process evaluation may focus on a broad range of factors relating to the roles of different agencies within a scheme, the decision-making processes underpinning policy formation and barriers encountered during strategy delivery. The types of questions that can inform a process evaluation are listed in Box 5.2. This is not a definitive list and answering any one of them can raise even more questions and issues.

BOX 5.2:   ISSUES TO CONSIDER

- Was counselling being provided to target groups?
- Were burgled houses target hardened?
- Were young people at risk referred into the program?
- Was information being provided?
- Did target groups attend educational classes?
- Were parents following the advice of healthcare workers?
- Was data being shared between partners?
- Did practitioners follow advice relating to best-practice?
- Did all partnership agencies fulfil their commitment to a strategy?
- Was there adequate funding to support the delivery of the strategy?
- Was technical support in place to assist with strategy planning?
- Was there political support for a strategy at central and local levels?

The importance of ensuring that crime prevention reviews include an assessment of the process of implementation cannot be overestimated. An outcome evaluation may find that a particular intervention did not achieve its objectives and hence deem it ineffective. However this does not mean that the intervention's underlying theory or aims were misplaced. Rather, this lack of success may reflect the fact that the program was not implemented properly. A number of studies in the crime prevention and community safety field have highlighted how implementation failure can confound program outcomes (e.g. Berman & Fox 2010; Braga, Hureau & Winship 2008; Homel & Homel 2012).

A number of criminologists have acknowledged the need for a more systematic knowledge base about the process of implementation (Homel 2005; Homel & Homel 2012; Laycock 2006; Tilley 2006). One reason for this is that implementation failure is a universal and constant problem that plagues crime prevention policy and practice internationally (Homel 2006; Homel & Homel 2012). The evaluation of implementation should not simply be concerned narrowly with logistical or managerial issues relating to whether key outputs of a strategy were delivered. It also needs to consider the broader political context in which the strategy is being implemented.

A number of studies have demonstrated that political factors are often more important in accounting for implementation failure than mere incompetence on the part of prevention practitioners or program personnel (Crawford 1997; Hough 2006; Homel & Homel 2012). For example, Cherney's (2004b) review of the implementation of the Victorian Safer Cities and Shires strategy found that the program began to flounder in its implementation because the broader political support for the scheme at the state level was withdrawn. This had a ripple effect down to the local level, where agencies also began to prevaricate about commitment to local community safety partnerships.

Various research methodologies can be employed when conducting a process evaluation. Quantitative and qualitative approaches can be used, ranging from surveys and focus groups involving program participants about their involvement in a scheme, the use of checklists that quantify the number of outputs, interviews with policy officers responsible for managing a program, participant observation of program staff, documentation reviews of strategy plans, and analysis of written minutes arising from crime prevention committees and partnerships. A popular method is that of conducting interviews with key informants (such as policy officers, program staff and local practitioners) about obstacles faced in translating policy into practical action. These key informants are the most familiar with the program in question and the contexts in which it operated, and hence are in an advantageous position to know why a program took the particular form it did, how well it was managed, what problems were encountered in implementation and what the strategy actually achieved.

Such methods do run the risk of being criticised as inherently subjective in nature, given they rely on the interpretive accounts and judgments of policy makers, program personnel, stakeholders or target groups, who may be reluctant to admit that a strategy did not go to plan. With such methods, sample size does matter; in the sense that it is important that the perspectives of various crime prevention personnel at state and local levels are canvassed as broadly as possible so any assessments can be cross-validated. Besides such qualitative approaches major advancements have been made in the use of quantitative methods for measuring implementation (e.g. Fagan et al. 2009; Payne & Eckert 2010), with there emerging what has been termed a 'science of implementation', which is concerned with understanding the dynamics of program delivery and how various contextual factors impact on this process (Flaspoher et al. 2008; Homel & Homel 2012).

Developing an evidence base

One of the key objectives of evaluation is to develop an evidence base that can inform policy developments. This relates both to guiding the design of current and future crime prevention programs and to assisting decisions about which crime prevention approaches are worth replicating. As outlined earlier in this chapter, there has been intense debate about the types of methodologies that should inform an evidence-based approach to crime prevention. Some criminologists prefer the use of randomised control trials and systematic reviews, while others advocate alternative methods, such as 'realist' frameworks concerned with stipulating the context, mechanism and outcome configurations that constitute a particular program (Laycock 2002; Tilley 2006; Lum & Yang 2005; Pawson & Tilley 1997; Farrington & Petrosino 2001). The former is concerned with developing a body of evidence premised on scientifically valid observations of tested programs that have consistently shown powerful net effects, while the latter is more concerned with developing a body of knowledge about causal explanations that help explain why a program worked.

Evaluation methodologies (such as randomised control trials) are one of the best ways to control for any selection bias resulting from the allocation of control and treatment groups, and help to rule out possible alternative explanations for how outcomes were achieved. They are not the only valid evaluation methodology that can inform an evidence-based approach to crime prevention. We raise this because in the design and replication of crime prevention programs, experimental methods may not always provide the types of insights and answers that policy makers or practitioners need or desire (Laycock 2002; Tilley 2010).

Within the crime prevention field there can be few opportunities to conduct randomised control experiments (Eck 2006; Laycock 2002). This is due to such practical reasons as resource constraints, program timelines, skill deficits, pressure on evaluators from program sponsors to produce quick results, ethical concerns, problems in accessing data and random allocation of control and treatment groups. Criminologists often have to choose 'weaker' forms of evaluation (for example, quasi-experimental designs and over-randomised control trials) due to such pragmatic reasons (Lum & Yang 2005). This is not to deny the fact that randomised control trials can be one of the best ways of testing novel or new interventions and can help to encourage innovation by promoting experimentation (see Sherman & Strang 2004; Sherman 2011). They are also becoming more widely adopted across different fields of crime prevention (Welsh & Farrington 2012b). However despite their scientific rigour, criminologists, policy makers and practitioners need to be mindful of the limitations of using randomised control trials to inform policy and practice (Hough 2011).

For instance, while having high levels of internal validity, randomised control trials can have low levels of external validity; that is, their results may not be highly generalisable. As pointed out by Eck (2002b), Ekblom (2010) and Hough (2011), the strict controls imposed in an experimental evaluation that aims to control for any intervening variables (i.e. variables that threaten the internal validity of the evaluation) may not reflect what occurs in everyday practice, and hence can be far removed from the pressures and constraints practitioners face. Replication helps to build the validity of results that have been achieved through randomised control trials. For their results to be transferable across contexts, however, other agencies have to implement them in exactly the same way. Under normal practical conditions and circumstances, this may be unrealistic (Eck 2006; Ekblom 2010). The issue of replication is discussed further below.

As Ekblom (2002, 2010) argues, rather than seeing intervening variables as nuisances that need to be controlled for, they should be seen as part of the game of real-world evaluation, with evaluation methods needing to uncover the various types of intervening variables that influence the success and failure of crime prevention strategies. This relates to understanding how particular conditions in which programs are implemented influence program outcomes. Such conditions include understanding the unique nature of the crime problem being addressed, as well as the central and local capacity to address the problem; and the organisational, political, economic, social and geographical contexts in which a program operates. Such contexts influence how the theory underpinning a particular intervention is translated into practical action. Goodnow (2006), in reference to developmental crime prevention, makes clear that social contexts (such as those that provide particular pathways and routes out of crime) have a direct bearing on the forms of prevention that should be adopted. Understanding these factors helps researchers and policy makers identify conditions relevant to selecting particular interventions and that influence the successful implementation of those interventions.

A number of researchers have argued that alternative forms of evaluation such as non-experimental designs or case studies can be far better at uncovering the types of contextual conditions that impact on program outcomes (Eck 2006; George & Bennett 2005; Ekblom 2002). Even Cook and Campbell (1979), early practitioners and doyens of experimental designs, recognised the need for flexible and varied techniques involving both quantitative and qualitative approaches to policy evaluation.

The limitation of evidence produced via randomised control trials also applies to systematic reviews, particularly the use of meta-evaluations to provide guidance for policy making (Pawson 2006). The core of these concerns relates to the fact that meta-analysis, using aggregated results from various studies to calculate a particular effect size (i.e. the magnitude of the increase or decrease in crime achieved), ignores the contexts and mechanisms that underpin program outcomes. That is, while meta-analysis might make a statistically meaningful calculation about the effectiveness of a certain crime prevention technique, it provides little insight into how and under what conditions a particular intervention subclass was implemented. Meta-analysis only provides insight into one aspect of effectiveness relevant to policy decision-making, and leaves policy makers and practitioners in the dark about whether the particular intervention under review is relevant to the nature of their crime problem, or the context in which they have to implement the intervention.

This is not to say that systematic reviews do not provide useful insights into the overall outcomes of a particular crime prevention approach. They rely on a series of studies rather than simply drawing conclusions from the results of a single study – which on their own may not be valid – but when aggregated with other similar studies can provide a strong indicator of an intervention's overall impact. A number of meta-analyses have also indicated that crime prevention can have a differential impact across target groups and contexts (Cherney 2009; see Welsh and Farrington 2004 as it pertains to the differential impact of street lighting and CCTV in London and the US). Also, meta-analytical reviews have provided potent ammunition for questioning the effectiveness of particular crime prevention programs that are politically popular, but whose overall efficacy remains questionable, such as Petrosino, Petrosino and Buehler's (2003) study of Scared Straight programs outlined in Case study 5.4. The results of such systematic reviews illustrate the inherently subjective and political nature of crime prevention evaluation, because despite negative – and, in the context of Scared Straight programs, detrimental – outcomes being identified for target groups (that they led to more offending behaviour), results can be ignored, questioned and resisted by agencies and politicians.

While it is problematic to rely on the results of a single case (i.e. the outcomes of one particular program) when deciding whether to implement a particular crime prevention approach, single case studies can provide important insights. Descriptive case studies can illustrate how different jurisdictions have addressed particular crime problems and help in the development of new ideas and responses (Yin 2003).

Case study evaluation involves the analysis of an individual program or policy to identify the ways different variables impacted on and determined program outcomes. Tracing or mapping the links between variables can identify why particular outcomes resulted under certain conditions, and how the theoretical assumptions underpinning a strategy were achieved in practice (George & Bennett 2005; Yin 2003). This includes examining factors relating to levels of cooperation between partner agencies, the skills and capacity of program personnel, and the quality of planning underpinning a strategy.

Other issues assessed could include the receptiveness of target groups to changing behaviour or the levels of support from central government (such as capacity building assistance relating to training, the provision of data, and leadership that generates agency and community support for a strategy). Stipulating whether such variables are present can provide useful knowledge for practitioners wishing to adopt a similar intervention (Ekblom 2010; George & Bennett 2005; Pawson 2006; Yin 2003). Eck (2006) states that the use of case studies in crime prevention process evaluations would improve the quality of knowledge derived from such assessments.

Measuring successful outcomes is only one part of the equation in promoting an evidence-based approach. Once strategies have been evaluated the next question is, how best-practice can be replicated and mainstreamed more broadly. This is a challenging task because there are problems in abstracting successful strategies from their original context and translating them to other settings (Cherney 2009; Ekblom 2010). Successful mainstreaming demands systems of change management that ensure the necessary processes are in place to adjust relevant policies and practices required when a new policy or program is adopted (Cherney 2009; Cherney & Head 2011; Homel & Homel 2012). This necessitates efforts to identify conditions that made the original program or policy successful. This is why we have advocated the use of dynamic and flexible forms of evaluation discussed above, which can help uncover such factors. Replication also demands investigation of whether the same conditions exist in the replication site. Ekblom states that:

> if a certain intervention needs, to make it work, the context of good community structures in terms of mutually-supportive relations between neighbours, then part of the ground work of any replication would involve trying to establish these conditions, for example, by setting up residents' associations. (Ekblom 2002, p. 161)

Various questions that need to be asked by policy makers and practitioners when replicating a particular crime prevention strategy are outlined in Box 5.3.

BOX 5.3:   QUESTIONS TO HELP INFORM DECISIONS

- In what context was the original program implemented? For example, was it an area characterised by low socio-economic status or a particular housing type?
- What was implemented? Was it target hardening or family support? What features of these approaches were adopted?
- Has any form of evaluation been done; for example, impact or process evaluation that can inform decision-making about whether to adopt the program?
- What causes (proximate/distal) did the intervention aim to affect? For example, did the program address crime opportunities or particular risk factors, or did it look at both social and situational factors?
- What factors appeared to ensure the success/failure of the original strategy? Were there functional partnerships, did partners follow through on commitments, was there ongoing funding, was there a dedicated coordinator, and was there stability in the program staff?
- Do any of the conditions/factors identified above exist in the replication site? For example, is the cause of the crime problem the same and is there the same level of ongoing funding?
- Do any features of the original program need to be modified or additional components added to accommodate differences in context between the original program and the replication site?

Building capacity for implementation and evaluation

Sherman (2006) argues that many of the most successful demonstrations of effective crime prevention programs have involved close collaborative partnerships between researchers and practitioners, in which researchers have played a major role in both program development and evaluation (also see Homel and Homel 2012). The Queensland Pathways project that has pioneered developmental crime prevention in Australia involves a close working partnership between criminologists and key service providers in the design, implementation and evaluation of the Pathways Project (Homel et al. 2006a; also see chapter 3). Evidence indicates that crime prevention programs are more likely to be effective when they involve evaluators in the development of the program. Examples from the UK (Matassa & Newburn 2003) and the US (Braga, McDevitt & Pierce 2006; Petrosino & Soydan 2005) indicate that enhanced outcomes can be achieved in comparison to the more traditional model of having a clear separation between the evaluator and program participants (Sherman 2006).

What this points to is the important role that collaborations between criminologists and state and local agencies can play in enhancing the quality of evaluation research and also the process of strategy development and delivery (Cherney 2009; Nutley, Walter & Daves 2007). Assessments of the UK Crime Reduction Programme indicate that when such 'productive interactions' are absent it can undermine successful program development (see Homel et al. 2004; Nutley & Homel 2006). Under the UK program, the Home Office awarded project evaluations to external contractors, with evaluation teams directed not to interact with any project teams. This maintained their independence and ensured project outcomes were not contaminated by any assistance provided by the evaluators. However, as highlighted by Nutley and Homel (2006), evaluators often had information and data that could help stakeholders refine their implementation plans, but were constrained in their capacity to directly assist projects because of the emphasis placed on the traditional arm's length evaluation by the Home Office. Hence many opportunities to improve program outcomes were lost.

Adopting a model of developer/evaluator collaboration described above is essential to local capacity building because it promotes within program learning (Sherman 2006; Nutley & Homel 2006; Nutley, Walter & Davis 2007). This facilitates a more evidence-based approach. It ensures that assessment becomes an institutionalised part of crime prevention planning, which provides opportunities for key lessons to be fed back into the ongoing process of implementation, which then allows strategy adjustments to be made. For this to be successful, though, processes need to be in place to ensure sufficient feedback is provided to project personnel in a timely and usable form (Nutley & Homel 2006; Laycock 2002; Tilley 2006). In this regard central agencies can play a key role.

Building capacity around implementation and evaluation is perhaps one of the most important roles that central agencies can play. This is particularly critical if central policy units want to increase the success rate of their crime prevention strategies. Skill development around implementation and evaluation can help local practitioners as well as the development of 'tool kits' that assist in problem diagnosis (e.g. see Ekblom 2010; White & Coventry 2000). One of the most helpful capacity-building functions that central policy unit 'experts' can undertake is to connect local and regional project teams who may be tackling similar crime problems, and who can share experience and pool knowledge.

Such knowledge can encompass not just specific crime reduction techniques, but the best ways to go about developing and implementing a crime prevention plan.

Practitioner networks can promote cultures of learning by promoting reflection through the process of lesson learning and the exchange of experience (Fung 2004; Nutley, Walter & Daves 2007). They can help to spread knowledge about successes and failures experienced when trialling different approaches and techniques in the context, for example, of a local crime prevention plan. Tapping such practitioner knowledge is important to expanding the knowledge base on how contingencies are addressed at the level of strategy implementation (Cherney 2004a; Coote, Allen & Woodhead 2004; Ekblom 2010; Tilley 2006). Both developer/evaluator collaborations and efforts to promote active lesson learning networks help to expand the 'toolkit' that central and local practitioners can draw on when developing crime prevention initiatives.

Tapping the political

One of the principal aims of the discussion above has been to outline many of the 'political' variables that impinge on the implementation and evaluation of crime prevention strategies. Uncovering such contingencies is important in the crime prevention field, given that so much crime prevention policy relies on some type of collaboration between agencies, whether at the state level through whole-of-government processes, or, more locally, through community safety partnerships. As indicated, when crime prevention policy draws on multiple partners problems do occur.

However, as we have argued, crime prevention's political element includes attempts to shift both the opinions and the actions of individuals, communities and governments away from 'law and order' to more inclusive responses to crime, changing social norms about crime control. Measuring the symbolic element of crime prevention is critical, because simply proving that crime prevention is more technically efficient than 'law and order' will not suffice to demonstrate its utility as a viable, alternative paradigm by which to frame crime control (Cherney 2002; Ekblom 2002, 2010; Freiberg 2001; Sutton 1997). As Laub (2004, p. 18) states, 'most policy issues are moral questions that cannot be answered by theory or for that matter by research ... the idea that scholarly knowledge and this knowledge alone should determine policy outcomes is naïve'. When it comes to developing crime prevention programs Ekblom (2010) argues that crime prevention experts ignore the symbolic element of crime prevention at their peril.

Responses to crime have an affective and emotional element that communicates particular messages about social cohesion (Freiberg 2001). Understanding how crime prevention taps into these elements is essential to evaluating its effectiveness because of the ways they determine broader support for particular crime control responses. These have a direct impact on the 'political' sustainability of strategies. Cherney (2002) outlines how many aspects of crime prevention have important symbolic dimensions. The proposal of strengthening protective factors within the context of early intervention resonates strongly with the ideal of investing in children and child-friendly institutions. Many forms of crime prevention aim to create more civil and secure environments through investing in neighbourhoods, family, schools, voluntary associations, sporting clubs and churches. The ideal is to create a sense of wellbeing and security, promoting values of connectedness and a sense of belonging. Rather than communicating the message that something has to be done to a person – as is evident in 'get tough' approaches – social prevention and environmental prevention requires that we do something for a person or community. All the above emphasise support, integration and protecting the most vulnerable.

The problem is that despite the communicative elements that underpin many crime prevention approaches, politicians focus expenditure on 'law and order', such as 'three strikes' (which involves the mandatory sentencing of an offender who has been found guilty of an offence on three or more occasions), due to popular demand for such 'get tough' policies. However, the attention given to punitive responses has actually contributed to this distorted view (Bishop 2006) and overshadowed many social benefits arising from investment in crime prevention.

In fact, research on the preferences of the public towards punitive compared to non-punitive crime control indicates the public are very supportive of the latter and recognise the benefits of crime prevention over punishment, particularly when it comes to addressing juvenile delinquency and recognising the benefits of early intervention (Cohen, Roland & Steen 2006; Cullen et al. 2007; Nagin et al. 2006; Piquero et al. 2010). This research is not limited to public opinion surveys, but has included examining the expenditure preferences the public makes between alternative responses to crime. Cohen, Roland and Steen (2006) found that when given options on how tax dollars should be spent on criminal justice, public preferences are towards prevention and drug treatment over prison (also see Cullen et al. 2007 as it relates to early intervention). Such research calls into question the popular support for punitive interventions and indicates that public support for crime prevention may be more widespread than assumed.

A key aim of developing and evaluating crime prevention programs should be to gauge support for crime prevention through qualitative and quantitative research methods, not only as it pertains to broad public support but also gauging whether people favour particular crime prevention approaches. As outlined by Ekblom (2010), policy makers and practitioners need to understand how to reconcile both the practical, rational elements of crime prevention as well as its symbolic and value-based dimension of ethics and justice. The success of crime prevention strategies is reliant on satisfying both aspects.

Apart from examining whether programs have been effective in shifting public attitudes towards offending and social control, crime prevention's political dimension also extends to examining whether the preferences of target groups have also been transformed. In the context of developmental prevention, France and Homel (2006) state that such programs need to examine the changed attitudes among individuals towards likely pathways into and out of crime. This requires integrating the voices of young people into the planning of developmental strategies so researchers can understand how they interpret opportunities provided by such interventions (France & Homel 2006). Such recommendations involve a political commitment to ensuring programs are inclusive of target group perceptions, which can actively shape program design and outcomes, rather than seeing such individuals as simply passive recipients of schemes.

Conclusion

The implementation and evaluation of crime prevention programs are complex tasks. Implementation requires a range of skills and knowledge and effective governance arrangements (i.e. partnerships). Given crime prevention programs are typically implemented through partnerships, agencies must be willing to collaborate and pool resources and expertise. Also, successful implementation requires leadership and support among key stakeholders and agencies involved in strategy delivery. Without such leadership or support crime prevention programs will founder.

A key message of this chapter is that when conducting evaluation we should not be inflexible or dogmatic about the types of evaluation methodologies that can best be employed to assess program outcomes. While particular types of evaluation methods are seen as superior (e.g. experimental designs), alternative forms of evaluation designs and approaches should not be dismissed as inadequate. In order to evaluate program outcomes and the implementation process, a mixed-methods approach to evaluation design is required. This also requires paying attention to the political, symbolic and affective dimensions of crime prevention. Understanding these broader parameters of evaluation will help improve the knowledge base on what works. This can only help to improve policy and practice.

CASE STUDY 5.5   EVALUATION AND PERFORMANCE MEASURES

Performance indicators are meant to examine progress made towards particular program goals (e.g., how far along are we in achieving what we set out to achieve?). **Performance targets**, on the other hand, refer to a specific end-point and relate to the particular outcomes that a program aims to achieve (e.g. reducing crime). In the context of developing both performance indicators and targets it is essential to identify both outputs and outcomes. This can include the components of a program that need to be implemented (outputs) and measures identifying whether or not progress is being made in relation to specific goals or outcomes (e.g. number of police arrests, number of ambulance call-outs). Measuring program performance can also involve a focus on:

Quantity
- measuring performance in terms of 'how many' and 'how often' (e.g. numbers of crimes reduced, frequency of delinquency).

Quality
- measuring performance in terms of 'how well' (e.g. opinions on program delivery, feedback from target groups).

Time frame
- measuring performance in terms of 'how long' (e.g. time taken to deliver a program, length of time to observe change in target groups).

Cost
- measuring performance in terms of 'how expensive' (e.g. money spent on a program, equipment purchased, costs of staff wages).

Resources
- measuring performance in terms of 'how much' and 'what was contributed by whom' (e.g. agency contributions, cash and in-kind contributions, use of volunteers, funding base).

Participation
- measuring performance in terms of 'who was involved' (e.g. members of target group, project organisers, funding agency, community residents).

(see also White 2013a).

QUESTIONS

Questions for further exploration

1. Consider the hypothetical scenario below and respond to the questions relating to the topic of implementation and evaluation:

Police data reveals that a particular street in your local area is subject to repeated break and enter. The houses are usually burgled during the day and items stolen include televisions, CD players, laptops and jewellery. Thieves force doors and windows open and witnesses report that they operate in pairs. The houses back onto parkland and none of the houses are fenced. The front yards of the houses are overgrown with grass and trees and neighbours report they do not know one another. The street is a mix of privately owned houses and rental properties.

- What type of crime prevention strategy would you put in place to address this problem?
- How would the strategy be implemented and by whom?
- What challenges/issues might you encounter when implementing your strategy?
- How would you evaluate the initiative?

2. When conducting an outcome evaluation of a situational or social crime prevention scheme what types of data would you need to collect and what outcomes would you consider?

3. Complete a search on the internet for a particular situational or social crime prevention program. If it has been subject to an evaluation examine how that evaluation could have been improved. If the program has not been evaluated, design an evaluation plan and outline what type of evaluation method (i.e. experiment, quasi-or non-experimental) should be adopted.

EXTENSION TOPICS AND REFERENCES

1. Consider the types of knowledge and skills relevant to designing and implementing crime prevention programs. How might these vary by particular crime problems?

References

Clancey, G., Lee, M. & Crofts, T. (2012) ' "We're not Batman" – roles and expectations of local government community safety officers in New South Wales', *Crime Prevention and Community Safety: An International Journal*, vol. 14, no. 4, pp. 235–257.

Ekblom, P. (2010) *Crime prevention, security and community safety using the 5Is framework*. Basingstoke: Palgrave Macmillan.

2. A number of problems plague the implementation of crime prevention programs. How might the implementation process in the field of crime prevention be improved?

Reference

Homel, R. & Homel, P. (2012) 'Implementing crime prevention: good governance and a science of implementation', in B. Welsh & D. Farrington (eds), *The Oxford handbook on crime prevention*. Oxford: Oxford University Press.

3. Randomised control trials (RCTs) are seen as the gold standard of evaluation research. What would need to occur for RCTs to be more widely adopted in the field of crime prevention?

Reference

Welsh, B.C. & Farrington, D.P. (2012) 'Science, politics and crime prevention: towards a new crime policy', *Journal of Criminal Justice*, vol. 40, no. 1, pp. 128–133.

PART

2

PRACTICE

6

FROM RESEARCH TO POLICY

Introduction

This chapter will discuss how crime prevention evolved in:

- France
- the Netherlands
- the UK
- Australia.

We also suggest ways in which crime prevention policy can be enhanced through:

- a shared vision
- local crime prevention plans.

Contemporary politicians and other policy makers talk about the 'rediscovery' of crime prevention. Such language is misleading. As chapters 2, 3 and 4 have shown, crime prevention has been around for a very long time. Concepts and principles of social and environmental prevention do not need to be rediscovered or reinvented. Like tool-making and speech, they are capacities that all humans can exercise, given the right conditions.

If anyone has forgotten about crime prevention, it is politicians and policy makers. To maintain and enhance their legitimacy, parties and their leaders need to be seen playing direct roles in protecting the public. Crime prevention, however, often works best when it is not so obvious: when it is subtly embedded in everyday routines and activities. Families, preschools, schools, sports clubs and vocational training centres all can contribute to the reduction of offending. Major prevention benefits also can flow from sound urban planning and environmental design, and from appropriate management of shopping centres, entertainment centres, malls and other facilities (see chapters 2 and 7). Again, there is no need for relevant practices always to carry the crime prevention label. Overemphasis on target hardening and other conspicuous security measures can merely intensify fear.

This helps explain why politicians in most late-modern democracies have tended to neglect crime prevention in favour of law and order. While more police and tougher penalties may not be the most cost-effective responses, they do bear a direct and obvious relationship to crime. At the symbolic level, they help governments articulate a simple and unequivocal political message: that they will act decisively to protect the public from offenders and other 'disruptive elements'.

Since the 1980s, however, governments in Western countries have begun to recognise that the politics of law and order also has difficulties. Recruiting more police and putting them 'on the beat', and building additional prisons to cope with offenders serving longer terms, involves major budget outlays at a time when business is demanding that governments try to reduce the tax burden to ensure that national and regional economies can be globally competitive. Some politicians on the left of the political spectrum have been concerned about the human costs associated with locking up more and more people from disadvantaged backgrounds. This in particular has been raised as a concern for Indigenous Australians who continue to be over-represented among those arrested and imprisoned (Weatherburn & Holmes 2010).

Faced with evidence that prevention 'works' and can be cost-effective, governments therefore have sought – albeit tentatively and intermittently – to develop strategies based on this theme. However, reintroducing prevention into official policy has not been easy. The problem is not just that prevention often works best when embedded in other social practices. By its very nature, this 'alternative' agenda also requires involvement from a much wider range of players than does law and order. Each group of participants will have their own values, interests, skills and priorities. In a federal system of government like Australia's, stakeholders also are likely to have differing and often conflicting lines of political and bureaucratic accountability. Persuading national, regional and local governments to endorse general statements about the need for a whole-of-government approach has been relatively straightforward. The real challenge has been finding ways to translate such 'in principle' agreement into strategies and programs that transcend political and administrative rivalries and engender genuine cooperation at the grassroots.

It is no accident, therefore, that the earliest and most ambitious attempts by late-modern democratic states to foster the development and implementation of national and regional crime prevention occurred in countries where systems of government are less complex than Australia's federal model. Examples include the so-called Bonnemaison program, implemented in France in the early 1980s, the Society and Crime strategy developed and implemented in the mid-1980s by the Netherlands' Ministry of Justice, and the Crime Reduction Programme in place in England and Wales from 1999 to 2002 (see also the Victorian Drugs and Crime Prevention Committee 2012 for an overview of these programs).

France: the role of politics and social inclusion

The Bonnemaison program derived its name from Gilbert Bonnemaison, chair of a national commission of enquiry into crime and ways to respond that was established by a new Socialist government shortly after it had been voted into power in France in May 1981. While in opposition, the Socialists had been critical of their predecessors' reliance on repressive 'law and order' policies. However, soon they were confronted with their own challenges. During the long summer vacation of 1981, Lyon and other major cities experienced extensive crime and disorder, including some rioting. Disadvantaged young people, including some teenagers from immigrant backgrounds, had resorted to various illegal activities including drag-racing in stolen cars, to 'keep themselves amused'. Violent clashes with police ensued (De Liege 1988).

Bonnemaison's committee comprised mayors of major towns and cities from throughout France as well as representatives of key national agencies. It had significant political influence. Bonnemaison himself, for example, was a Socialist deputy in the national parliament as well as being the mayor of a town near Paris. The committee's final report, *Confronting Crime: Prevention, Repression and Solidarity* (Bonnemaison 1983), built on ideas developed by previous expert groups but found ways to apply them in political and policy contexts.

The report emphasised three key concepts: 'solidarity', 'integration' and 'locality'. Working from the premise that people subject to social dislocation and exclusion from mainstream social life and opportunities were more likely to resort to crime, it argued that prevention strategies should concentrate on addressing the problems experienced by disaffected young people, immigrants, the unemployed and other at-risk groups, and strive to reintegrate them into their local communities (Crawford 1998). An immediate response, implemented in 1982 even before the committee had delivered its final report, was a summer camp (or 'étés jeunes') scheme for those aged 18 and under, designed to ensure that even the most disadvantaged would be able to take part in structured recreational activities during the summer months. During its first year of operation 10 000 young people became involved in such camps, while a further 100 000 participated in some form of organised program (King 1988). North African immigrant communities in particular were targeted, with young leaders from these backgrounds recruited and paid to help run programs and encourage peer participation.

Advocates claim that by channelling the energies of previously disaffected youngsters into more constructive outlets, 'étés jeunes' helped bring about significant reductions in youth offending. However, there was much more to Bonnemaison than a series of summer camps and other special initiatives. The committee's report recommended a nation-wide infrastructure dedicated to the continuous development and implementation of crime prevention.

This infrastructure operated at three levels. Nationally, the French Government established an 80-member National Council for the Prevention of Crime, chaired by the Prime Minister and comprising mayors of key towns and cities and representatives of relevant government ministries. Regionally, Departmental Councils for the Prevention of Crime, chaired by the chief administrator of each region, helped facilitate liaison between national and local authorities and ensure a coordinated approach. At the local level, all cities and large towns were encouraged to set up a Local Council for the Prevention of Crime. Chaired by the mayor and comprising representatives of national and local government and community groups, local committees had responsibility for developing and monitoring the implementation of a coordinated crime prevention plan. Such plans were to be based on systematic assessment, not just of the town or city's crime and safety problems and their causes, but of the resources and institutions that might help effect solutions.

Local prevention plans were to give attention to the needs of crime victims as well as actual and potential offenders. Emphasis was on agency-based prevention (see chapter 3) with key institutions (such as schools, housing authorities, and employment and youth support centres) working together with police to identify groups drifting or being driven towards society's margins, and finding innovative ways to draw them back. Initially, city plans were for 12 months, but this was later extended to three years. As Crawford (1998, p. 222) points out, the Bonnemaison approach stressed flexibility at the grassroots level, and in this context there was an attempt to ensure that the national bureaucracy – which traditionally had been highly centralised – devolved resources and decision-making powers to the local stakeholders. To facilitate this, a system of 'prevention action contracts' was developed. Contracts were between the national government and the various local crime prevention committees, and became a key mechanism for re-affirming the prevention scheme's guiding philosophy – fighting crime through the reduction of social exclusion and urban segregation – as well as its operating principle of improved inter-agency cooperation and responsiveness at the local level.

As noted, the Bonnemaison program proceeded on the basis that crime was a product of economic and other social and cultural marginalisation. Its emphasis therefore was on social prevention. In addition to étés jeunes, relevant schemes included community development programs on public housing estates and more than 100 youth centres ('missions locales') in towns and cities throughout France dedicated to helping unemployed and unqualified people in the 16 to 25 age group meet accommodation, money management, literacy and employment challenges. Missions locales were highly innovative, sponsoring small business ventures as well as public sector based schemes, such as a teachers' aide program to help rebuild links between migrant groups and the education system. It should be noted, however, that local crime prevention plans also had scope for situational and other forms of environmental prevention. Examples include the upgrading of security doors and alarm systems by public housing authorities, and enhanced protective measures for older citizens in some regions.

From the outset Bonnemaison was perceived as more than a set of procedures for generating local prevention projects. It was also a political program: a concerted attempt to present a coherent and convincing alternative to law and order. Crime prevention councils, plans and contracts were all designed and used as vehicles for reaffirming the message that social inclusion rather than exclusion should be the key to reducing offending. As noted, prior to the 1980s, post-war French crime policy had emphasised *repression*: 'strict enforcement of the criminal code by the police and the judiciary and the widespread use of imprisonment' (De Liege 1991, p. 125). Youth and other social welfare programs had been treated as entirely separate, and of little or no relevance to order-maintenance.

Grassroots stakeholders in the provision of educational, welfare and other services often do not object to such a division, because they are wary about negative consequences that can occur when their work is labelled as crime prevention. One of the strengths of the Bonnemaison approach was that it helped overcome these inhibitions. The prevention contract and planning process ensured that while local institutions, such as schools and employment centres, could dedicate additional resources to outreach initiatives for 'at risk' groups, they could do so in ways that were non-stigmatising. Social prevention could remain embedded in mainstream organisations and routines, and need not become the overriding concern of program providers or recipients. Only at the level of the local plan would these additional efforts be 'disembedded' and assessed for ways they might help reduce offending and other disorder.

Another advantage of local contracts and plans was that they helped ensure that resources earmarked for prevention were apportioned in disciplined and systematic ways. As previous chapters have emphasised, the term 'crime prevention' embraces a vast range of activities, from the installation and monitoring of CCTV systems to enhanced support for disadvantaged infants and their parents. Local stakeholders charged with implementing a prevention program will have to make choices and, as US experience showed (Skogan 1988), can have trouble reaching agreement on priorities. Indeed, competition over access to government resources can exacerbate local conflicts and divisions. The Bonnemaison program, with its clearly and forcefully articulated philosophy and its infrastructure of national and local committees chaired by dominant political figures, reduced these tendencies by establishing from the outset the parameters within which all parties must work.

Some commentators argue that Bonnemaison was too political, and insufficiently based on research evidence. Following its implementation, France's rates of recorded crime, which had been on the increase, began to steady and even decline. Effects seemed to be strongest in regions with crime prevention plans. However, such broad-trend assessment falls well short of rigorous evaluation. In the absence of strong empirical evidence that the strategy had worked to reduce offending, commitment to prevention as a distinct policy alternative was difficult to sustain over the long term. By the late 1990s, even the Socialists were endorsing law and order, and prevention again had been relegated to a background task.

The Netherlands: a genuine alternative?

Too much emphasis on politics, and not enough on the evidence-base and evaluation, is an accusation less easily levelled against the Netherlands' approach. *Society and Crime*, the government white paper that provided the basis for Dutch prevention strategies launched in the mid- to late-1980s, was well-informed by criminological theory. It began by reviewing trends in increases in reported crime, and decreases in police clear-up rates, since World War II. Like most consumer societies, the Netherlands had seen considerable growth in property offences: a trend that had not been stemmed by boosting resources for police and other criminal justice agencies or by increases in the number of offenders apprehended and prosecuted. *Society and Crime* argued that the main reasons for the growth in less serious, but highly frequent and often troubling, forms of offending were increased opportunities (brought about by higher population mobility) and a weakening of traditional social values and constraints. It concluded that, used in isolation, criminal justice responses would never be adequate to deal with such problems. They would always need to be supplemented by other measures.

Specifically, the report advocated three major approaches:

- improving the physical design of urban environments to improve opportunities for surveillance

- reintroducing people with professional or 'functional' surveillance responsibilities into environments where offending was more likely to occur (e.g. housing estates, public transport, public malls and shopping centres). Such people can include concierges, train and bus conductors, sports coaches and youth workers

- finding ways, in contexts such as family, school, leisure activities and work, to strengthen ties between young people and society.

Unlike most other jurisdictions, the Netherlands made an effort to assess whether the general public would understand and respond positively to its prevention schemes. Findings from a Ministry of Justice survey contested widespread assumptions that public opinion only favoured repression (e.g. more police, tougher sentences):

> Dutch people have no special preference for a mode of tackling crime geared to prevention or geared toward corrective action. A majority of those surveyed were of the opinion that both approaches were of value. [Some] 70% thought that the imposition of harsher penalties was a good way of tackling crime. Even higher percentages, however, favoured measures

requiring offenders to pay compensation and improving surveillance in buses and trams, flats, schools and shops (84% and 74% respectively). A majority of those questioned favoured increased surveillance in public transport, shops, etc. even if it was to mean additional costs to themselves. (Netherlands Ministry of Justice 1985, p. 25)

To coordinate strategy implementation the Dutch Government established a National Interministerial Standing Committee on Crime Prevention. It comprised representatives of key departments and was responsible for allocating approximately $30 million to national and local projects over a five-year period (1986–1990). All initiatives were to be evaluated by Ministry of Justice or academic researchers, with 10 per cent of the funds set aside for this purpose.

Schemes funded included the introduction of a 'concierge' system in public housing to reduce damage and disorder and help deter offences such as breaking and entering, schemes to address vandalism and graffiti, and an award-winning initiative to address concerns about young people's behaviour at a major shopping complex in Rotterdam. This last program involved traders from more than 100 shops and stores forming a local crime prevention committee made up of representatives of the shopkeepers' association, police, public prosecutors and local government. The committee's key tasks were to improve understanding and goodwill between local retail business and young people, to enforce minimum rules and to promote young people's involvement in constructive leisure activities. Committee representatives persuaded young people to help develop and publicise an agreed code regarding behaviour within the centre. In return for this agreement two separate areas were set aside for their exclusive use and the committee provided funds for organised sport and other leisure activities. It also employed a detached youth worker to organise events and to help teenagers frequenting the centre address their employment, educational and other problems.

Another key initiative supported by the Interministerial Standing Committee was the so-called 'Halt' program. Implemented on a national basis, Halt was a court-diversion initiative that involved extensive cooperation between police, prosecutors and social workers at the local level. In lieu of being subject to court proceedings, young people alleged to have been involved in less serious forms of crime were required to provide direct or indirect compensation for victims; for example, by repairing vandalised property or removing graffiti. Halt also involved helping young offenders deal with educational, employment and homelessness issues.

Research in the Netherlands has confirmed a strong association between school failure and delinquency (Van Dijk and Junger-Tas 1988). In light of this, yet another national program focused on reducing truancy and improving academic achievement in secondary schools. Trialled first in a large college with high rates of absenteeism, the first step was to update attendance record systems to ensure that authorities became aware of non-attendance by 'at risk' pupils, and could make early contact with their parents. A specialist officer was also employed to work with these students and their families. Finally, aspects of the school curriculum were revised to make them more relevant and accessible to these students.

Results at the experimental site were compared systematically with a control school of similar size and student composition. Effects of each intervention were measured separately, and a modified program then implemented on a national basis. Similar close evaluation characterised a national project based on the public transport system. About 1300 'security, information and control' (SIC) officers were recruited to patrol trams and trains in three cities. Young people from disadvantaged backgrounds, people from minority ethnic groups and women were specifically targeted for recruitment. The idea was that a greater presence of people with formal control responsibilities would reduce vandalism and threatening or violent behaviour and deter fare evasion. Evaluation indicated that the main impacts were in the last of these areas. Contrary to the hopes of those who designed it, the SIC program did not significantly improve feelings of security among transport users. However, it did make major inroads against fare evasion. Approximately one-third of the cost of the program was recouped in additional fare revenues (van Andel 1988).

In developing the SIC program, Dutch policy makers recognised that previous efforts to improve the transport system's efficiency and reduce costs often had involved 'stripping out' employees, such as conductors and information officers, whose presence or absence could be of major relevance to safety and security. Police departments had attempted to fill the gap, but police themselves had been under pressure to rationalise the allocation of personnel and resources. In practical terms, this meant that not all public and semi-public areas could be covered by routine patrols. Faced with this development, the business sector was relying more and more on private security firms.

The 'City Warden' (or 'City Guards') program, first trialled in the city of Dordrecht in 1989 and later extended to more than 26 cities (Crawford 1998, p. 233; Hofstra & Shapland 1997), was a response to these developments. Its key aim was to develop a second tier of public policing that would help maintain routine surveillance in public space, while at the same time providing work opportunities in a service industry undergoing rapid expansion. Recruitment policies focused on young people and those who had been unemployed for an extended period. Key roles for city wardens included intervening to prevent minor offending (e.g. littering and disorderly conduct), providing a reassuring presence and serving as 'ambassadors for the city'.

While wardens did not have formal police powers, they were equipped with two-way radios and in appropriate circumstances could call for police backup. City wardens underwent formal training and after 12 months were eligible to sit for a public examination, with successful completion qualifying them for entry-level positions in the private security service. By 1994, a total of 650 wardens were employed throughout the Netherlands. Evaluations (Hauber et al. 1996) indicate the program did help improve public perceptions of security, and had helped reduce offences such as bicycle theft and causing public nuisance. Most city wardens had been able to find employment in the private security sector within two years (Van Dijk 1995, p. 9).

Society and Crime and its constituent programs were presented always as a supplement, rather than a distinct alternative, to law and order. As noted, the focus was on a range of relatively minor offences occurring in public space, with crimes such as family violence receiving comparatively little attention. Commentators such as van Swaaningen (2002) argued that local implementation structures, which involved mayors working in partnership with police and prosecutors, limited the strategy's capacity to address social problems, such as unemployment and social exclusion. Programs launched in the early to mid-1990s, such as the Integrated Safety Policy and the Major Cities Policy, attempted to address these issues. The Integrated Safety Policy involved cooperative action on community safety by five national departments: Interior, Justice, Welfare and Employment, Transport and Public Works, and Housing and Environmental Planning. Annual surveys of fear of crime and perceptions of security were used to help these departments work with local authorities in implementing safety programs. The Major Cities Policy, which came after the Integrated Safety Policy, involved every major city developing an inventory of the crime and security problems confronting it, and articulating a major plan for dealing with them. On the basis of the plan, the city then concluded a 'safety covenant' with the national government and could be offered additional funds to help implement it (van Swaaningen 2002, pp. 268–269).

In embracing integrated regional plans, the Major Cities Policy moved away from the project-by-project approach that had informed Society and Crime. This reflected acknowledgment of the need to ensure that prevention became embedded in mainstream social institutions and processes. Despite this development, van Swaaningen (2002) argues that prevention in the Netherlands still has not addressed underlying structural causes of crime and insecurity. In part, this is because national governments have been reluctant to devolve resources and decision-making powers: 'local authorities are in fact invited to do more with less money' (p. 279). This, in turn, reflects the absence of strong commitment to a political and policy discourse that could be seen as a genuine alternative to law and order.

The United Kingdom: an attempt at an evidence-based approach

Similar problems apply to British attempts to implement crime prevention and community safety. As Waller (1988) points out, Britain has a long history in this field, with the government establishing a Standing Conference on Crime Prevention in 1966. The Standing Conference brought together representatives of the Confederation of British Industry, the National Chamber of Trade, the British Insurance Association, the Trades Union Congress and the Association of Chief Police Officers. One of its key functions was to convince the business sector to give more attention to crime prevention. Among other things it:

> [p]ersuaded British industry to fit steering column locks, reduced losses from robberies of cigarette trucks by 25%, developed a security code on the security of dwellings and produced materials on law and order for schools ... By 1986 it had working groups on car security, residential burglary, shop theft, commercial robbery and violence associated with licensed premises.
> (Waller 1988, p. 16)

The Home Office Crime Prevention Unit, established in 1983, also has a well-earned reputation as a pioneer of theories and techniques of situational prevention. In a series of reports, it has summarised experiments to reduce offences ranging from shop theft to armed robbery. Not all British prevention has been situational, however. In partnership with not-for-profit organisations, such as Crime Concern and the National Association for the Care and Resettlement of Offenders (NACRO), governments in the mid- to late-1970s also sponsored a variety of demonstration projects on high-crime housing estates that combined situational and social prevention (see Hope & Shaw 1988; Ekblom 1987). The Safe Cities program, implemented in the 1980s, embodied a similar mixture of approaches.

The most ambitious and controversial initiative, however, has been the Crime Reduction Programme (CRP), which ran in England and Wales from 1999 to 2002 and which was originally intended to receive government support for 10 years. At the time of its announcement, the CRP was to be the exemplar of evidence-based, whole-of-government crime prevention (Homel 2004). It was developed after a Home Office review had documented an inventory of approaches worth pursuing (Goldblatt and Lewis 1998). The program began in April 1999, with £250 million allocated for expenditure over the first three years. A further £150 million was later added, for the installation of closed-circuit television (CCTV) systems in town centres (Tilley 2004b).

Policy architects intended that the CRP would commence by piloting a range of initiatives identified as having potential to be cost-effective. Each pilot project would be evaluated by independent researchers, with 10 per cent of the initial allocation set aside for this purpose. Schemes whose effectiveness had been confirmed would then be implemented on a large scale, with independent researchers again being used to monitor whether cost benefits were maintained (Tilley 2004b, p. 259).

By the end of its first three years, CRP funds had supported more than 1500 separate initiatives managed by a variety of agencies at all levels of government, from central to local, and through community-level partnerships. Programs targeted problems ranging from violence against women to the need to reduce the social marginalisation of young people; also a major national scheme to try to reduce high-volume crimes such as domestic burglary (Homel 2004). Despite these 'runs on the board', the CRP was not extended beyond its initial 36 months and most commentators agree that it fell well short of expectations. Tilley (2004b, p. 255), for example, argues that the program 'eventually came to disappoint many of those who played a part in it', while Maguire observes that:

> [t]he CRP came up against problems in virtually every aspect of its design and implementation, and (though some less immediately obvious lessons and benefits may emerge over time) it is difficult to point to more than a handful of clearly successful projects, of conclusive findings, or of national 'roll outs' of practices endorsed by research. (Maguire 2004, p. 15)

Various factors helped cause these difficulties. One was a tension between the program's stated philosophy, of being evidence-based and only proceeding to large-scale implementation after an approach had been piloted and demonstrated to be cost-effective, and the political need for prevention to be high-profile and perceived by the public as providing an umbrella of safety and security. The first and most obvious symptom of this tension was the government's decision to set aside an additional £150 million for the installation of town-centre CCTV systems. This commitment was made in the absence of research evidence that CCTV always constituted the most cost-effective response to the problems confronting town centres (Welsh & Farrington 2002).

A key problem with the 'phase 1: pilot and evaluate; phase 2: implement success stories on a large scale' approach was that it made the roll-out of the CRP far too slow. Rigorous evaluation of crime reduction projects demands complex and time-consuming data collection and analysis – and even when such research had taken place, experts will not necessarily agree about what findings mean (Hope 2004). By the end of its first 12 months (1999–2000), only 13 per cent of the budget set aside for CRP expenditure in that year had in fact been committed

(P. Homel et al. 2004). Faced with the choice of either downsizing the program to a fraction of what originally had been intended or radically altering funding criteria, central authorities opted for the latter. Control of the program moved from the Research and Statistics Directorate, which had insisted on the evidence-based approach, to a higher-level body within the Home Office which gave priority to rapid implementation (P. Homel et al. 2004). Under the new regime, there was a:

> cutting back of plans to fund projects with innovative ideas and approaches, in favour of those based on established methods; and likewise a stronger focus on acquisitive ('volume') crime, which was the main driver of the increase in recorded crime figures. But perhaps most importantly, the central focus of the CRP began a clear shift away from the need for good research evidence about 'what works' toward an emphasis on delivering crime reduction outcomes as soon as possible. (Maguire 2004, p. 224)

In the context of accelerated program delivery, the CRP also drifted away from the whole-of-government approach. Initially, the Home Office was perceived as the lead agency in an initiative that would involve significant input from, and cooperation between, a wide range of government ministries. Oversight of the CRP had been made the responsibility of the ministerial group chaired by the Home Secretary, but also comprising Ministers overseeing Education and Employment, Environment Transport and the Regions, Health, Social Security, Trade and Industry, the Lord Chancellor's Department and Treasury. During the latter part of 1999, however, meetings of this committee ceased. Program management and fund allocation became the Home Office's exclusive responsibility (P. Homel et al. 2004, pp. 4–5).

With hindsight, most commentators agree that the initial design of the CRP was too ambitious. For the program to have been viable, its requirement that all project evaluations conform to an experimental or quasi-experimental design needed to give way to a more 'realistic' approach (Pawson & Tilley 1997 – see also chapter 5). Peter Homel, the first author of a major review of the program (P. Homel et al. 2004), has argued that enthusiasm for the whole-of-government approach also should have been tempered. Homel acknowledges that causes of crime are 'complex and various', encompassing issues in families and communities as well as 'social and structural factors such as access to and achievement of health, education, employment and housing opportunities'. He also agrees that to be addressed effectively, problems of this nature require cooperative input from several agencies. Nonetheless:

> [u]sing whole of government approaches to crime prevention is not easy and need not always be the strategy of first choice. There are significant overheads involved. For example, undertaking a whole of government approach requires significant planning, investment in management infrastructure and

> ongoing support, particularly at the centre. As such it may often be better to use a modified or scaled down approach based on effective bilateral partnerships or joint inter-agency arrangements. (P. Homel et al. 2004, p. 7 – italics in original)

The UK's CRP was unprecedented for the extent to which government and academic criminologists were involved in its design, implementation and assessment. In the context of this engagement the discipline has learnt much about adjustments and compromises that need to be made when theory and research translate into large-scale strategies and programs.

At the time the UK Government's (led by Tony Blair) 'Tough on Crime: Tough on the Causes of Crime' sloganeering never provided space for there to be a clearly articulated vision for crime prevention (Darke 2011). One of the CRP's five key aims, 'the development of more effective sentencing strategies', was as much about improving criminal justice as it was about prevention. Rather than emphasising alternatives to law and order, the British *Crime and Disorder Act 1998*, which provided the program's legislative framework, also introduced a system of Anti-Social Behaviour Orders (ASBOs), which in fact extended the criminal justice system's powers to target individuals and groups deemed troublesome or deviant – even in circumstances where no offence had been committed (Darke 2011; Crawford 2009; Hope 2001).

In the absence of an overall guiding philosophy, the Crime Reduction Programme was reliant from the outset on technical and administrative knowledge to provide it with authority and direction. Science, embodied in the design and evaluation of pilot projects, was to be the sole arbiter of what schemes should be rolled out on a larger scale. Administrative expertise, exemplified in doctrines of 'joined-up government' and 'governance at a distance' (Hough 2004), was to be the mechanism for steering program implementation at the local level. Once these knowledge systems failed to deliver, the program lost impetus and legitimacy.

Despite criticism levelled at aspects of the UK *Crime and Disorder Act 1998* (see Darke 2011), it is an important development. The Act gave crime prevention legislative backing by placing a statutory duty on police and local authorities (housing, health, education and councils) to work collaboratively in the annual development of local crime and disorder plans. Evaluations show that Crime and Disorder partnerships formed under the Act do vary in their performance and that despite its being a statutory duty for agencies to collaborate in the formation of plans, like all partnerships, problems are encountered in the levels of commitments and input among participating agencies (Phillips 2002; Kelman, Hong & Turbitt 2012). Also Darke (2011) argues that rather than promoting an alternative to criminal justice responses, the UK *Crime and Disorder Act 1998* has simply led Crime and Disorder Partnerships to adopt enforcement approaches to prevention (e.g. via imposing ASBOS). Despite how the provisions of the UK *Crime and Disorder*

Act have been realised in practice, the Act aimed to promote and institutionalise partnerships and crime prevention planning as part of the mainstream functions of police and other local agencies.

Australia: working together?

France's experience has highlighted the difficulties of sustaining national and regional crime prevention over the long term, purely on the basis of a political philosophy and commitment. Events in the UK have demonstrated, however, that expertise alone also cannot make a strategy succeed. Large-scale policies and associated programs need to combine both technical knowledge and political vision. To what extent has Australia been able to build on this understanding?

The short answer is, not greatly. It is now well over two decades since the crime policy agendas of Australian governments began to include prevention and community safety. Victoria was first to do so, with the Good Neighbourhood program, which commenced in 1988 (Sutton & Cherney 2002). South Australia followed, with the five-year $10 million Together Against Crime strategy launched in 1989 (South Australian Attorney-General's Department 1989). All other states and territories now have established initiatives (see Anderson & Homel 2005; Anderson & Tresidder 2008; Clancy, Lee & Crofts 2012; Clancy 2011; Victorian Drugs and Crime Prevention Committee 2012 – see Case study 6.1).

Australian crime prevention policy has been influenced by approaches taken overseas. Some states, most notably Victoria and South Australia, have tried to adapt the French model of a scheme designed and funded centrally but implemented at the grassroots level by multi-agency committees (Sutton 1997; Sutton & Cherney 2002). Similar partnership approaches have been adopted in New South Wales, Western Australia and Queensland (Anderson & Homel 2005; Anderson & Tresidder 2008; Clancey, Lee & Crofts 2012). Commonwealth Governments have been more influenced by the 'what works?' philosophy that underpinned prevention in the UK and the Netherlands. For example, early initiatives – such as the National Community Crime Prevention Program (see www.crimeprevention. gov.au) – focused on commissioning expert reports on best-practice in fields such as fear of crime (Tulloch et al. 1998a), school bullying (Rigby 2002), family violence (Cashmore et al. 2001a), violence prevention in Indigenous communities (Madjulla Incorporated 2004; Memmott et al. 2001; Blagg & Valuri 2003), developmental and early intervention (Cashmore et al. 2001b), ways to avoid clashes between young people and other users of public space (White 1999b) and residential burglary (Henderson, Henderson & Associates 2001). Work also focused on identifying promising developments (Grabosky & James 1995; Grant & Grabosky 2000).

The fact that state and national policy makers took inspiration from strategies implemented overseas does not, of course, mean that they have not tried to adapt and modify them for local conditions. This has not proven easy. For example, while Victoria and South Australia tried from the outset to encourage local authorities to play key coordinating roles in the prevention planning process, achieving this in practice has been impeded by the fact that in Australia the 'third tier' of government's direct responsibilities in relation to crime have tended to be minimal. As a consequence, local authorities have wanted to use funds for broader purposes than simply the prevention of offending. In Victoria, concern about this aspect has caused state governments continually to abandon established strategies in favour of new ones (Sutton & Cherney 2002). Victoria's Safer Streets and Homes program, launched in 2002 amid confident pronouncements that henceforth policies would be evidence-based and strategic, in fact was wound up in 2006 and the government's commitment to prevention was significantly downgraded (Cherney & Sutton 2007). More recently there has been renewed effort to bring crime prevention back to centre stage in Victoria, with the formation of a Community Crime Prevention Unit within the Department of Justice and appointment of the first ever Minister for Crime Prevention (see Victorian Drugs and Crime Prevention Committee 2012).

In South Australia problems over priorities at the community level and within the central coordinating unit erupted within a year of Together Against Crime's unveiling. This led to the abrupt departure of the strategy's first director (one of the authors of this book – Sutton 1997). After a highly critical and controversial assessment of the work of his successors (Presdee and Walters 1998), the South Australian Government abandoned the plan-based approach altogether.

Commonwealth government involvement in crime prevention and community safety emerged some years after the states. The decision to opt for a project- rather than plan-based approach has largely remained intact to this day (see www. crimeprevention.gov.au). When launched in 2004 there was considerable time and money invested in researching and documenting crime prevention and community safety best-practice, with the then Prime Minister announcing a $64 million funding package. However, much of the National Community Crime Prevention Program has been driven by grant applications from community groups, with a proportion of funds being used to help local governments and traders' associations install CCTV systems in shopping malls and town centres under the guise of a Safer Suburbs program. As noted earlier, it is far from clear that closed-circuit surveillance constitutes the most cost-effective way of dealing with the problems such locations can face. In an effort to provide some coherency and direction, the Australian Institute of Criminology has developed a blueprint for a National Crime Prevention Framework, which draws on a range of best practice principles and outlines the roles and responsibilities that state/territory and federal governments should adopt under a national approach (see www.aic.gov.au/crime_community/crimeprevention/ncpf.html). This framework was developed for the Australian and New Zealand Crime Prevention Senior Officers' Group, which is a national forum comprising senior crime prevention staff from state and territory governments and police, as well as Commonwealth and New Zealand governments. The aim of this group is to exchange and share information about crime prevention practices (see Australian Institute of Criminology 2012). One hopes that this framework and the Senior Officers group will at last provide some leadership and direction that has been so lacking at the national level in Australia (Homel 2009b).

After promising beginnings in the late 1980s, government-led crime prevention in Australia has been subject to turn-over and cyclical developments, which has impacted on the sustainability of programs. The dilemma is well-summarised in a review by Peter Homel (2005) who, before being seconded to Britain's Home Office to work on a review of the UK Crime Reduction Program, had been director of crime prevention in New South Wales. Homel argues that Australian attempts to develop and implement coherent and consistent strategies have been bedevilled by much the same problems that undermined the UK's efforts: lack of effective leadership, inflexible top-down program design and poor communication between local and central stakeholders.

It is important, however, not to be too pessimistic. In specific fields, such as the reduction of motor vehicle theft (National Motor Vehicle Theft Reduction Council 2006), encouraging and facilitating multi-agency interventions in disadvantaged communities, violence in and around pubs and clubs (Homel et al. 2006a; Homel & Homel 2012) and addressing family violence, Australian policy makers and researchers have made significant advances (Homel & Homel 2012 – see also chapters 7 and 8). When problems occur, they have been more at the policy and strategy levels than at the grassroots. The key difficulty has been finding ways for central governments to commit to crime prevention in a wholehearted way and to ensure that this commitment is understood, reciprocated and reinforced by grassroots stakeholders, the mass media and the public. Clearly, such commitment requires political vision, leadership and effective communication. These are the qualities that have been absent in Australia. To conclude this chapter, we outline ways to overcome the deficit, and what this might mean for the ways crime prevention schemes are designed and implemented.

The way forward

In stating that large-scale crime prevention strategies need leadership and vision, we mean they must go beyond 'how to' exhortations; for example, about being 'evidence-led' and embracing principles of 'joined-up government'. Both principles are important, but experience in the UK, the US, the Netherlands and Australia has made it clear that technique alone will never make crime prevention work. By their very nature, ambitious prevention strategies require input from a wide range of interest groups in the government and non-government sectors. Left to their own devices or instructed simply to rely on 'expertise', such participants will, at best, be like a group of enthusiastic musicians brought together for the first time and expected to perform without the benefit of a conductor or a score. They will be sorely tempted to fall back into playing their own favourite tunes – and, as a result, to generate more discord than harmony. To be able to work together effectively, diverse groups must share a common vision and sense of purpose.

Of course, specifying the vision for governments to convey goes beyond research and into the arena of value judgments and politics. Earlier chapters have made our own preferences clear: we are convinced that the unifying theme for crime prevention should be public acknowledgment of, and reinforcement for, forms of social control that reduce offending and fear without having to resort to punishment and social exclusion. We agree with Hough (2004) that exclusionary, 'tough on crime' rhetoric is incompatible with many elements of crime prevention best-practice. It favours stereotypical 'forceful' responses rather than problem solving and systematic analysis. Its oversimplified understanding of the causes of offending implies pre-emptive dismissal of the idea that more inclusive institutions and processes (such as family, education and work) may also have preventive potential. As noted earlier, one of the reasons Western governments began to 'rediscover' prevention was concern about the human and economic cost of increasing reliance on high-profile policing, tougher laws and stricter sentencing (see also Crawford 1998, 2002; Crawford & Matassa 2000).

Having made these points, we acknowledge that it is both politically and technically feasible for governments to articulate and gain public support for strategies that also emphasise punishment and social exclusion. The one course not available, however, is for central authorities to be ambivalent on these issues. Slogans such as 'tough on crime, tough on the causes of crime', first coined in Britain but quickly echoed in Australia, seem astute because they enable politicians to avoid appearing 'soft' on crime while gesturing in the direction of prevention. Such political cleverness has a price, however. Associated strategies and programs become nightmares to implement.

Once central governments have articulated a vision for crime prevention, the next step is to put in place administrative arrangements that will enable this vision to be translated into grassroots programs and projects. Like Peter Homel, we see a partnership model as essential. As UK and Australian experiences make clear, partnerships must be flexible: it is important to avoid a 'one-size-fits-all' approach. The challenge is to ensure the right mix of administrative structures at the central, regional and local levels to facilitate strategy implementation (Homel 2004, 2010;

Homel et al. 2004; Homel & Homel 2012). Within such flexible partnership frameworks, local or regional stakeholders can work with the centre to develop, implement and evaluate prevention plans.

Consistent with the partnership model, locally-based prevention should take the form of coordinated plans rather than project-based interventions sponsored by individual organisations. Local plans should involve a combination of both shorter-term (e.g. situational) and longer-term (e.g. social) measures. As noted, local prevention planning was a key feature of France's Bonnemaison scheme and the Netherlands' Major Cities Policy, and also was part of the UK Crime Reduction Program. It has also been attempted in a number of Australian states, including New South Wales, Victoria and Western Australia.

In Australia, however, failure by the centre to provide strategic direction has stymied the development process and undermined the cohesion of plans. In the context of a properly conceived plan, local stakeholders can tackle strategic goals in systematic ways. It is essential, though, that prevention planning provides scope for problem solving and flexibility. This has not always been the case. As mentioned, the UK *Crime and Disorder Act* included a statutory requirement that local authorities develop crime and disorder plans. However, instead of being used as a vehicle for dialogue between the centre and local authorities and community groups, this statutory obligation seems to have become a mechanism for imposing fixed targets (e.g. specified reductions in certain volume crimes). Flexibility and independent problem identification and solving at the local level were not encouraged (Hughes 2004; Homel et al. 2004).

From preceding chapters it should be clear that we are not the first to identify problem solving as a key to success in crime prevention. Ron Clarke (1997) locates this at the heart of situational prevention (see also Clarke & Eck 2005). Community development theorists (e.g. Toumbourou 1999) also stress the need for an open-minded, problem-solving approach. In many respects, use of a data gathering and analysis 'audit' to clarify priorities, identify stakeholders, specify intervention techniques and formulate evaluation strategies and outcome measures exemplifies scientific rationalism.

Compared with standard managerial or scientific rationalist approaches, however, problem solving in the context of a large-scale national or regional crime prevention strategy needs to be much more reflexive and reiterative. From the stage of prioritising issues to be addressed right through to developing and implementing solutions, local practitioners will be confronted with a raft of challenges (see also Clarke & Eck 2005; Laycock 2005b). To succeed, the prevention framework must find ways to endow grassroots practitioners with the authority and skills to identify and overcome these obstacles.

This has been confirmed by research on the UK's Burglary Reduction Initiative. Tim Hope (2005), a leader of one of several consortiums commissioned to evaluate aspects of the scheme, found that the projects that were more successful had the capacity to adapt to changing circumstances rather than persevering rigidly with principles prescribed by the Home Office (also see Homel et al. 2005). Research in Australia also confirms that when crime prevention practitioners have freedom to adapt to contingencies encountered in the day-to-day management of programs, they appear to be far more satisfied with the results achieved (Clancy, Lee & Crofts 2012; Cherney 2004a; Sutton & Cherney 2003).

A problem with top-down rationalist approaches is that they assume expert knowledge invariably is superior to lay assessments. Our starting point, however, is that crime prevention is a basic human competence. As research by Wynne (1996) has shown, even in areas that might seem more technical and esoteric, expert risk assessment that ignores local knowledge about specific variations can fail dismally.

Capacity to blend expert knowledge with local expertise is also essential if crime prevention plans are to promote and incorporate innovation. Experience over the last three decades now has made it abundantly clear that attempts to transplant 'successful' projects to fresh locations without first assessing their applicability to these new contexts have failed dismally (Ekblom 2010; Hughes & Edwards 2001; Sansfacon & Waller 2001). As noted, Australian national and some state governments have invested considerable resources on project trials and evaluations and on improving the knowledge base on 'what works'. However, the most critical challenge for governments and their advisers lies in finding ways to help grassroots practitioners develop the ability to use this knowledge in specific local contexts. Overly-prescriptive 'recipe book' approaches by the centre governments work against flexible problem solving and stifle innovation (see Homel et al. 2004; Homel 2009b; Hope 2005; Maguire 2004).

The flexible approach to crime prevention planning requires that governments also be prepared to engage in dialogue with local stakeholders, to help clarify what the key problems are. If the centre is to enlist local support in strategy implementation it is critical that it be prepared to invite and engage in discussions that will help all parties make the essential first step – agreeing on problems and priorities. Skogan's (1988) research on community-based prevention in the US highlights the problems that tend to erupt when governments try to omit this first step. Of course, openness to dialogue also has dangers: if the centre is too weak, the strategy may end up being coopted and subverted by local vested interests. This is less likely to occur, however, if prior to and throughout the process of dialogue, the centre articulates a strong vision for crime prevention and makes the parameters for negotiations clear. In this context, we see some value in a formal crime prevention contract between central and local stakeholders. Properly designed, a formal contract can help ensure that the funding source is explicit both about its vision for prevention and about the ways activities in a specific region can help achieve that vision.

A problem with contracts is that they can become overly formal and prescriptive. The key objective of such formal agreements between central governments and local stakeholders should not be to set targets and to make renewal of prevention funds dependent on these targets being achieved. A good crime prevention plan must include long-term objectives, and progress in relation to these objectives will not always be easy to demonstrate within the life of a particular contract. If central authorities are serious about promoting a culture of innovation and learning, the planning and implementation process must allow scope for failure as well as success. The key factor for central governments in deciding whether to enter into a fresh contract with a specific region should not be whether all outcomes specified in the preceding plan have been achieved in detail, but whether progress on that plan reflects a genuine commitment to realising the vision and principles articulated in the relevant contract.

Such commitment will not be achieved unless there are dedicated personnel at the local level who understand the interests of all players and have the capacity and skills to steer a plan through the complexities of development and implementation. Many attempts to apply crime prevention at the local level have failed because of a dearth of local staff with relevant understanding and expertise (Knutsson 2003; Laycock & Webb 2003). Such personnel are critical for ensuring that key stakeholders maintain an interest in crime prevention and help it become sustainable (Clancey, Lee & Crofts 2012; Hedderman & Williams 2001). Central governments that want to build a local culture of crime prevention should see it as in their interest to foster and support such practitioners. Their role is akin to the community safety officer (CSO) and community safety auxiliary work already widespread within local government and police agencies in Australia and in the UK and other parts of Europe (Cherney 2004a; Clancy et al. 2012; Hughes & Gilling 2004 – see chapter 5). CSOs can act as key intermediaries between the central and the local. However, their role must go far beyond designing and implementing projects that 'work' in a technical sense. If crime prevention is conceived as a series of dialogues, the core of the CSO role lies in enhanced communication and interpreting. Even if the centre has taken the trouble to articulate an overall vision for its strategy, one cannot assume that local stakeholders will immediately understand this vision and see it as relevant to their own specialisations and interests.

Those whose main interest is in repressing and excluding those perceived as deviant or potentially disruptive – Skogan's (1988) 'preservationists' – may well be happy to have their projects labelled 'crime prevention'. However, individuals and groups whose preference is for more inclusive strategies will tend to be less comfortable. Often, they will argue that educational, employment and other relevant social initiatives deserve support in their own right and, not without reason, will be concerned that too close an association with crime prevention may be stigmatising and counterproductive. Working within the context of a crime prevention plan, properly trained CSOs can help overcome such concerns. They can help ensure that central government funds are used to enhance the prevention potential of ongoing practices (such as urban planning, education, vocational training and recreation) while still enabling such activities to remain 'embedded' in mainstream institutions (local schools, job search centres, etc.).

However, in assisting local stakeholders to develop, implement and assess these plans, a CSO also can help ensure that relevant investments are recognised in a broader context as contributions to helping preserve order and reduce offending. Such recognition is of critical importance for politicians and other interests under constant pressure to 'do something' about crime at the local, regional and national levels.

Overseeing the development, implementation and assessment of plans that embed and disembed crime prevention in ways that meet the needs of both central and local interests is the core task for CSOs and other crime prevention specialists. Establishing and maintaining the proper balance in this respect is far more important than identifying and initiating projects that 'work' in a purely technical sense. Their capacity to do so, however, always will depend on a program's central sponsors articulating a vision of crime prevention as an alternative to law and order and establishing the ground rules for the dialogue with and between local stakeholders. To the extent that it relies on these broader parameters, local and regional-level crime prevention will always be political. Denying this element, and treating crime prevention purely as a matter of expertise, will doom it to failure.

Of course, we are not arguing that large-scale crime prevention strategies are entirely political, and that there is no place for research and the dissemination of best-practice. On the contrary, such expertise can and should play a critical role in ensuring that goals are achieved and momentum maintained. One of the key roles for central government policy units, for example, should be to connect local and regional teams who may be tackling similar problems, and help them to share experience and pool knowledge. Such knowledge can encompass both specific crime prevention techniques and the best ways to go about developing and implementing a prevention plan. Practitioner (e.g. CSO) networks can promote cultures of learning (Fung 2004) by spreading knowledge about successes and failures experienced when trialling different approaches and techniques in the context of a local plan.

These learning cultures should not shun the use of complex and rigorous evaluation designs – there is scope for them to be incorporated into the development of plans. As noted in chapter 5, we need to be wary about over-reliance on the experimental model. Often, to reduce threats to what theorists term 'internal validity' (i.e. confidence that a specific intervention has been responsible for reducing a particular form of crime), programs aimed at assessing the impact of a specific form of prevention try to impose strict controls on the ways that intervention is delivered. However as Eck (2002b) has pointed out, over-strict controls result in situations that seldom occur in everyday practice. This in turn will affect the external validity (i.e. transferability) of the program itself. Evaluation purists need to acknowledge that insistence on experimental or even quasi-experimental designs can create dilemmas for practitioners keen to ensure that local plans include 'embedded' social as well as discrete situational approaches. Faced with demands that they deliver prevention in ways they perceive as artificial, stigmatising and counterproductive, such practitioners can be sorely tempted to accept program funding, but defer and resist demands for evaluation.

Conclusion

For many of its advocates, the advantages of crime prevention appear self-evident. As far as they are concerned, intervening before offending occurs rather than relying on expensive police and other criminal justice reactions is simply commonsense. Experience in Australia and other countries demonstrates, however, that translating such 'commonsense' into large-scale government strategies and programs involves major challenges. At the purely pragmatic level prevention may, indeed, be the most rational thing to do. Yet as Durkheim (1984) pointed out, when an entire society defines and tries to find ways to deal with crime, it is always doing more than implementing a series of practical measures; it is making major statements about the ways it sees its present, past and future.

This chapter has outlined a framework that governments could adopt, if they wanted to make prevention a key component of crime policy. In our view, an approach based on contracts and plans is the key to ensuring success at the political and policy levels. Whether this approach will be implemented is, of course, open to question. It would require central governments to devolve significant resources and decision-making powers to grassroots stakeholders, and evidence that they are prepared to do so is not strong. Nor is it clear that politicians have the capacity and vision to initiate and sustain the dialogues about key social values and preferred approaches to social control, which we see as the starting point to any prevention scheme. Whatever the challenges, crime prevention is worth doing. Strategies launched in countries like France, the Netherlands, the UK, and in Australia, may have encountered obstacles, but they have also yielded significant benefits. We now should be able to learn from this experience.

CASE STUDY 6.1   AN EXAMPLE OF CRIME PREVENTION PARTNERSHIPS AND CAPACITY BUILDING

In the Australian state of Queensland in 2002 the Labor government implemented a nationwide Strategic Framework for Community Crime Prevention. As part of this program, eight pilot regions were chosen in which local government was funded to form community safety partnerships, or what were termed BSCATs (Building Safer Community Action Teams). Like many crime preventions programs (see chapter 1), BSCATs were required to develop action plans and involved partners drawn from local government, business, community services and the police. Two important components of the Queensland Strategic Framework were that it involved the delivery of training to BSCATs and also the appointment of Senior Community Support Officers, whose role was to assist BSCATs in developing and implementing local community safety plans. Both these elements were aimed at local capacity building. BSCATs faced a number of problems, such as finding a common focus among partners, engaging youth and Indigenous groups, accessing police data and deciding how best to deal with the complexity of crime. In many circumstances Senior Community Support Officers were essential in helping BSCATs overcome such problems. The program was subject to a review (which involved one of the authors – Cherney) and it was found that there was disenchantment at the local level about the program, given there was no commitment from the State government to extend funding for BSCATs. Also there was little evidence the program had been effective in reducing crime or improving community safety, mainly because there had been little investment in evaluation. Responsibility for the Strategic Framework was eventually shifted from the Queensland Department of Communities to the Queensland Police Service, where it was subject to redevelopment.

QUESTIONS

Questions for further exploration
1. What are the similarities and differences in the way countries abroad have designed and implemented crime prevention programs?
2. What problems have plagued crime prevention programs in Australia?
3. If you were to make one key recommendation on how to improve crime prevention policy and practice in Australia, what would it be?

EXTENSION TOPICS AND REFERENCES

1. The UK Crime Reduction Programme was perhaps one of the most ambitious and well-funded attempts to implement a national approach to crime prevention. But why did the UK Crime Reduction Programme fail to achieve its objectives?

References

Homel, P., Nutley, S., Webb, B. & Tilley N. (2004) *Investing to deliver: reviewing the implementation of the UK Crime Reduction Programme*. London: Home Office Research Study 281.

Hough, M. (2004) 'Modernization, scientific rationalism and the crime reduction programme', *Criminal Justice*, vol. 4, no. 3, pp. 239–253.

2. State governments have taken a lead role in the development of crime prevention policy in Australia. Review how different Australian states have implemented crime prevention initiatives. What have been the strengths and weaknesses of the different approaches adopted?

References

Anderson, J. & Homel, P. (2005) *Reviewing the New South Wales Local Crime Prevention Planning Process*. Canberra: Australian Institute of Criminology, www.aic.gov.au/publications/previous%20series/other/61–80.html.

Anderson, J. & Tresidder, J. (2008) *A review of the Western Australian community safety and crime prevention planning process. Final report*. Canberra: Australian Institute of Criminology, www.aic.gov.au/publications/previous%20series/other/61–80.html.

Victorian Drugs and Crime Prevention Committee (2012) *Inquiry into locally based approaches to community safety and crime prevention. Final report*. Drugs and Crime Prevention Committee. Melbourne: Parliament of Victoria, www.parliament.vic.gov.au/dcpc/inquiries/article/1842.

7

PREVENTION IN PUBLIC PLACES

Introduction

This chapter will discuss the following topics:

- the notion of community constructed around where we live and shop
- the involvement of youth in crime prevention
- crime prevention and community spaces – planning, management and social development
- shopping centres and people-friendly environments
- cyberspace as public space and cyber-bullying.

The aim of this chapter is to discuss crime prevention in relation to the use of public spaces. More specifically, the chapter is premised on the fact that very often the notion of community, and of community safety, is constructed around where we live, shop and engage in leisure pursuits. Perceptions of safety in our residential areas and local neighbourhoods, and how security is provided for in shopping centres and shopping strips, have a concrete and immediate bearing on how people experience their everyday lives.

When we speak of community crime prevention and community organisations it is essential to bear in mind that 'community' incorporates many different interests, groups, struggles, agendas, strategies and relationships to the state (Carson 2004a, 2004b; White & Perrone 2005; Hughes 2007). This has to be taken into account when considering specific crime prevention measures.

Communities can initially be delineated by territorial boundaries. These may include:

- **geography** (local, regional or international): people living in the same area
- **power structures** (federal, state, local government): defined by electoral boundaries
- **services** (transport line, school): defined by service providers, such as local councils.

The essential link here is one of locality – a collective identity is shared simply due to the physical fact of where people live.

The so-called 'bonds of community' may include more than just a geographical community (Currie 1988). Such bonds can be conceived in terms of interconnected and deeply embedded institutional influences and interests (e.g. work, religion and communal associations), broader structural contexts (e.g. housing policy, employment opportunities) and social factors (e.g. gender, race and class). They may be related to:

- people's **social profile** that leads individuals and groups to share similar backgrounds (e.g. as it relates to income, class, age, ethnicity, gender and religion)

- **self-defined interests** (e.g. communal associations and networks comprising like-minded people with a common concern)
- **industry or employment profiles** relating to what people do for a living (e.g. if they work in retail outlets, commercial trades or factories)
- **organised political lobby groups** (e.g. residential groups, unions and business groups).

To speak of community crime prevention, therefore, we need to have a sense of which particular 'community' we are referring to at any particular time, and how and why this particular community is relevant to the design and implementation of a crime prevention strategy.

In this chapter we want to move from general contextual analysis of crime prevention towards specific matters of practice. In doing so, we emphasise, again, that crime prevention ought to bear a positive relationship to the notion of social inclusion, that it necessitates a modicum of planning and thinking ahead, and that it should be incorporated as much as possible into everyday practices. Good crime prevention should be relevant to how people live their everyday lives, and yet – in its own way – be more or less innocuous.

This chapter examines issues relating to crime prevention at the local neighbourhood level, participatory approaches to crime prevention (especially those that emphasise social inclusion), the planning and management of public spaces, and crime prevention in the context of shopping centres and malls. The next chapter will continue the discussion of crime prevention in public spaces by examining instances of social disorder and unexpected disruptions to community life.

Community participation and social inclusion

Perhaps the most well-known local crime prevention initiative that specifically targets residential living is that of Neighbourhood Watch (NW). It is useful, therefore, to discuss the strengths and limitations of NW in order to illustrate the diverse political and social issues pertaining to crime prevention practice.

Community safety and community crime prevention is frequently expressed in terms of three key objectives: reducing crime, reducing fear of crime and restoring a sense of community (White & Coventry 2000). As with crime prevention in general, it is legitimate to ask of NW whether it is effective in regards to these objectives, and what it actually achieves or does (see Fleming 2005; Victorian Drugs and Crime Prevention Committee 2012). In the main, NW tends not to give priority to social crime prevention and its emphasis on distal causes of crime (such as poverty, unemployment and racism). Rather, the main concern of NW tends to be with situational crime prevention, and in particular opportunity reduction (e.g. use of target-hardening devices, such as locks, surveillance, property marking and use of better lighting). The main focus, in fact, has been on burglary reduction, and thus with a relatively narrow range of crimes and offensive behaviour.

Theoretically, NW is potentially a way of making a police service more democratically responsive and responsible through citizen participation in oversight activities. In practice, however, it tends to mainly reflect police priorities and emphases in crime control, with the community playing an auxiliary function. There is no real direct community input and prioritising of 'local' crime problems. This can, in turn, reinforce the culture of 'law and order' as the focus is on police priorities and action. We can also ask whether or not the presence of a NW scheme might lead to the potential displacement of crime away from the NW areas to other areas or even to other types of crimes. Questions can also be asked regarding whether or not the presence of NW schemes themselves lead to an increase in fear of crime at the local level (see Crawford 1998).

criticisms

The language of NW is that of promoting 'community spirit' and 'partnerships' and 'participation'. Such language tends to gloss over who is *not* included in these terms, and what is actually meant by community participation at a local level. As Box 7.1 illustrates, there are diverse meanings to 'community participation'. NW tends to fit within the more selective and top-down forms of participation.

BOX 7.1:   TYPES OF COMMUNITY PARTICIPATION

- Market research (polls, telephone interviews, surveys, etc.): aimed at tapping into what people think about certain issues or social problems.
- Appointment to decision-making bodies (representatives of the community sit on advisory boards and committees): focused on capturing what representatives think about certain issues or social problems.
- Incorporation of opposition groups (inviting diverse community leaders into a central decision-making forum): can be concerned with making public matters confidential or silencing an opposing view by positioning it as simply one voice among many.
- Social therapy (neighbourhood clean-up campaigns): the community actually takes part, but does work or provides services that are determined by other third parties.
- Grassroots activism (street watch or pollution watch committees): people or groups decide themselves how to intervene in certain local problems.

(Source: Sandercock 1983)

There are, of course, major differences *between* and *within* communities. As Crawford (1999) observes, community responses to crime are easiest to generate in exactly those areas where they are least needed (neighbourhoods characterised by social cohesion and low crime rates), and they are hardest to establish where the need is greatest (neighbourhoods characterised by disorder and crime). The poor and the rich are socially divided by 'security differentials' that increasingly become significant characteristics of wealth, power and status. Community safety activities like NW are easier to sustain in homogenous, middle-class suburbs than in heterogeneous, lower-class neighbourhoods. One consequence of the combination of affluence and security consciousness is 'gated communities', which may include physical perimeters and controlled access, often guarded and controlled by private security police (see Atkinson & Blandy 2005).

For these communities, people may well become imprisoned within security arrangements to which they have actively contributed. Areas with low crime rates, most notably middle-class suburbs, do not display the characteristics traditionally associated with 'community', such as intimacy, connectedness and mutual support: they tend not to rely on informal social control mechanisms, but on formal 'external' control mechanisms, such as the police (Crawford 1999).

For other, disadvantaged, neighbourhoods, the community itself may be blamed for 'their' crime problem. How people in such areas perceive social issues, however, will influence how they respond to crime concerns. For example, residents who define the problem in terms of local poverty, drug abuse or unemployment may be less inclined to support a 'watch-type' program than residents who feel that the problem is attributable to the presence of suspicious strangers in their neighbourhood. Nevertheless, the 'moral voice of a community' may come to be dominated by unrepresentative elites who, 'in the name of the community', focus on the exclusion of undesirables (Crawford 1999; Carson 2004a; Miller 2008). Indeed, as seen in chapter 3, US research has shown big rifts at the local level between the conservative better-off 'preservationists' and the less well-off 'insurgents' (Skogan 1988). Whose voice gets heard by those in authority is contingent on how 'crime prevention' itself is construed and conceptualised.

In many cases, the definition of 'undesirable' tends to be centred on specific groups within the community, who are targeted on the basis of age, race, ethnicity, class or other forms of social identification. In this way, the social interaction that occurs around 'crime prevention' matters may lead to increases (rather than decreases) in fear of crime, and racial targeting and other skewed crime-related perceptions (Rosenbaum 1987). As such, they may contribute to social fragmentation (rather than the often hoped-for feeling of collective community spirit). In addition, the 'us' versus 'them' mentality reinforces the idea that crime and criminals are external 'others' and that the 'community' is somehow under attack from the outside: there is little sense in which offenders are members of communities, as neighbours, husbands, wives, sons or daughters. Yet we know that property crime, in particular, is concentrated in poor areas, and that both the victims and the perpetrators are from the same community. Crime, like wealth and poverty, is spatially distributed along the lines of political and economic inequality (Currie 2013; Vinson 2004).

The commodification of security – as manifest in the market for security doors, burglar alarms and security company patrols – can reinforce fear, risk and danger. This runs counter to the language of community, which is about connection, trust and solidarity. Thus, there may be an inherent tension between 'feeling secure' and 'being social', in the sense that the need for personal security may undermine the public sphere and people's experience of it, particularly as people withdraw from community spaces into private, regulated environments (Crawford 1999; Zedner 2010).

From our perspective, it is important to respond to these issues by emphasising a broader concept of crime prevention that includes measures that relate to the reduction of criminal events, as well as 'quality of life' issues. Consistent with arguments presented in this book it is important that there be less emphasis on deficits, problems and outsiders, and more on capacities, competencies and participation. The main issue is how to build 'social cohesion' and 'social capital' in ways that promote collective and inclusive responses to local crime and safety problems.

Crime prevention, we argue, ought to therefore be informed by principles of social inclusion and popular participation. But crime prevention is not only about social inclusion as a *goal* (i.e. to foster policies and practices that ensure people are included in most facets of social life). Crime prevention is also about a *process* that is socially inclusive. To illustrate what this might mean in practice, we will briefly consider the ways in which young people – so often the targets of coercive street intervention – can be directly involved in positive crime prevention activities.

Involving youth in crime prevention

While by no means universally applied, there has nevertheless been a proliferation of positive and innovative practices and strategies that not only respect the rights and wishes of young people, but that directly involve them in decision-making processes (e.g. see Crane 2000; Salvadori 1997; White 1998; Wood & Bradley 2009). And, vice versa: many older people who previously did little to recognise the special needs and common rights of young people now do so as a matter of course – whether this is shopping centre managers, local council representatives or urban planners.

To address potential and existing social problems it is essential to create social spaces that are convivial and safe. This requires a careful assessment of particular sites, and a weighing-up of potentially competing objectives. For instance, when public space is over-regulated and 'sanitised' it tends to be less frequented, to the detriment of citizens and businesses alike. Public space that does not convey a sense of security and safety, on the other hand, will also tend to be less frequented and to be reserved for the select few who claim it as their own.

Diffusing potential tensions on the street – between groups of young people and other groups of young people, and between young people and older people and authority figures – can initially involve a series of audits of a particular local environment (see Malone 1999; Robinson 2000; White 2001; White & Sutton 2001). These resemble the CPTED site surveys discussed in chapter 4. Briefly, these audits might focus on:

- the **physical environment** (identifying sites considered to be unsafe or threatening)
- the **social environment** (different users and uses of public space)
- the **regulatory environment** (the nature of police and security approaches)
- types of **amenity** (youth-specific and youth-friendly)
- **movements through public places** (flow of people through particular areas).

The purpose of such mapping exercises is to gain accurate information on how public spaces are used at different times and by different groups. They have also been used to provide an avenue for youth participation in planning and design of communal spaces (see also NSW Department of Urban Affairs and Planning 1999; Malone 1999). Different perspectives and the contributions of diverse sections of the wider community can provide useful insights into how local environments can be modified in ways that reassure and restore confidence. Suggested measures may be as simple as providing better street lighting, through to more intensive community forums on conduct associated with skateboarding.

In various government and commercial circles, there is an increasingly expressed view that making everyone feel welcome in a space is important to the creation of a sense of communal wellbeing and collective sharing. Social inclusion also refers to the provision of various ways in which young people can participate in decisions relating to a particular site; that is, decisions over use, regulation design and planning. In recent years, for example, conflict between authority figures, such as police and security guards, and young people has led to a recognition that solutions need to be more strategic in orientation rather than simply tactical. That is, rather than using certain tactics (telling young people to move on, asking them their name and address) as a means to exclude young people from certain streetscapes, a problem-oriented approach attempts to devise a strategy that deals with underlying issues.

What happens at the local government level has major implications for the nature of street life. For example, policies and perspectives within local councils that emphasise young people as a problem tend to lean towards coercive measures that aim to control the activities and behaviour of young people through curfews, skateboard bans and other exclusionary means. Alternatively, local councils can emphasise the place of young people in the community as social participants, and thereby ensure that they have a say in formulating and implementing local council policies (even those that do involve some restriction on their activity, as in the case of skateboarding protocols). Fostering respectful and healthy relationships between young people and other members of the local community can be enhanced through youth participation and youth policy initiatives at the local government level (see White 1998; Glenorchy City Council 2003 for examples).

The significance of youth policy development within local government circles is that it provides for a climate in which dialogue and negotiation with young people about perceived and actual social problems can take place. It allows for potentially volatile situations to be 'cooled out' before escalating due to misinformation, over-reaction or political machination. Open lines of communication and a strong commitment to social inclusion can serve to diffuse tensions, while allowing for a serious assessment of, and practical responses to, anti-social behaviour. This can lead to a number of gains, such as the development of more youth-friendly spaces and an understanding of how and why certain public spaces are used by young people. This can help generate more effective place management that emphasises social inclusion.

Balancing the spontaneity and civility of urban spaces

Crime prevention involves a range of specific techniques and intervention measures. It is necessary to develop a certain cultural climate and material infrastructure if crime prevention is to be effective. In particular, and as discussed in chapter 2, crime prevention planning requires:

- knowledge of local problems and community needs
- understanding of the different approaches to crime prevention and choosing the most suitable for a specific area or problem
- coordination of various groups, agencies and individuals around crime prevention objectives
- training and education of appropriate personnel in problem solving, crime-prevention techniques and partnership approaches
- ongoing evaluation of crime prevention initiatives and strategies.

The challenge is to devise crime prevention plans and strategies in a manner that embeds good practices at the local level. This needs to be done in ways that enhance, rather than diminish, the social life of communities.

It is important to be aware of both the limits of crime prevention in general, and of specific measures in particular. A fixation on dealing with a perceived 'crime problem' can lead to the adoption of overly repressive measures, which can generate further fear of crime.

Public spaces such as malls and 'nightlife' streets can be attractive in the first instance precisely because of the unstructured, unorganised nature of these spaces (this is discussed in greater depth in chapter 8). Part of the attraction, in fact, is that certain public spaces are exciting and interesting, and this may occasionally include minor incivilities in such spaces. The over-regulation of public spaces can deter people in much the same way as a lack of appropriate social regulation can make people reticent to visit some places. Thus, crime prevention in public and community spaces always involves a trade-off. This entails making decisions about the extent to which one prioritises preventing crime, in relation to other kinds of social objectives, such as ensuring that people have access to public spaces and public events, which they wish to attend because they hold the promise of something out of the ordinary. This could consist of simply having the chance to observe and have contact with a diverse array of people, with varying types of clothes and appearance, and engaging in a range of activities and behaviours.

Effective crime prevention planning, therefore, not only requires a thorough analysis of local crime problems, but sensitivity towards the concerns, priorities and rights of people likely to be affected by the adoption of particular measures. Planning a crime prevention strategy is more than simply a matter of choosing the right technique, for these techniques are never neutral in application and they always have certain social and economic consequences. It is important, therefore, to consult with local interests and users of a certain space to determine what they see as the priority issues and to closely consider the potential effects of specific measures on how a certain public space is used, and its attraction to particular people or groups.

Shopping centres and public malls

Shopping centres and malls are a big part of our lives in the 21st century. These are essentially commercial spaces, but they are also public spaces, in that, ostensibly, they are open to the public, even though many are in fact privately owned and managed. A number of studies provide useful overviews of good practice across a wide range of locations, crimes and activities. For present purposes, we cite examples drawn from the US, Canada, Australia and the Netherlands – each of which deals with shopping centres or malls.

Inclusive planning processes

In the US city of Santa Monica, the local council was concerned to revitalise an old, run-down mall which was perceived to be blighted and unsafe (Sandercock 1997). The mall was redesigned in such a way as to encourage different types of activity, from shopping to strolling, to sitting and meeting, to parades and community celebrations. Ample space was allowed for public seating, trees and banners made for a visually interesting environment, footpath cafes were encouraged as well as street performers, and people from all social backgrounds and interests were encouraged to congregate in the mall.

The public space was planned and designed from the start as a 'community space'. The emphasis was on a mix of activities, a low-level and tolerant police presence, promotion of street performers without controlling them (they do not have to audition) and improvement in the general streetscape. The result: a convivial atmosphere that is socially inclusive and has very little street crime (Sandercock 1997).

Another example of how changing the environment can affect human interaction, especially criminal and offensive activity, is the case of a shopping plaza in Ontario, Canada. In this instance, the police undertook a CPTED survey of the area around and including the plaza. They identified a 'leftover' space adjacent to the mall that was isolated and visually disconnected from it, and that seemed to be the site for assaults and other incivilities. The police recommended that the space be opened up visually to the street and passers-by. With physical changes made to the space, the level of loitering, vandalism and other kinds of crimes was reportedly lower than before the changes. Thus, commercial land uses can be investigated from the point of view of creating safer places, by increasing surveillance through the transformation of unsafe spaces (Schneider & Kitchen 2002, pp. 174–175).

Development of management protocols

In Australia, the Brisbane City Council undertook a major project designed to improve safety in major centres, including shopping centres and malls (Heywood et al. 1998). As part of the recommended courses of action, attention was directed at management practices within centres, including security arrangements.

It was recommended that centres develop clear, fair and non-discriminatory rules, which applied to all users. Protocols were to be developed to deal with a variety of problems, as experienced by various stakeholders, including centre management, shop owners and young people themselves. Such protocols were to provide for the involvement of youth services in responding to the needs of young people. They were to provide substantial guidance for managers, police, security, youth services and young people in dealing with difficulties, such as conflicts between young patrons and security staff. In addition to these general protocols, it was recommended that there be developed a specific 'code of practice' for security personnel regarding engagement with young people, and that security staff undertake specific training. Centre management was encouraged to shift to a more 'customer-oriented' style of security provision, away from a strict 'law enforcement' approach.

The Myer Centre Youth Protocol was developed in 1998 as a means to deal with any potential problems that might arise from young people's use of that particular centre, located in Brisbane, Queensland. The protocol was developed as a collaborative effort involving a local government authority, a major retail centre and the youth sector. Some of the principles underpinning the protocol included transparency and accountability, health and safety, access and equity; involvement of young people, minimally intrusive security provision, customer service, and redress in the case of complaints (Crane & Marston 1999). The idea of protocols has surfaced in other places as well. For example, in New South Wales a guide was developed that provides a step-by-step outline of how to devise an agreement (protocol) between key people involved in managing, maintaining the security of, accessing or using a shopping centre. The guide is intended to assist people at the local level to develop a protocol that best suits the specific needs of their particular community and particular shopping centre (NSW Shopping Centre Protocol Project 2005).

Participation and service provision

In the Dutch city of Rotterdam there were serious forms of youth crime and vandalism at the Zuidplein shopping centre in the early 1990s (Hoefnagels 1997). Attempts to deal with this by applying harsher, repressive measures only led to further problems with young people.

A broad-based community committee was set up to address the issues. The main outcomes included the adoption of 'rules of conduct' for the centre, which were conveyed to the young people of the district by the police through the local school. Second, a street youth worker was appointed, who was financed 75 per cent by the city, and 25 per cent by the employers' association. The youth worker operated independently from the police, the courts and the shop owners. Two so-called 'tolerance' locations were established at the shopping centre, and the youth worker organised support and activities for the young people who used the centre. When problems arose, the worker discussed them directly with the people involved, leading to improved communication between shopkeepers and young people. As a consequence of these measures, both vandalism and shoplifting declined in appreciable terms (Hoefnagels 1997).

Similar types of intervention have been tried in Australia. For example, in Perth, Western Australia, the manager of a suburban shopping centre was confronted with vandalism, abuse of shoppers, and conflicts between security guards and young people, among other things. He approached a local youth organisation for assistance, and a committee was established to look into the issues. The committee included representatives from the centre management, local council, local youth service, state and Commonwealth government departments, local businesses, police and community groups. A survey was conducted to understand the situation better and to develop a program that would attempt to address the needs of the young people and the community. In the end, a part-time youth worker was hired for the centre, paid for jointly by the centre and a government department. The role of the youth worker was to engage with young users of the centre, to link them into existing support and information services, and to act as a go-between for the young people and centre management. The result was a marked change in the atmosphere of the shopping centre, from adversarial to consultative. Such an accommodating approach also led to initiatives, such as regular monthly rock concerts, and greater appreciation of the place of the centres in the social life of young people (White 1998).

These examples provide insight into measures that can be adopted by commercial retail centres that emphasise inclusion and in doing so are potentially more effective at reducing crime and safety problems in these centres due to them involving young people who are typically seen as the problem, rather than part of the solution. In the next section, we explore in greater depth two of these interventions – one that involves crime prevention in a publicly-owned mall, the other in a privately-owned shopping centre.

Crime prevention and community spaces

As indicated above, there are two approaches to crime prevention associated with shopping centres and mall spaces. These are not necessarily mutually exclusive, although they do tend to reflect opposing philosophies:

- the *exclusionary* focus on minimising the presence of people or groups perceived as potential troublemakers usually translates into an increase in the number of security guards and in investment in security tags for merchandise, possibly restricting public transport to ensure a more affluent customer and an increased use of closed-circuit television cameras and store detectives

- the *inclusionary* focus on ensuring that these spaces meet the needs of diverse groups and users. This might include the employment of youth and community workers within the shopping centre complex, the setting up of counselling and welfare services, and media campaigns designed to make people take pride in their local shopping centre.

The last few decades have seen Australia and other countries undergoing rapid and far-reaching economic and cultural transformations. Many people feel uncertain about their own jobs and futures and about prospects for their children and grandchildren. A tendency to gravitate towards physical settings that provide visible evidence of being well-maintained, well-controlled and 'predictable' may be part of attempts to compensate for such stresses. Yet, as mentioned, there is simultaneously a desire for public spaces that are in some way unpredictable in order to be exciting. Addressing this tension requires some thought into how best to achieve the right balance between 'order' and 'spontaneity'.

We also have to be aware that different people perceive things quite differently when it comes to safety and security concerns. For example, while some studies have indicated that older people are fearful of the young when it comes to their use of public transport (Tulloch et al. 1998a), studies specific to analysis of seniors in shopping centres suggest that such users are not fearful of young people as such (White 2007a). Rather, older people have their preferred times at which to visit the shopping centre (in the morning), and they 'avoid' younger people not because they are afraid of them as such, but because they congregate in particular ways (e.g. big boisterous groups that take up space and make lots of noise). Once you understand these informal rules of non-engagement (leave the shopping centre to us in the morning, and we'll leave it to you in the afternoon), then you'll see that the issue is more one of convenience than perceived threats of crime and disorder (White 2007a). In this way, crime prevention as an everyday practice is about inclusive *and* exclusive spaces, since both are necessary and both depend on immediate social context. Self-exclusion that is passive, and by choice, is an important aspect of constructing public places that do cater for a wide variety of interests and age groups.

The public mall

Box 7.2 describes an ideal mall environment in cases of publicly-owned and managed properties. The guiding principle is to steer relevant authorities within local councils away from seeing themselves simply as commercial facilitators and managers, and towards the role of sponsoring mixed business and community involvement and activity within public spaces. The basic idea here is that mall development should be based on inclusionary policies that celebrate diversity and difference, while simultaneously holding out the promise of safety for all users of the public space. For those who are interested in transforming public spaces into 'community spaces', the principles and practices outlined here constitute at least one example of the kinds of issues that future planning of such commercial spaces might wish to consider.

BOX 7.2:   THE IDEAL OPEN-AIR MALL

Future planning could put emphasis on malls being recognised and used as a community resource, and as a community meeting place. The unifying theme for its uses could be that the mall provides social and physical links: links between different generations and genders, between different ethnic groups, between people from different parts of the city, and between people with very diverse social backgrounds and personal interests.

It is desirable to have one or more 'community' facilities located in the mall – for example, a public library, a youth drop-in centre or an adult education facility. A separate area could also be set aside as a designated children's playground. Regular use of the mall for community purposes – for example, for regular 'Sunday markets' and free concerts – could also be encouraged.

As a community space, the mall could be made accessible to a wide range of activity and interest groups, whether for displays or for specific events. Chess clubs, neighbourhood houses, ethnic community associations and clubs, graffiti artists, skateboarders and others all could be encouraged to use this venue for educating and involving the public, and to provide a forum for displaying skills and expertise.

Community and commercial uses of the mall should be seen as mutually reinforcing, rather than as competitive. Success in establishing the mall as a preferred meeting place – somewhere people actively choose to congregate – would help stimulate demand for commercial outlets (such as cafes, coffee shops and boutique stores).

Malls should be made more amenable as an environment in which to congregate, walk and sit: through physical design local councils could ensure that the mall provides a convivial atmosphere that is safe, inviting and secure for sections of the community.

The physical structure and design of malls influence how people use such space, and their perceptions of safety. Priority could be given to providing systematic protection from the elements – preferably in the form of a fixed structure (either a roof or 'sails'). Enclosing the mall space in this way would add to the feeling of security, as well as comfort. A semi-controlled environment of this nature would offer users a sense of reassurance not dissimilar to that offered by the closed environment of the 'hard-top' establishments.

Clear sightlines also need to be established in order to ensure both natural and occupational surveillance. Appropriate low-level shrubs and non-screening trees could be provided to ensure a 'cool' and 'green' offset to existing or proposed paving. Similarly, bright banners placed strategically throughout the mall could help instil a sense of vitality and celebration.

There should be comprehensive signage of amenities, and at least some of these signs (when in written form) should be not just in English but in languages spoken in the countries of origin of recent immigrants to the local area. Conscious effort could also be made to ensure that street furniture, sculptures and other fixtures reflect and celebrate the cultural diversity of the region.

A stage area amenable to multiple purposes could be provided. Any furniture and special-event materials should be constructed in durable, graffiti-proof materials. Furniture, paving and coverings need to be well-maintained at all times. Widespread experience has shown that one of the most effective ways to prevent vandalism and other forms of anti-social activity in public space is to ensure that the relevant environment is both well cared for, and looks well cared for. Basic crime prevention principles dictate that maintenance and cleaning in and around the mall should, in future, receive high priority.

The mall should be well-managed and regulated, but in a low-key, friendly and inclusive manner, and local councils should provide that the security of the mall's environment be undertaken primarily through the use of 'community information officers'.

Healthy, vibrant, community malls are those that, while being effectively monitored, are highly tolerant of diverse activities, diverse groups of people and diverse types of uses of public space. Security should therefore be visible, but as unobtrusive as possible. The point of intervention (both passive and active) is to facilitate harmonious community relations, rather than constantly to remind those present that rules and laws may be transgressed.

Security of the mall environs could be undertaken primarily through the use of community information officers. These officers would provide users with information (e.g. directions and events) and assistance; would liaise with police, private security providers, ambulance personnel and other emergency services; would work with maintenance and cleaning staff to ensure that any damage or other problems were addressed quickly and effectively (identify dirty sites, dangerous materials); and would provide information on community services and agencies in the local area (e.g. schools, neighbourhood houses). They could also help to arrange and manage special events and permanent exhibition sites within the mall precinct.

The community information officers could be recruited locally, and should visibly reflect both a local council's commitment to community safety and the mall's role in linking diverse groups and communities. For example, they could be comprised of young and elderly people, Anglo-Australians and ethnic minority Australians. It is important that young people, in particular, be strongly encouraged to apply for and take up these positions: peer-led security has been shown to be one of the most effective ways to minimise conflicts and clashes between young people and other users of public space.

A formal management committee could be developed to manage and monitor safety and security within the mall, with a membership drawn from local police, business establishments, community groups and young people who use the mall. The committee would be a key forum for discussing and reviewing mall safety and security on an ongoing basis, and for ensuring a coordinated approach to prevention issues. There should also be regular meetings between this committee and the community information officers, for the purposes of feedback and discussion on current performance, present and emerging issues, event planning and suggestions for future priorities. As well, committee liaison with members of the local press on issues concerning the life of the mall would be useful from the point of view of encouraging use and reducing any potential security concerns among groups who might visit the mall, also ensuring that there was informed public comment about mall events.

(Source: White & Sutton 2001)

On the other hand, many shopping and congregating spaces are privately owned and managed, for private commercial purposes. In this instance, a different approach to crime prevention and community safety may well be required. Given that the main 'problems' from shopping-centre management points of view tend to be associated with young people, the next section mainly concerns itself with positive, non-coercive forms of youth crime prevention in shopping centres.

Youth-friendly shopping centres

There are a growing number of documented cases of shopping-centre management strategies that involve the adoption of youth-friendly approaches. As indicated previously in this chapter, these approaches generally include dialogue between interested parties, including youth advocates and young people, support for youth services and youth workers, and the reliance on low-key inclusive management procedures (see also White, Kosky & Kosky 2001; Crane & Marston 1999). We concentrate here on one particular case in order to tease out the complexities of crime prevention in these kinds of places.

In February to May 2000, the MCS Shopping Centre Youth Project examined youth–community centre relations at several shopping centre sites in Queensland and Victoria (White, Kosky & Kosky 2001). At the time, MCS Property Ltd owned

24 shopping centres throughout Australia, the majority of which were medium-sized, food-based, sub-regional or neighbourhood shopping centres. The project's aims were to examine youth–community relations at shopping centres; to explore a pro-active approach to creating youth-friendly and socially-inclusive spaces and practices at shopping centres; and to assess how such an approach can not only provide useful community spaces, but can be demonstrated to deliver real benefit to the centre by reducing overheads and generating greater business.

Through a case study of the Festival Faire shopping centre at Manoora, a suburb of Cairns (Queensland), the project documented the processes through which centre management established a sense of community engagement, especially in regard to local young people. The study found that Festival Faire had a potential youth problem that was well-managed (White, Kosky & Kosky 2001). What might be considered trivial (schoolchildren running or in high spirits) or minor (shoplifting or more serious misbehaviour) incidents occurred fairly regularly. These were generally handled on a low-key basis and in a way that remained largely unnoticed by most customers.

The general youth issues or problems found in sub-regional, food-based shopping centres (SRFB centres) usually mirror the issues or problems found in the local community surrounding the centre's catchment. The types of problems that emerged at various times over the past 15 years at Festival Faire included:

- vandalism
- theft
- unruly behaviour
- break-ins
- and, for a short period, groups of youths fighting other youths.

The nature of youth-centre management relations at any time is shaped by a range of diverse factors. In the case of Festival Faire, specific *characteristics of tenancy* had a profound effect on the way in which young people were perceived, interacted with other centre users, and were dealt with in terms of specific anti-social incidents. For example, it is highly significant that during the period of review, the shopping centre tenants included an 'alternative educational campus' within the centre precincts. This refers to a special school designed for students who for one reason or another find it difficult to attend ordinary local schools or who have been expelled from other schools. These students are routinely seen by members of the general public as the most difficult, rough and troublesome of young people that mainstream institutions cannot handle. Shopping centre tenancy was also bolstered by the presence of a police shopfront that incorporated community liaison officers. The 'Police Beat' shopfront was the first of its kind in Queensland, and comprised general operational duties as well as liaison officers.

Individual young people were liable to be recognised and to have a certain social status in the eyes of other centre users due to local knowledge of families living in the district and through existing centre networks, including the alternative school. The combination of teachers and community police in the centre meant that it was generally easy to identify young people who were engaged in particular kinds of activities. The preferred method of centre regulation was low-level intervention. For example, the security staff tended to let particular young people with a history of occasionally being troublesome know that they were being watched. This was done in a friendly way: 'Good morning, we know you're here, so please behave' (accompanied by a smile). In this proactive, but benign manner, efforts were continually made to forestall anti-social or illegal behaviour in the least confrontational way possible.

Security guards were encouraged to become familiar with family members of centre users, across generations (e.g. parents, children, grandparents) and kinship networks (e.g. aunts, uncles, nephews, nieces). Importantly, cultural sensitivity was seen as an important element of security staff responsibilities. On some occasions, family members were involved in the policing of misbehaviour. For example, elders were consulted and were asked to step in under certain circumstances, such as when certain youths were chronically misbehaving. Also, older youth tended to informally police younger youth through the form of stories relating to 'acceptable' and 'unacceptable' behaviour.

Insulting and nuisance behaviour – such as swearing, abusive language, spitting and excessive noise – was regularly targeted by security staff. Importantly, showing respect for other people was touted as an appropriate and desirable centre norm for security staff to follow, and young people and adults alike viewed this positively and as something to be encouraged among themselves.

This attitude was also reflected in how retailers generally responded to shoplifting. The approach taken by many shopkeepers (and the centre's security officers) was to deal with young people sensitively and carefully, as indicated in Box 7.3.

BOX 7.3:   GUIDELINES FOR DEALING WITH SHOP STEALING

- Treat young people caught shop stealing with respect.
- Be seen to be dealing with offenders in a firm but fair manner.
- Do 'favours' for the young persons, if they didn't shop steal again.
- Issue multiple warnings.
- Ban persistent offenders from shops.
- Refer to police only in serious and repeat cases.

Generally speaking, the response to shoplifting outlined in Box 7.3 was informed by a culture of negotiation and dialogue. The idea was to develop an ongoing rapport with young people, and to only involve police after a number of warnings had been issued.

The precise manner in which traders dealt with 'youth issues', including incidences of shoplifting, varied, however. On occasion, some traders tended to take security and other dealings with young people into their own hands. This was not encouraged by management if it involved coercive intervention, such as grabbing a young person by the arm or ordering young people to leave the centre. Such responses may be understood as 'spontaneous' reactions to particular and immediate situations. But they often involved measures that were inappropriate and that could lead to defiance and increased unruly behaviour by young people at the centre. It is recognised that close liaison between traders, security officials – and education about prevention and security matters – is essential if youth-related issues are to be dealt with sensitively and legally (e.g. see Sarre & Prenzler 2005).

The preferred method of centre management and regulation was prevention. This involved a range of players, including centre management, security guards, maintenance personnel and traders. For instance, often there were two cleaners who were constantly working in the public areas of the centre. They had two-way radios and were in contact with the centre management office. They could thus provide 'early warning' of any potential incident. Vandalism did not appear to be a problem, due to the deterrent effect of active night patrols. This patrol activity involved random checks of the premises. It was accompanied by use of full alarm systems, and the exclusion of young people from the centre grounds after hours.

Interestingly, specific incidents of vandalism and graffiti tended to be dealt with informally. If an offender was not apprehended by security guards or the police, there was a good chance that some of the local young people would nonetheless know who they were. Those young people who attended the alternative school appeared to have a strong sense of ownership of, and attachment to, the centre. This was because of the school's location in the centre; the young people's connections with the wider community via the diversity of centre patrons; the specialist provision offered by the school (i.e. dealing with issues such as health, hygiene, domestic violence and so on); and a general positive appreciation of the school and the centre among youth.

The net result of this positive experience was that frequently it was the young people in the community, including students from the alternative school, who identified those who defaced centre walls and property. A typical response – to graffiti, for example – was for a young person or other community member to identify the source of the graffiti, which would be reported to community workers, teachers, community elders or police liaison officers. The elders or community workers might then arrange for the offenders to apologise to centre management and then clean up the graffiti. In this way, the problem was handled informally, but effectively, and the harm repaired without recourse to (official) police or court action.

While security and regulation of the centre environment was weighted in the direction of low-level, non-coercive intervention, this was not always possible or desirable (depending on the circumstances). There was a period in which there was extensive damage to the premises, with certain young people engaging in gang-like behaviour in the centre, which intimidated other patrons. The response included the selective use of intensive security patrols. This was temporarily adopted in order to put a halt to the serious vandalism and group aggression occurring in the centre. This tactic was used as a circuit breaker, to establish clear boundaries of behaviour, and was targeted at a defined, known group of troublemakers.

An important aspect of the centre's approach was that centre management provided strong leadership in fostering the attitude that use of the centre was based on the notion of community inclusion, and accommodated the needs and wishes of diverse groups of people in the local community. For example, the centre held a regular 'seniors week', during which older patrons were encouraged to spend time at the centre and gain various discounts on beverages and other goods. A 'seniors card' was also available to elderly patrons. The centre also ran a 'Kids Club' for children under the age of 13. The sense of community and customer care was also fostered by the employment of local young people as 'courtesy crews' to assist shoppers with trolleys, packing and gift wrapping during the Christmas period.

Cyberspace as public space and cyber-bullying

New information technologies are rapidly having an impact on people in ways unheard of only a few short years ago (Collin et al. 2010; White & Wyn 2013). While digital information technologies may have had a significant effect on older people's lives, their impact on young people is even more profound. Young people use the internet for personal communication (e.g. email, blogging, Facebook and Twitter); as a medium for seeking information; and for shopping, banking and organising travel. They expect to use a wide range of digitally produced and mediated leisure and communication devices (including mobile phones, iPods, MP3s and CDs) and enjoy television programs and films that are increasingly produced and distributed digitally. Moreover, they increasingly produce as well as consume these media. Personal publishing and blogging are now commonplace, gradually shifting the balance from using the internet as a source of information to using it as a tool for communication.

One of the key aspects of new information technology use is social networking. Young people are enthusiastic users of Social Networking Services (SNS), with the majority engaging on a daily basis with SNS via a computer or mobile phone. SNS include services outlined above, as well as Bebo.com, Twitter.com and MSN (texting using a phone). It has been pointed out that Australia's young people are 'the world's most prolific users of social media, and young people under 25 are the most active group when it comes to creating, updating and viewing social media' (Collin et al. 2010: p. 10), that 90 per cent of 12 to 17 year olds and 97 per cent of 16 to 17 year olds use SNS, and SNS is basically the number one online activity for 16 to 29 year olds. Their use has been enhanced and facilitated by the advent of mobile phones that access the Internet.

Cyberspace in its many dimensions thus constitutes another form of community space. It is accessed by many, and for many it is a vital platform for communication and interaction. Not everyone, however, is welcome to the internet party – for many reasons, including criminal ones (see chapter 9). For instance, there are patterns surrounding who is or is not welcome to participate in social networking. West et al. (2009), for example, found that for US university students, parents are rarely reported to be Facebook friends and there is a view that in general they would not be welcomed. More generally, the students did not appear to conceive of there being two distinct realms, the public and the private – rather, the 'public' appeared to be the individual's private social world. Facebook is both a public and private community space, where one can be public to one's friends but private to one's parents (West et al. 2009).

Cyber-bullying

Another issue that pertains to how private and public spaces are socially constituted in cyberspace is that of cyber-bullying. In simple terms cyber-bullying has been described as a covert form of bullying that is carried out through the use of technology (Australian Institute of Criminology 2010; Price & Dalgleish 2010). Covert bullying 'can be understood as any form of aggressive behaviour that is repeated, intended to cause harm, characterised by an imbalance of power and is hidden from, or unacknowledged by, adults. It can include the spreading of rumours or attempts at socially excluding others' (Australian Institute of Criminology 2010). It is presented as a significant social problem for children and young people today.

Bullying has become a ubiquitous term to describe all manner of conflict between individuals and groups, with particular emphasis on bullying among adolescents. Definitions of bullying have changed over time to include indirect forms of bullying, such as exclusion (Rigby 2003). This change also includes reference to the commonly held belief that bullying involves one individual bullying another individual. However, it is recognised that there is also a group basis to bullying (Rigby 2003). Thus, the definition of a bully has expanded from traditional perceptions of the bully as primarily individually-based, to include the group as the source of bullying behaviour.

Situations arise whereby young people are members of a group that is more powerful than another group. Bullying may be motivated by a grievance or prejudice, rivalry or simply to have fun at the expense of another. These acts of bullying are typically initiated and sustained by the connection with a group rather than driven by individual motives. The type of bullying undertaken and the motives for bullying are dependent upon the context within which it occurs. Typically, schoolyard and cyber-bullying is where the normal rules of restraint do not apply. Bullying is not restricted to settling a gripe or asserting status in a one-off opportunistic situation but is the systematic, ongoing persecution of another over time (Rigby 2003).

As mentioned, the specific context for what appears to be cyber-bullying requires careful appraisal. For instance, recent research into the patterns of text messaging among high school students in the US provides an interesting interpretation of the content of such texting. It was pointed out that:

> [a]s with emails, text messages can be forwarded to others, increasing the possibility of having private, damaging, or hostile information disseminated to multiple recipients. Additionally, text messages lack context and are thus subject to misinterpretation and misconstrued meanings, which can contribute to interpersonal conflict and damaged relationships whether intentional or not. (Allen 2012: p. 99)

Text messages can also involve aggression in the form of cyber-bullying, seen here as the wilful and repeated harm inflicted through the medium of electronic text.

Importantly, though, the prolific use of texting, combined with relatively high levels of hostile text messaging, manages to both routinise and increase the harms associated with cyber-bullying. This occurs because of the frequency of text messaging, and the opportunities it provides for gossiping and the spreading of malicious rumours, all of which may contribute to conflict. This, in turn, can see the bullying proliferate online to include other third parties and associates.

There are a number of recognised challenges to SNS and other uses of the Internet that simultaneously pose challenges for crime prevention (see also chapter 9). However, as Collin et al. (2010) argue, the positioning of SNS use within an online risk-management paradigm that over-emphasises the potential harms and risks is inherently limiting because it ignores the range of benefits associated with online practices. They observe that the benefits of SNS include:

- media literacy
- formal educational outcomes
- informal education and learning
- creativity
- individual identity and self-expression
- strengthening of social relationships
- belonging and collective identity
- building and strengthening of communities
- civic and political participation
- self-efficacy and wellbeing.

The benefits of social networking revolve around the participatory nature of the contemporary digital environment, including creative content production, dissemination and consumption (Collin et al. 2010). Crime prevention that misconstrues the positive benefits of new information technology, and the status and nous of young people as digital natives, will inevitably present as unwanted, coercive and ineffective. As with real world community spaces, intervention involving the internet requires application of strategies that involve the active participation of the key users. Knowing what is actually going on, rather than assuming the worst, is a good place to start.

For example, some 'top tips for teens' to prevent cyber-bullying include advice such as educating oneself about what it is, safeguarding your passwords, not opening messages from people you do not know or from known bullies, logging out when finished with a computer or mobile phone and restricting access to your online profile to trusted friends (H. Jinduja & Patchin 2012). Parents are advised to know the sites that their children visit and their online activities, to ask for their passwords in case of emergency and to encourage their children to tell them immediately if they, or someone they know, is being cyber-bullied (US Department of Health & Human Services 2013). Generally speaking, raising awareness of the issue is crucial to its prevention.

Given the immersion in cyberspace by young people today, it is not that surprising that the threat of restricted internet and technology use is viewed as having an important deterrent effect on offenders. Clear rules with enforced penalties and ongoing prevention awareness programs form the backbone of crime prevention approaches relevant to this kind of behaviour (Kraft & Wang 2009).

Conclusion

There are no simple solutions to the issues raised in this chapter. One key message is the need to create and sustain community spaces in ways that neither provide for simplistic understandings of the notion of 'community' nor dismiss its importance in how we live, shop and play in our everyday lives. Good crime prevention is essentially about how best to regulate specific environments in ways that enhance feelings of safety, without unnecessarily excluding any people or groups from participating in local public life. For this to occur, it is necessary to evaluate existing regulatory mechanisms and practices to ensure they do not exacerbate exclusion. In general the creation of a positive, regulatory environment within community spaces rests on active consultation and incorporation of groups who use these spaces into the decision-making process. As this chapter has demonstrated, a participatory and inclusive crime prevention process can lead to plans that build positive social relationships in various community spaces.

CASE STUDY 7.1 **PREVENTING CYBER-BULLYING**

Systematic reviews of cyber-bullying prevention strategies have identified a wide range of initiatives (e.g. Kraft & Wang 2009). Some of these include:

- no computer use in schools or the bedroom of young people
- parents taking away an offender's computer and mobile phone
- barring access to social networking sites
- offender(s) attending netiquette classes
- informing students about what to do if bullied online
- having clear rules for preventing cyber-bullying and enforcing penalties on cyber bullies
- schools having a zero-tolerance policy for bullying, including online bullying
- programs involving student participation in activities to help raise awareness about cyber-bullying and enhancing individual coping skills to prevent the occurrence of cyber-bullying and minimise its impact.

QUESTIONS

Questions for further exploration

1. What is the relationship between public and private when it comes to the ownership, accessibility and control over public spaces? What are the implications for the development of crime prevention strategies?

2. Why is youth involvement in crime prevention seen to be relevant to issues of social inclusion?

3. How do we make public spaces safe for the elderly and young people taking into account the differences in how they use public spaces and why?

4. Digital information technologies offer liberating, emancipating opportunities for the creation of new communities and spaces where young people can belong, yet they can be constraining and oppressive as well. Discuss.

EXTENSION TOPICS AND REFERENCES

1. The shopping mall and consumption have become defining features of contemporary life for young people. What are the implications of this when it comes to thinking about community safety and crime prevention?

References

Chatterton, P. & Hollands, R. (2003) *Urban nightscapes: youth cultures, pleasure spaces and corporate power.* London: Routledge.

White, R. & Wyn, J. (2013) *Youth and society: exploring the dynamics of youth experience.* Melbourne: Oxford University Press.

2. Cyber-safety issues have tended to dominate and skew public debate away from what the experts – young people themselves – are actually doing in regards to digital technologies. Accordingly, what can be done to ensure that social analysis incorporate the direct experiences of young people in negotiating and navigating the cyber world?

References

Collin, P., Rahilly, K., Richardson, I. & Third, A. (2010) *The benefits of social networking services: literature review.* Melbourne: Cooperative Research Centre for Young People, Technology and Wellbeing.

Third, A., Richardson, I., Collin, P., Rahilly, K. & Bolzan, N. (2010) *Intergenerational attitudes towards social networking and cybersafety: a Living Lab Research Report.* Melbourne: Cooperative Research Centre for Young People, Technology and Wellbeing.

Wood, J. & Bradley, D. (2009) 'Embedding partnership policing: what we've learned from the Nexus policing project', *Police Practice and Research: An International Journal*, vol.10, no. 2, pp. 133–144.

Zedner, L. (2010) 'Security, the state, and the citizen: the changing architecture of crime control', *New Criminal Law Review*, vol. 13, no. 2, pp. 379–403.

8

DEALING WITH SOCIAL DISORDER

Introduction

This chapter will discuss the following topics:

- multipronged approaches
- the ambiguities of public space
- graffiti and social disorder
- youth gangs and social conflict
- alcohol-related street violence
- unexpected disruptions to the community.

Much public consternation about crime stems from experience and perceptions of disorder or anti-social behaviour in public places. Indeed, when people think of 'crime', very often they mean 'street crime' – activities generally associated with street-level interactions, events and situations.

As discussed in chapter 4, the implementation of CPTED measures has generally revolved around crime prevention in public places. This is because many perceived and actual crime problems that local government and the police are required to address relate to contestations over public and community spaces. The high profile of social disorder in public places, in both popular consciousness and crime prevention agendas, means that relevant measures warrant further discussion.

The aim of this chapter, therefore, is to explore further how crime prevention applies to public spaces and, in particular, cityscapes, such as streets, public buildings and parks. Building on discussions in the last chapter, we want to demonstrate that crime prevention is basically about making life safer and better, and that we can do this by taking a holistic view of social contexts and interactions. Ensuring community wellbeing demands an appreciation of the physical, social and cultural dimensions of local environments. Understanding the dynamics of 'place', the ebbs and flows of urban life, the variety of cultural forms in which people express themselves, and the importance of 'ambiguity' in shaping people's experiences and enjoyment of place is crucial to this task.

The chapter begins with a brief review of the benefits of undertaking planned, multipronged approaches to crime prevention. This is followed by analysis of the ambiguous nature of public spaces, the phenomenon of graffiti, and youth gangs. We use this chapter to demonstrate that our approach to crime prevention allows for a certain degree of tolerance at the same time as it addresses issues relating to social disorder.

Multipronged approaches

For some people, crime prevention simply consists of finding ways to exclude unwanted groups from access to your property. The problem with this approach is that while it might work well in selected communities for selected crimes and for selected purposes, too often it can also actually make things worse for other sections of the community. In other words, the protection of the security and peace of mind of the better-off in society is frequently premised on displacement of crime to the worse-off, and the social exclusion of certain categories of the population from mainstream social life. In other words, some forms of crime prevention can actually lead to the creation of 'unsafe' places, and may foster unhealthy social practices among those who have been dispossessed of the safety and security provided to the middle classes.

Consider for a moment the phenomenon of motor vehicle theft. We know that a combination of situational crime prevention measures and environmental design measures can radically reduce certain types of car theft, and more generally the volume of cars stolen in any given locality. However, we also know that prevention of car theft is also very much a matter of social relationships as well as situational changes and modifications of physical environments. This is because a proportion of car theft is intrinsically related to the social situation of the car thieves, including their class backgrounds, levels of access to public transport and their status as young men (see White 1990; Walker 1998; Walker, Butland & Connell 2000).

An integrated approach to car theft must, therefore, incorporate various dimensions and techniques (see Box 8.1). This is explicitly acknowledged in the National Motor Vehicle Theft Reduction Strategy, which has involved strategic planning, the bringing together of diverse interest groups, and the adoption of a combination of crime prevention techniques and approaches (see, for example, National Motor Vehicle Theft Reduction Council 2006). The council is a joint initiative of Australian governments and the insurance industry. It works actively with police, insurers, the motor trades, vehicle manufacturers, registration authorities and justice agencies, as well as providing information and educational materials to local communities. The council employs a wide range of strategies to reduce car theft and, as the dynamics of car theft change over time, it remains open to new strategies.

BOX 8.1:   DEALING WITH MOTOR VEHICLE THEFT

Situational techniques that focus on the offence:

increasing the risks and efforts; e.g. fitting alarms and tracking devices, engine immobilisers, steering column locks and data dots

CPTED measures that focus on the physical environment:

designing out crime opportunities; e.g. improved lighting, improved design of car parks, installation of entrance barriers and electronic access

Social crime prevention approaches that focus on the offender:

addressing motivations and social circumstances; e.g. comic books and other educational materials to help young people become more aware of the risks and social and legal consequences of vehicle crime, and intensive trade-based training for young recidivist car thieves.

The importance of multipronged approaches that draw on social and situational measures is one of the key themes of this chapter. That is, our concern is to demonstrate how various kinds of perceived harms and dangers require close analysis of particular sorts of social interaction, and sensitivity to the human element in whatever measures we adopt. We also need to acknowledge that there are indeed particular urban areas, and particular types of group behaviour, that are generally perceived as threatening and potentially dangerous.

It is the ambiguities of social life and social order that form the key concerns of this chapter. That is, we wish to explore how our particular crime prevention perspective informs our views of certain types of social phenomena – such as graffiti, youth gangs and gatecrashing – and our preferred social responses to them. From our point of view, analysis and action ought to proceed in ways that capture the volatility, dynamics and contradictions of social life in the same moment that we strive to make things better by engaging in the crime prevention process and dialogue.

We start the next section, ironically enough, with the observation that a modicum of disorder in fact can be good and desirable. Contrary to many approaches that see disorder as inherently bad and as something to contain and manage (often through ruthless and draconian means), we view some forms of disorder and some kinds of cultural activity as part and parcel of the excitement associated with city life. Acknowledgment of this means that crime prevention needs to be framed more widely and more sensitively than is often the case. In particular, in our vision of social control, we encourage the use of an accommodating approach that is founded upon, and promotes, positive dialogue between a wide variety of public space users.

Ambiguities of public space

We begin this section with the tale of the dancing man of Hobart (see Box 8.2). This is a true story, one that touched the lives of many people living in this city.

BOX 8.2:   THE DANCING MAN OF HOBART

The 'dancing man' died in Melbourne in May 2003. His death sparked spontaneous outpourings of grief, love and loss in Hobart, his place of residence and dancing for a number of years. Most people did not know his name (Anthony James Day); they only saw him dancing – in the main city mall, at civic events, in all manner of public spaces.

He died soon after leaving Hobart. He left Hobart shortly after being fined for failing to obey the direction of a police officer to 'move on'.

Tributes were written in the mall in chalk. Alas, the chalk memorial was hosed away by local council workers that same night. The next day, undeterred, friends, acquaintances and complete strangers gathered to celebrate his life by dancing in the mall.

Such are the contradictions and ambiguities of street life.

We introduce the story of the dancing man because, with the advent of controlled, air conditioned shopping malls, with a heavy security presence, there are fewer and fewer niches for eccentric characters like the dancing man. We believe that crime prevention that construes public safety in ways that eliminate such characters is actually counter-productive. Not only does it rob the social environment of interesting and exotic people, it can also breed resentment at both the uniformity of community spaces and how such spaces are regulated.

The mass privatisation of public spaces across many national contexts – and renewed interest in questions of public disorder and how best to control, manage and regulate this – are crucial backdrops to the story of the dancing man. How state and private security agencies respond to the unusual (people, activities, events) in public spaces reflects both differences in institutional imperatives (for state police, issues of public order and law enforcement; for private police, issues of consumer activity and order maintenance) and the differential treatment of people depending on social background and group affiliation (e.g. 'gangs').

Public space is a site for people to get together and do things. What they do, and how they do it, is intrinsic to the excitement and communal attributes of such spaces. They also contribute to the ambiguities of such space. People, especially young people, use public space to entertain themselves, to engage in disreputable (and reputable) pleasures, to connect with each other and to assert social identity (White 2012). The making, shaking and taking of public space is achieved through phenomena such as 'swarming', public dancing, making music, selling drugs, drinking alcohol and street fighting. It is also the key site for democratic struggle, street protests and resistance to oppressive government policies and political regimes.

Ambiguities of street life are reflected in the diverse ways in which people experience public spaces: the street is a source of fun, excitement and entertainment, and simultaneously a site in which there is considerable fear, trepidation and violence. These ambiguities are also reflected in the paradoxes of state intervention. On the one hand, concerted attempts have been made to include young people in public space projects. On the other hand, the state has engaged in aggressive efforts to 'clean up the streets' by targeting young people in general, with extra special measures being directed at particular groups of young people. Why and how this is the case is worthy of some consideration before we discuss public places and crime prevention as such.

The type of activities engaged in by people in public spaces is, in part, shaped by the ambiguous nature of such spaces, as well as by the specific environments of particular places. For example, much is said about the fear of crime and victimisation associated with public incivilities, crime and homelessness. However, little is said about how – for all generations – the appearance of some degree of 'social disorganisation' can itself be a source of pleasure. The contrast between highly sanitised, extensively regulated spaces (e.g. some shopping complexes) and urban environments with less overt structure and social control can make the latter desirable to visit for many people. For example, when we think of Sydney, we often think of Kings Cross; with Brisbane, of Fortitude Valley; and with Melbourne, St Kilda comes to mind. Certain night-time spots become poles of attraction, especially for tourists, precisely due to their tarnished reputation.

Use of some public places thus can carry with it a realistic assessment and expectation that to be exciting and interesting, street life often will include some 'negative' features. Just as lack of appropriate social regulation can make people reticent to visit some places, the converse – over-ordering and lack of spontaneity – can drive people away. The ambiguities of public spaces, therefore, can be an important part of their energy and attraction.

Potentially 'dangerous' spaces can, in turn, be contrasted with their opposite – the mundane spaces of the modern consumer. Large commercial facilities offer customers convenient access to a wide range of goods. Their self-contained, climate-controlled, closely monitored and well-maintained environments also provide users with a sense of order and predictability, which many people in contemporary society value for its own sake. Recent years have seen many groups demonstrating less and less appetite for 'street-level' interactions – with middle-class and more affluent adults gravitating instead towards more enclosed 'mass private space', such as office and shopping complexes, and secured apartment and housing estates (White & Sutton 2001). In part, this seems to be related to fear of crime (even though the incidence of stranger-perpetrated violence is low in Australia compared to, say, the US). It also signals a symbolic and material split between the 'haves' and the 'have-nots', that increasingly is reflected in spatial as well as financial terms, as in the case of gated residential developments (Atkinson & Blandy 2005).

Yet, as pointed out earlier, there is simultaneously a desire that public spaces be in some way unpredictable in order to be exciting. Addressing this tension requires some thought into how best to achieve the right balance between 'order' and 'spontaneity'. Sanitised spaces are boring spaces. Predictability can lend itself to routinisation, stagnation and lack of stimulation. How to provide public spaces that are full of vitality yet non-threatening is essentially a matter of how best to create 'community' spaces.

It is also important not to forget the 'simple' pleasures associated with public space, pleasures that are about human relationships, networks and non-commercial activities (see Worpole & Greenhalgh 1996). Activity in public spaces – such as beaches, malls, the street, bushland and shopping centres – is not entirely consumption-oriented. People of all ages are likewise prone to 'hanging out' in such spaces, regardless of the functional imperatives of commercial enterprises.

The feeling of connection, the sense of excitement and the exhilaration of being in and around others translates into enjoyable public spaces. Part of what makes public spaces so attractive is the sheer diversity of people, and activities, within them. 'People watching' is a pastime keenly engaged in by many of us. And it requires little in the way of money or action to do so. What we watch, however, are those with whom we have relatively little or no direct contact, except when we venture into the commercial centres of contemporary capitalism.

Public space, including the street as broadly defined, is one of the few havens for people who want to please themselves when it comes to what to do, when and with whom (even though they are nevertheless subject to numerous restrictions). As a place to hang out, public space refers to a wide range of specific locations; places where people have a degree of room to move, as well as to watch and interact with their peers and others (White 1990). Conversely, people complain about issues such as lack of adequate seating, no sheltered areas, a feeling that they had to purchase something in order to be there, bad lighting, inadequate transport, and harassment from other public space users, including at times authority figures, as factors affecting satisfaction with public places and venues (White 1999a). Suspicion, intolerance and moral censure operate in particular ways to limit the spatial world of young people in particular (Malone & Hasluck 2002), even as they explore the limits and boundaries of this world.

How young people, as a specific category of public space users, actually use these spaces is contingent on access to resources and amenities, the construction of youth-friendly venues and areas, and the social relationships that are built on the street. Different groups of young people use the street and other public venues in different ways. They also perceive the issues surrounding public space from a range of viewpoints. Issues of personal safety, for example, are not confined to older people. Young people, too, wish to have safe environments in which to socialise and move, and to be free from the threat of violence – whether from other young people, adults or authority figures (White & Wyn 2013).

Young people are not passive users of the street, nor are they reticent about establishing a public presence. Their active engagement with local environments frequently brings them to the attention of authority figures, including crime prevention planners. This is especially the case with graffiti, a phenomenon usually associated with youth.

Graffiti and social disorder

There are a number of reasons why graffiti has become a 'public issue' of some concern. To a certain extent the presence of graffiti has been linked to the 'fear of crime' in that it can become the visible signifier of disorder and unruliness: a threat to the 'quality of life' of residents and the private property of businesses. The pervasiveness of graffiti may lead people to be fearful of walking in their neighbourhoods, of becoming patrons at certain shops and of feeling safe and secure in their communities. One reason for this is the constant link that is made between graffiti work and criminal behaviour. This takes several forms. For example, at a concrete level, at least in the US, part of the fear generated by graffiti is that it is linked directly to criminal youth gangs (US Bureau of Justice Assistance 1998). There is some evidence that such linkages are periodically made in Australia as well, particularly through media portrayals of 'graffiti gangs' (see White 1990).

In theoretical terms, an association is also frequently made between graffiti work and more serious types of crimes. This has been described in terms of the so-called 'broken windows' metaphor (Wilson and Kelling 1982). This refers to the idea that if a broken window in a building is not repaired, then the sense that nobody cares or is in control will inevitably lead to more windows being broken. By analogy, some people feel that if activities such as graffiti are ignored and go unchecked, then the atmosphere of lawlessness implied by this will lead to even more serious crimes being committed.

Related to this idea is the feeling on the part of some that the anti-authoritarianism represented in graffiti is a threat to those in control (i.e. institutional authorities and political leaders), and thereby a threat to 'ordinary' law-abiding citizens. As such, what needs containment is not so much the crimes and potential crimes posed by graffiti work, but the subversive element that graffiti represents generally (see Ferrell 1997). Moreover, the threat is not only to existing institutional regimes of power, but to those wishing to shape cultural spaces in ways that reflect commercial objectives and consumption agendas. Graffiti can be seen to threaten the conventionalised and homogenised ways in which public places are being reconstructed to emphasise managed shopping spaces, where the impetus to act is based on consumption, not expression; the spending of money, not the spending of energy. Also objections to graffiti can include the costs of clean-up, and the presence of what some people deem to be unsightly art, or slogans or tags on public walls, trains and buses.

Graffiti takes many different forms, and is associated with different purposes – from political slogans to gang territoriality to artistic creation to identity tagging (White 2001; Halsey & Young 2002, 2006). For some young people, the graffiti 'gang' is a vital social connection in their lives. The graffiti experience represents an important 'identity-securing form of action', something that confirms who one is and their presence in the urban setting (McDonald 1999). The act of graffiti thus is also about constructing subjectivity that makes sense to the author.

BOX 8.3:   WHY DO GRAFFITI?

Graffiti can offer a number of specific benefits to participants. Some of these include:

- availability of technologies (e.g. spray paints) that allow *low-cost* ways to make a personal mark on the environment
- a sense of *defiance* against authority figures
- opportunities for *free expression* that are open to anyone regardless of background or skill, and the notion that power is within one's own hands
- experiences that are more *authentic* than either commercial activity or doing something for, or dictated by, someone else
- opportunities to experience an adrenaline rush and buzz of *excitement* that relates to doing something broadly perceived to be deviant or wrong.

It is useful to consider the perspective of 'cultural criminology' in regards to behaviour such as vandalism and graffiti. In this view, ostensibly anti-social behaviour like this is best interpreted as meaningful attempts to 'transgress' the ordinary, and the given (Presdee 2000). In a world of standardised diversity and global conformities, it is exciting and pleasurable to break the rules, to push the boundaries and to engage in risky and risk-taking activities. Transgressions of this nature are one way in which the marginalised can attain a sense of identity and commonality, in a world that seems to offer them so little. To transgress is to deviate. This does not necessarily mean violence and criminality (as illustrated by the dancing man of Hobart). A key idea of cultural criminology is that the 'seductions of crime' are about the 'moral and sensual attractions in doing evil' and that we need to appreciate fully the 'lived experience of criminality' (see Katz 1988). Thus:

> causal explanations of criminality that stress the importance of structural, environmental, genetic or rational choice factors, over and above the emotional and interpretative qualities of crime, are often guilty of stripping away and repressing key individual emotions such as humiliation, arrogance, ridicule, cynicism (and importantly) pleasure and excitement – emotions that, in many cases, are central to the criminal event. (Hayward 2002, p. 81)

In this framework, deviance offers the perpetrator a means of 'self-transcendence', a way of overcoming the conventionality and mundanity typically associated with the banal routines and practicalities of everyday 'regular life'. For example, the street cultures of youth (such as vandalism, drugs, cruising and peer-group violence) are seen as ways of exerting control and providing avenues of expression when traditional avenues of youthful stimulation and endeavour have long since evaporated. In a similar vein, it is argued that graffiti equals pleasure – and pleasure is intrinsically associated with the powerful affective and visceral aspects of graffiti writing (Halsey & Young 2006).

At another level, however, opportunities for young people to further develop themselves and their own relationship with the wider social world are often restricted by the actions of the institutional providers of amenities and public spaces. This can transform general community amenities, and even youth-specific amenities, into youth-unfriendly spaces.

For some young people, therefore, the illegality of graffiti is precisely the point. The thrill of graffiti work in this instance is premised on the rush of excitement from 'doing wrong', in breaking the conventions, in sending a message to those in authority that the rules will not be adhered to. We cannot underestimate the emotional attractions of, and fun attached to, behaviour that transgresses conventional norms and values. This observation certainly complicates the question of crime prevention in relation to graffiti.

Some forms of crime prevention focus on ways to deter graffiti through manipulation of the physical and social environments. The emphasis here is on removing the opportunities for graffiti work by modifying the environment within which graffiti takes place. A number of measures have been developed along these lines (Clarke 1997; Geason & Wilson 1990; US Bureau of Justice Assistance 1998; Weisel 2002). They include the following examples.

Graffiti removal campaigns

The rapid removal of graffiti has been demonstrated to have an impact in some circumstances (e.g. New York Transit System – see Clarke 1997; Weisel 2002), as it removes the incentive for those graffitists who want an audience for their work. Graffiti removal may involve policy decisions within government departments, such as a transport organisation. It may also entail the introduction of laws that require private property holders, both businesses and home owners, to remove graffiti within a specified time limit.

Target hardening

Target hardening refers to measures taken to make it more difficult for graffitists to make their mark. Specifically, in addition to increasing visible signs of surveillance (e.g. closed-circuit cameras, security patrols), the idea is to use materials that are resistant to graffiti and/or that are easy to clean. Dark surfaces are also seen as discouraging graffiti. Better lighting is also cited as a factor influencing perceptions of risk in undertaking graffiti work (Weisel 2002).

Discouraging and/or displacing graffiti

The idea of this approach is to forestall potential graffiti work by covering a potential target surface with something else, such as replacing footpaths with landscaped walkways or covering walls with climbing vines. Another measure is to reduce the availability of graffiti tools, such as restricting sales of spray paint, or stocking spray paint nozzles separate from the paint can. The use of chalkboards or whiteboards in toilet blocks is designed to encourage graffiti work within established boundaries, on surfaces that are relatively easy to monitor and clean.

Such technical approaches can help displace graffiti from very specific locations and circumstances. In recent years, however, more attention has been devoted to community-based strategies that target offenders and potential offenders in efforts to modify their attitudes and behaviour in relation to graffiti work.

Community-based strategies have several different dimensions. In some instances, the key focus of the intervention is on the whole community. In others, the focus is on working with graffiti groups directly (e.g. see Collins 1998; Halsey & Young 2002).

Community involvement

The emphasis of this approach is to encourage active community involvement in dealing with issues surrounding graffiti work. This might include school and community-based education programs that emphasise both the costs of (what is perceived to be) graffiti vandalism and the benefits of participating in structured graffiti skill workshops and projects. Education can also be directed to the community at large, to inform residents about the nature of graffiti culture, and to decrease any fears associated with graffiti production.

An important component of community-based measures is engagement in clean-up campaigns or, more proactively, participation in 'pride' campaigns designed to improve the appearance of local amenities. The latter is not only concerned with clearing litter and covering over certain types of graffiti but, as well, the creative sponsorship of graffiti to enhance community appearances.

Graffitists' involvement

In this case, the focus is more directly on the graffiti writers. It has been suggested that local knowledge is essential in determining who is doing graffiti and why. Furthermore, the idea is to orient existing graffiti towards pro-social, legal community projects, and away from illegal, graffiti vandalism. This can be accomplished by assisting young people in their skill development, providing avenues for the undertaking of community projects, increasing the prospects of writers or artists receiving an income from involvement in commercial projects. By positing 'positive' versus 'negative' forms of graffiti work, the intention is to foster a graffiti culture that is essentially self-policing. This assumes certain standards of judgment regarding what is acceptable and unacceptable behaviour within a graffiti culture and the community at large.

The point of community-based interventions such as these is less to eradicate graffiti than to contain and redirect it. Such approaches assume that, for some graffiti writers, the movement from 'tags' to 'pieces' is firmly grounded in a local graffiti culture. The intention, therefore, is to shift the nature of this culture in ways that will channel the graffiti production along more socially acceptable lines, as determined by authority figures.

The crime prevention measures described above are not mutually exclusive. Indeed, most practitioners in the field recognise the importance of adopting multipronged approaches in dealing with graffiti (see Weisel 2002). Questions remain, however, as to the costs and desirability of enacting comprehensive anti-graffiti programs. For a start, many who engage in graffiti are simply not interested in 'converting' to legal programs or to have their work evaluated as 'art'. The whole point is to evade and challenge mainstream rules and constraints, whether legal, social or aesthetic. Under these circumstances, a situational crime prevention approach may well be the most viable option for guiding and reshaping spontaneous graffiti behaviour and minimising associated costs and harms (see also chapter 4).

It is fundamental to acknowledge that tackling graffiti is not simply about responding to 'disorder' or 'crime'. Our response to graffiti has to be tempered by the realisation that it can have an important social and political place in our society. Zero-tolerance policies on graffiti can be extremely difficult for enforcement authorities to apply, and insensitive to the sociological realities of graffiti production. There are nevertheless specific instances in which dealing with graffiti does demand an answer of some kind. It can be profoundly disturbing, annoying and threatening. It can affect our sense of neighbourhood pride, our public services, our shop trade, our collective identity. How then should we proceed?

A good starting point is to deal principally with graffiti at the local level. This is reaffirmed in the literature (Iveson 2000; Weisel 2002). It is essential to map out the precise nature of the problem. This means gathering information about types of graffiti, the extent of graffiti, who is directly affected by graffiti, locations of graffiti, methods of graffiti, times when it occurs, and so on. We need to gain some idea of whether it is a problem, which types are perceived to be the problem, for whom it is a problem, and why it is a problem.

Action to deal with graffiti may be required in specific circumstances (e.g. graffiti-covered classroom walls at school; racist graffiti in the local cemetery). In thinking about possible solutions to the problem, it is useful to adopt a problem-solving approach (see chapter 2 – also Weisel 2002) that involves collecting relevant information not just about the potential offenders and causes, but about the nature of the victims and their possible contribution to the problem (where appropriate and applicable). For instance, an escalation in train graffiti may be due to the presence of a new cohort of taggers or artists in the locality. But it also may have something to do with more authoritarian and interventionist styles of station management or train security. School graffiti may likewise raise questions about the experiences of those who currently attend or in the past attended the school, but feel disempowered by and/or resentful about the experience. Perhaps the answer in the latter case might be to open up the school as a community resource, and to offer art classes to those who might benefit from a different type of learning experience.

Graffiti is a complex phenomenon, and there are numerous ambiguities surrounding its production, its consumption and the ways in which we might wish to respond to it. The options available to us include attempting eradication, instigating new ways to manage graffiti production, tolerating graffiti in whatever form it takes, and expanding the alternative cultural spaces available to those who are already stretching the boundaries of convention and mainstream meaning. What is appropriate, necessary or 'do-able' depends on local circumstances, the nature of the graffiti and graffitists, the process and outcomes of analysis and dialogue, and the diversity of interests and values that have to be considered in any decision-making process.

It is important to acknowledge the limitations of crime prevention, at the same time as recognising how certain crime prevention frameworks can enhance community safety and wellbeing. In some instances, however, perceptions of danger and social harm can lead to pre-emptive strategies that have the potential to poison relationships and to reinforce the very things that were deemed to be problematic. This is frequently the case in regards to the group behaviours of young people.

Youth gangs and social conflict

In recent years considerable media attention has been given to the alleged problem of 'youth gangs' in Western cities (see Klein et al. 2001; Gordon 2000; White 2006a; Hagedorn 2007; Goldson 2011; White 2013b). Ironically many young people group together for *safety*; yet such large groups can in turn be intimidating to other young people and residents. It is interesting to note that youth gangs can serve to protect young people against threats to their own sense of security in public spaces (White et al. 1997).

Very often 'gangs' occupy a rather ambiguous position within local communities. As indicated in Box 8.4, this is so for several different reasons. Nevertheless, the image of 'gangs' is a powerful one, and has engendered varying kinds of negative social reactions. For example, the social status and public perception of young people in groups very much influences the regulation of public space. Many groups of young people, some of which might be labelled 'gangs', tend to hang out in places like shopping centres. However, in light of the connections between community circumstances that give rise to gangs and community relations that sustain them, community processes are most likely to provide the best opportunities for their transformation (Spergal & Grossman 1997)

BOX 8.4:   THE PLACE OF GANGS IN LOCAL COMMUNITIES

- Frequently there are close ties between gang members and other members of their community, whether through family, religious or cultural linkages.
- Gang members do not solely engage in criminal activities, but in a wide range of conventional activities that bring them in close contact with other people in the local community.
- Gang membership (however loosely defined) may be a continuous feature of some communities, and thus have a measure of traditional legitimacy attached to it.
- Gang-related activity may tap into underground or criminal economies that provide benefits to local residents in poorer working-class neighbourhoods (in that they provide a source of income and purchasing power that allows money to circulate within community agencies and businesses).
- Gang membership may be viewed by adult members of a community as an important way in which to protect each other, and to maintain a particular social identity important to the community as a whole (visible expression of ethnic pride and strength).

(Source: White 2007b; see also White 2013b)

Community-based approaches have a number of dimensions that include both direct service provision and efforts to build pro-social relationships at the local level. Some are directed at youth specifically; others are designed as whole-of-community strategies that benefit people across a local area. An example of youth-oriented strategy is the employment of detached youth and community workers to provide supervised recreation and leisure activities and after-school programs, by targeting young people and intervening in a low-key fashion.

US research has demonstrated the importance of detached youth worker programs in influencing individual gang membership and group processes, particularly when youth workers are ex-gang members themselves (see Howell 2000; Spergal & Grossman 1997). Some of these studies have suggested that interventions, in fact, can enhance gang cohesion by helping to foster joint activities, common identification and overall group cohesiveness (see especially Klein 1995). Whether through welfare or suppression programs, the inadvertent effect of direct intervention with street groups can be to increase gang cohesiveness. This is problematic so far as 'The more cohesive gang usually is the more criminally involved' (Klein 2002, p. 247). Regarding the development of groups such as the 'Glenorchy Mafia' in Tasmania, this observation provides an important cautionary warning to practitioners. What was once a sports team for 'disadvantaged kids', jokingly referred to as the GM, has over time evolved into a publicly identified 'youth gang'.

Another example is having youth facilities available that provide young people with safe places in which to hang out, while simultaneously providing an opportunity (through adult and youth mentors) to develop an alternative sense of belonging, identity and self-worth compared to belonging to a 'gang'. This is a youth service approach, in which the young people come to the centre.

Services for youth, whether youth-specific or for the community as a whole, must acknowledge social differences within communities. For example, specific spaces and facilities could be reserved, perhaps at designated times, exclusively for certain young people (e.g. swimming pools, rooms that could be used for prayers), in order that religious and cultural practices be acknowledged and respected (White 1998).

Community-based approaches also include those that involve large-scale, and often non-youth specific measures. Urban renewal projects, for example, are meant to increase work opportunities for, and civic participation among, local residents. The intention of such interventions is to change the material situation and infrastructure of specific sites and neighbourhoods and to change perceptions and attitudes among residents and non-residents about these areas. For instance, the Tasmanian suburb of Bridgewater (and its neighbouring suburb, Gagebrook) had a very negative image, was linked to extensive crime and anti-social behaviour in Tasmania, and was rated as one of the unhealthiest communities in Australia.

The Bridgewater Urban Renewal Programme (BURP) was designed to change this situation, by changing the circumstances of the community. Four main avenues for change were identified (see Whelan 2001):

- **Marketing and promotion**: through creation of a local newspaper that explicitly attempts to provide positive stories and coverage of the area, and through the employment of a public relations firm.
- **Community leadership and community involvement**: through conscious efforts on the part of community and state agencies to work together rather than independently, and the use of initiatives that involve citizens (such as creation of local sports teams).
- **The building of pride and aspirations**: through continual assertion that local residents deserve and ought to expect the best in the way of living standards, with an emphasis on people taking responsibility to make the neighbourhood something to be proud of.
- **Physical renewal and design**: through projects such as tree planting, mural painting, landscaping of parks and shopping complexes, and painting of homes by tenants, and initiatives such as establishment of a local garden club.

Community reputation – especially if accompanied by stigma associated with gangs, crime and anti-social activities – can have a dramatic impact on life within particular locales. Young people who live in stigmatised areas are more likely to suffer the consequences in the form of reduced job opportunities and difficulties in moving out of their neighbourhood (e.g. see Lee 2006). A 'bad' community reputation may occasionally translate into a gang mentality based on defensiveness and reassertion of worth in the face of a hostile 'outside' world. Changing the community's reputation through communal development is one way in which to address these issues (Spergal & Grossman 1997).

In broad terms, a community approach to gang problems has, at some stage, to grapple with issues of social justice and social inequality. Addressing the hard issues that so often appear too big to handle requires vision and political will (see Canada, National Crime Prevention Council 1996). It also requires a strategic plan (see chapter 6). One way in which local government, in particular, can contribute is to foster action across three areas of intervention, as outlined in Box 8.5.

A community strategy ought not to be confused with a neighbourhood approach (focusing on geographically-defined physical environments), although the two are obviously interrelated. Changing local social environments is ultimately what counts, and this means engaging and involving young people and their communities in finding solutions to their own problems, with the support of expert advice and contributions by different tiers of government. Also essential to this task is giving particular attention to those young people who are at risk of becoming gang members or who are presently gang members, so that they too

---

BOX 8.5:   BUILDING COMMUNITY AS AN ANTI-GANG
           INTERVENTION

1. Framing anti-gang strategies in terms of what particular communities need in order to break the cycle of crime and violence, rather than solely concentrating on control and punishment of individual offenders.
2. Transforming the conditions that give rise to gang membership by giving practical weight to concepts such as solidarity and cooperation via encouragement of pro-social neighbourhood groups.
3. Lobbying governments for more assistance in the redevelopment of local neighbourhoods while simultaneously mapping, and utilising, existing assets, capacities and skills of local residents, including young people.

---

have a meaningful role to play in the regeneration of their neighbourhoods (see Davies 1995; Diacon 1999).

Encouraging youth participation is not as simple as it may seem. This is especially so if the object of the exercise is linked to anti-gang strategies. For example, the background of program staff can influence levels of participation. An evaluation of an intervention in the US found that, while the project incorporated opportunity enhancement and youth participation principles, a major difficulty was that the 'case workers were all white, middle-class adults working with lower-class adolescents' (Pappas 2001, p. 10). Assessment of the program demonstrated the need for, and importance of having, local people from within the community to serve as case workers and organisers. This case also highlights the potential of peer mentors in addressing local youth issues.

Finally, it needs to be reiterated that dealing with real or imagined gang problems is a challenging task. It embodies different ideological perspectives and conflicting viewpoints. Making urban areas safer places in which to live and work means tackling a wide range of social disorders and incivilities. It means trying to strengthen the bonds that link people to their families, schools, workplaces and communities.

Alcohol and street violence

Street violence associated with alcohol and other drug use is a major social issue in many Western countries today including Australia (Winlow & Hall 2006; Graham & Homel 2008; White & Wyn 2013). A leisure culture that links alcohol use with a good time, combined with a culture of violence, generates risks for young people.

Public portrayals of these issues tend to emphasise particular moments, events and features of the night-time economy and culture. Some of these include widespread binge drinking, 'glassing' (smashing glasses or bottles into someone's face or head) and what appears to be mindless thuggery involving groups of young men.

Alcohol-related violence is a growing problem in Australia. Many factors contribute to the problem and it is not surprising, therefore, that a multifaceted response is needed to address it. Above all, it is essential to de-normalise alcohol-related violence, if genuine and effective responses to the problem are to be found. The main concern of this section is to map out the relationship between alcohol and public violence, and to review both the key dimensions and dynamics of alcohol-related street violence, and recommended courses of action in relation to this.

Not everyone drinks the same way

Whether it is binge drinking among teenagers (or, as sometimes is forgotten, adults of any age) or the drug habits of gang members versus non-gang members (White & Mason 2006), the fact is that different people drink differently, and that drinking varies according to occasion and to congregations of people. Careful analysis of drinking patterns and cultural contexts, especially in regards to young people, has identified a number of relevant social dynamics. It has been suggested, for example, that lack of appropriate leisure options can result in drinking as relief from 'leisure boredom' for some young people (Roche et al. 2008). Once started on this pathway (to initial use of alcohol), the major issue then becomes how alcohol is consumed.

The shift from 'just drinking' to 'risky drinking' has been associated with several different factors. For instance, *features of social settings* found to encourage risky drinking include, among others, large group size (especially in relation to home parties and gatecrashing), presence of intoxicated people, drinking games (where the intention is intoxication), and pre-gaming or pre-loading (drinking in order to get drunk before going to an alcohol-free event or setting where alcohol will be expensive) (Roche et al. 2008). Related to these factors, studies have found that those young people who drink at their own or at a friend's house prior to attending city nightlife venues reported significantly higher total alcohol consumption over a night out than those not drinking until reaching bars and nightclubs. They are also much more likely to have been involved in a fight in the city's nightlife than those who did not start drinking at home first (Hughes et al. 2007). The intensity of access to communication technologies has also been positively correlated with heavy use of alcohol, through, for example, facilitating the organisation of 'big nights out' (Roche et al. 2008).

Drinking heavily is socially constructed and very much depends upon the interplay between the individual, culture and society. What to drink, when, how, and how much are subjects for deliberation, not simply left to random chance. *Cultural explanations* point to important shifts in attitudes and thinking about drinking. For example, drinking heavily has been associated with the notion of 'calculated hedonism'; that is, a calculated and planned, rational hedonism in which young people plan to 'let loose' (Brain 2000; Roche et al. 2008). Related to this is the idea of a 'culture of intoxication', a culture that is informed by a tradition of 'weekday restraint and weekend excess' (Measham 2006, p. 258).

Culture is influenced by social setting, and vice versa. This is illustrated, for example, in the way in which the emergence of shots, aftershots or shooters, heavily promoted in bars, have become an established and popular part of an evening's drinking during weekend nights out (Measham & Brain 2005). Their consumption is related to consumer objectives of getting drunk quicker and treating friends (since shots are cheaper than other forms of alcoholic beverage).

How much one drinks is linked to violence and aggression, and the injuries arising from these. A study on the *association of hostility to drinking pattern* has shown that hostility is directly related to variables such as total monthly intake of alcohol, drinking frequency, drinks per drinking day, and heavy episodic drinking (Boyle et al. 2007). Research on persons hospitalised for assault in the Canadian province of Ontario found that the risk of being a victim of serious assault increases with alcohol sales, especially among young urban men (Ray et al. 2008).

Alcohol has been linked to serious injuries that are enough to warrant presentation at a hospital. In a NSW study, one-third of the injured patients interviewed reported consuming alcohol prior to the injury and almost two-thirds of these patients stated that they had been drinking at licensed premises. Moreover, alcohol consumption was found to be more prevalent among patients presenting with injuries resulting from interpersonal violence, with almost two-thirds of these patients reporting that they had been drinking prior to the injury (Poynton et al. 2005).

The *type of alcohol consumed* also has social consequences. For example, a Western Australian study showed that cask wine and high-strength beer consumption were significantly associated with rates of night-time assault (Stockwell et al. 1998). Research has examined the different types of drinkers and the probability of committing offences depending upon how one drinks. How much, and the way in which, one consumes alcohol is directly related to probability of committing disorder across a number of dimensions: drink-driving, verbal abuse, creating a public disturbance, stealing property, damaging property and physical abuse (Makkai 1998). Moreover, the frequency of engagement in social disorder increases according to propensity to drink heavily, to binge drink, and to drink in harmful ways.

Licensed venues and patterns of alcohol consumption

There has been considerable research that has examined the specific relationship between licensed venues and levels of violence. A key finding is that there is a correlation between late trading hours, increased levels of alcohol consumption (compared with hotels with earlier trading hours) and significant increases in assault rates (compared with hotels with earlier closing hours) (Chikritzhs & Stockwell 2002; Graham & Homel 2008). People who live in areas with greater densities of bars and pubs report greater norms for alcohol-related aggression, and greater peak drinking levels were directly related to greater levels of hostility (Graham & Homel 2008; Treno et al. 2007). Similarly, those postcode residential areas that have a higher alcohol sales volume have higher rates of assault, malicious damage to property and offensive behaviour than those with a lower sales volume (see Briscoe & Donnelly 2001a).

Studies have shown that there is a positive relationship between outlet density and assault rates (i.e. the more licensed premises in a particular area, the more likely an increase in assault rates), and that this relationship is non-linear, which implies that there are potential threshold or saturation densities at which point the likelihood of violence is dramatically increased (Graham & Homel 2008; Livingston 2008; see also Chikritzhs et al. 2007)

A small number of problematic licensed premises are associated with a disproportionate amount of violence, with hotels and nightclubs being most problematic. Hotels with extended or 24-hour trading recorded a greater number of assaults compared with those trading standard hours (Briscoe & Donnelly 2001b). Certain categories of licensed premises (e.g. nightclubs, hotels and taverns) are associated with increased likelihood of the risk of alcohol-related harm compared to others (clubs and restaurants). Moreover, within and across the types of licensed venues, those deemed to be high 'risk' exhibited features such as the continued serving of intoxicated persons, the offering of discounted drinks and the permitting of overcrowding (see Briscoe & Donnelly 2001a; Graham 2009; Graham & Homel 2008).

It has been found that a range of environmental variables associated with the physical aspects of the drinking establishment increase the potential for alcohol-related violence, including such things as uncleanliness, uncomfortable settings, poorly designed seating and bar access, and poor ventilation (Graham 2009;

Graham & Homel 2008). Violence around licensed premises is also associated with things such as queues in clubs, pubs and nightclubs, and frustrations associated with patron perceptions of unfair and delaying processes of entry.

The proliferation of vertical drinking establishments has been linked to increased levels of alcohol-related harms. These consist of establishments in which patrons are forced to stand while drinking and have nowhere to place their glasses. This is associated with an increased pace of drinking and consequential social harms (Graham 2009; Nicholas 2008). The alcohol served/consumed also has a bearing on alcohol-related assaults, with consumption of cask wine and high-strength beer significantly associated with night-time assaults and alcohol-related harm generally (Briscoe & Donnelly 2001a; Chikritzhs et al. 2007).

Responding to alcohol-related violence

Crime prevention aimed at reducing or preventing alcohol-related violence needs to address various factors simultaneously, as indicated in Table 8.1.

Specific suggestions with regard to how we might reduce alcohol-related crime include those aimed at changing alcohol consumption patterns, those oriented towards the licensed premises and those based upon educational provision.

Alcohol consumption

It has been argued that what is needed is enforcement of existing prohibited drinking laws (e.g. alcohol-free zones) insofar as a reduction in the number of intoxicated persons on the street could have an impact on crimes such as assault (Briscoe & Donnelly 2001a). Increasing the minimum legal drinking age or minimum legal purchase of alcohol has also been put forward (Nicholas 2008). Related to these is the idea of ensuring adequate liquor licensing legislation so as to address such issues as inadequate definitions of intoxication (which curtail the ability to prosecute licensees for serving intoxicated patrons) and inadequate scope (Nicholas 2008).

Other measures have included restricting the sales of specific beverage types, such as cask wine and full-strength beer (Nicholas 2008), and to systematically reduce the levels of alcohol consumption in existing sites by an increase in tax on alcohol, restricting outlet sales hours or reducing the number of outlets (Briscoe & Donnelly 2001a). The imposition of strategic taxes on alcohol that penalise the high-alcohol product and reward the low-alcohol product – and that could be channelled into programs that reduce alcohol-related harms – have been suggested

Table 8.1   Matrix for organising protective factors in relation to violent behaviour

Level of observation	Temporal proximity		
	Predisposing	Situational	Immediate
Social and economic forces (macrosocial)	Customs related to drinking Reconstructing masculinity and its link to violence Liquor licensing laws Anti-racist and anti-sexist campaigns	Special event planning that offers regulation of and alternatives to alcohol consumption Shortened trading hours for licensed premises Limit exposure to violent entertainment, especially in public venues Dispersal of licensed premises in specific geographical areas	Limited availability of alcohol Enhance responsible alcohol service provision
Encounters between people (microsocial)	Promotion of a culture of peace rather than conflict Closing of violent pubs and drinking establishments Promotion of 'safe' drinking practices and places	Bouncer as mediator not enforcer Separation of potential protagonists Displacement / exclusion of violent persons from public spaces and venues	Street level liaison between public and private security operators and police services Effective crowd dispersal techniques and strategies Zero tolerance to expressions of violence and threats of violence
Psychosocial	Campaigns around responsible drinking	High profile given to principles of Step Back Think	Change in type and number of alcoholic drinks available
Neuro-behavioural	Public information on health implications of alcohol consumption during pregnancy	Availability of emergency medical services	Availability of breathalyser equipment

Source: drawing from and expanding on Roth 1994a, 1994b.

as well (Nicholas 2008). However, it has also been pointed out that National Competition Policy is committed to liberalising the restrictions on the sale and availability of alcohol and promoting competition in this industry, and this can undermine strategies based upon restriction (Fleming 2008).

Licensed premises

Measures that deal with licensed premises include identifying problematic licensed premises that are most associated with alcohol-related harm (Nicholas 2008), and establishing a venues-rating system in which patrons rate establishments on the basis of safety and good practice. Staggering hotels' and clubs' closing times, ensuring better transport is available to move intoxicated patrons out of these areas more efficiently or police monitoring of bottlenecks where several licensed premises are located have been put forward as intervention strategies (Briscoe & Donnelly 2001a).

A number of commentators speak about the importance of regulatory issues. These include limiting the intoxication levels of patrons who drink on licensed premises by enforcing policies promoted by responsible drinking campaigns (Briscoe & Donnelly 2001a). Consideration is given to implementing licensing accords, as a means to promote communication, but it is acknowledged that these also need systematic enforcement activity (Nicholas 2008). Moreover, the targeting of liquor law enforcement activities on those most likely to reduce alcohol-related harms, such as more attention being given to licensees rather than patrons by police, has been suggested (Nicholas 2008).

Another recommendation is for the introduction and enforcement of late-hour entry restrictions, which involve not allowing new patrons into a venue beyond a set time. Lockouts vary in terms of type of venue, number of venues in particular area, times in which they come into effect, and whether exceptions are allowed and, if so, under what conditions (KPMG 2008; Mazerolle et al. 2012).

Police use of front-line strategies that involve keeping a visible police presence on the streets and that involve a range of enforcement options (such as walk-throughs; intelligence-based activity, e.g. identification of hot spots and problematic premises; and task forces or 'grog squads') have also been noted (Fleming 2008).

Education

Various kinds of education programs and projects have been put forward as one way in which to change the culture surrounding drinking, and the culture surrounding public violence. For example, there is peer education that strives to break down culturally ingrained attitudes towards violence and to highlight the negative consequences of alcohol and other related forms of violent behaviour. This is illustrated by Step Back Think, a youth-generated intervention that involves young people talking to other young people about real life cases of harm and violence.

There are also mass campaigns directed at young people, especially high school and university students, with the objective of enhancing their self-cognition and encouraging them to take responsibility for both 'high-risk' drinking (a health issue) and irresponsible behaviour associated with consumption of alcohol (a social issue) (see Moore 2000). In the Australian context, these include media campaigns, such as 'Don't Turn a Night Out into a Nightmare', that attempt to demonstrate the violence and indiscretions associated with too much alcohol consumption (Toohey 2008).

There are also systematic forms of school-based alcohol education that include strategies and models such as information approaches (that emphasise the risks associated with drinking), affective approaches (that seek to build self-esteem of young people so that they are less vulnerable to peer pressure to drink in certain ways) and social influence approaches (that involve many messages and multifaceted action) (Hughes 2008). The social norms approach adopts what might be described as a positive strategy in order to reassure school students that sensible approaches to alcohol are in fact 'the norm'.

Other measures have included provision of adequate transportation (e.g. taxis, trams, trains and buses) in areas with concentrations of licensed premises, and the expansion of measures that directly impact on the social harms associated with alcohol consumption, such as sobering-up units and night patrols (Nicholas 2008).

Integrated approaches to alcohol-related violence

An integrated model of intervention is crucial to the success or otherwise of strategies designed to reduce alcohol-related violence. This is acknowledged in the specific literature on alcohol-related public violence. For example, a roundtable discussion and analysis of violence in public places held in Victoria in October 2008 brought together participants from a range of organisations and with a broad spectrum of expertise in alcohol, youth and violence related issues (Eckersley & Reeder 2008). As a whole, the forum offered the view that an integrated approach to alcohol-related anti-social behaviour and violence is essential. Key policy areas and recommendations included:

> *Business regulation*
> e.g. stronger regulation of licensed premises alongside better education of venue staff

Law enforcement

e.g. increased randomised policing of premises

Medical services

e.g. improved responses by, and communication between, police, ambulance and hospitals

Judicial system

e.g. development of a peer court to allow young people to be involved in court processes

Education

e.g. school programs that include conflict management skills and an emphasis on the social and emotional wellbeing of students

Technology and media

e.g. greater regulation of media and communication technologies to minimise adverse effects of portrayals of violence

Community and culture

e.g. encourage greater community participation in crime prevention activities.

In the specific area of alcohol-related public violence, recent work has focused primarily on the relationship between alcohol, harm and the licensed environment (McIlwain & Homel 2009). In developing an effective operational model of intervention this project has emphasised the combination of:

- targeted police enforcement (TP)
- staff training based upon the Safer Bars Program (SB) in Canada
- community mobilisation (CM).

Importantly, it is asserted that longer term reduction in social harms requires the sustained implementation of strategies, and strategies that encompass the myriad of factors that lead to aggression and violence. Successful intervention depends upon establishing a combination of partnerships and community engagement, embedded within the local context, and both informal and formal styles of regulation.

The issues covered in this section raise a number of important questions relating to addressing alcohol-related violence. These include how to deal with the attractions of alcohol and alcohol-related violence to, especially, youth, and, in particular, young males; how to develop policing approaches that do not simply create resentment among club or nightclub patrons and thus generate more violence; and how to identify third parties who should take responsibility for dealing with alcohol-related violence. While an integrated approach makes sense, actually developing and coordinating this can be challenging given the competing interests of various parties and the normalisation of alcohol consumption in countries like Australia. Generating a cultural shift in relation to alcohol consumption will be difficult.

Unexpected disruptions to the community

What happens in local neighbourhoods, malls and shopping centres is hard to predict, or manage. This is certainly true of episodes of group 'swarming' and one-off events such as Schoolies Week. These, too, can be disruptive of communities and neighbourhoods. They also demand our attention from the point of view of community safety and crime prevention.

Swarming refers to the unexpected gathering of large numbers of people in particular public locales (see White 2006b). Swarming may or may not feature violence. It does, however, involve large crowds – crowds that may occasionally transform into 'mobs'. The size of the crowd is what also transforms a private home or private party into a public event via the spilling out of people onto footpaths and surrounding streets and lawns. The sudden gathering of large numbers of people in public spaces may be organised or be spontaneous; it may engender or be associated with violence, or it might not. Such a gathering may include riots (situations in which large numbers of people seem to spontaneously engage in unlawful, anti-social and violent behaviour) or mob violence (where the key variable is 'the crowd', and the transformation of the crowd into a mob).

Gatecrashing, as one particular form of swarming, likewise can involve events that are sparked largely by immediate crowd dynamics rather than intent to harm. Across Australia the presence of hundreds of gatecrashers at some parties has been facilitated by new communication technologies, and the search for venues that do not rely on security guards and bouncers to keep order. Not all gatecrashed parties end in violence. Again, this largely depends on the atmosphere of the event, who is there, the quantity of alcohol consumed, and how order is maintained by hosts. Investigation of previous instances of gatecrashing – and experience gained from dealing with 'fixed' events, such as Schoolies Week – allow for pre-planning; even where the exact location, numbers and timing of events, such as gatecrashing, are not known.

Swarming types of social gatherings are by their nature more spontaneous than planned events, such as Schoolies Week or Australia Day celebrations or New Year's Eve. Nevertheless, analysis of planned events can give us insights into, and some pre-planned responses to, some types of swarming. Box 8.7 provides a snapshot of measures that have been adopted to deal with events such as Schoolies Week in some jurisdictions.

BOX 8.6:   PLANNED EVENTS, SUCH AS SCHOOLIES WEEK

Philosophy of 'community safety' rather than 'law enforcement':
* preparation of communities and assessment of what worked in the past (but not generating panic about the risks of events),
* increased service staff (e.g. crisis and health workers)
* increased number of support workers (non-uniformed) to assist students
* use of students as events 'staff'
* culture of collaboration that includes dialogue with a wide range of stakeholders, including young people.

Emphasis on safe fun:
* use of plastic bottles
* advertising and information pamphlets on health aspects (e.g. not to swim and drink)
* structured events, with a focus on entertainment not alcohol or drug use
* reduction of overcrowding at particular sites and services;
* available food and alternative (i.e. non-alcoholic) drinks.

Explicit rules and behaviour boundaries:
* registration and 'tagging' of schoolies;
* designated areas and contained spaces;
* adequate transportation and accommodation;
* 'friendly' but firm security and police presence;
* exclusion or diversion of 'toolies' (over-age young adults who may attempt to gatecrash an event);
* well-lit pathways, exit and entry points;
* signage for emergency venues and services;
* emphasis on clear rules of behaviour (i.e. 'dos', not 'don'ts').

(Source: White 2006b)

Successful implementation of these types of measures requires understanding of the theories and principles of CPTED, situational prevention and social prevention. Also, passive forms of social control should be emphasised so as to ensure that interventions remain innocuous and don't detract from the 'feel' of an event. Consider, for example, how crowds are managed in large venues such as 'theme parks'. One example of this is the regime of discipline in place at Disney World, as described by Shearing and Stenning (1992). Visitors who enter and then progress through Disney World have their conduct constantly shaped or ordered through various means:

- by the use of control staff who advise and direct, and through piped information tapes that play through speakers
- by a range of physical and architectural controls that limit where people can go, and in what way they can move
- by direct intervention of the controllers themselves, where failure to comply with the rules of use will invoke a punitive response.

All of these mechanisms are designed to induce compliance with the specified norms of behaviour in Disney World – by producing in the visitor a desire to behave in a particular way (i.e. self-discipline), by restricting the choices that visitors have available to them (i.e. by way of physical design and architecture) or by engaging staff whose role is to enforce compliance (i.e. direct intervention). These interventions are not informed by moral objectives (i.e. notions of behaviour as being intrinsically 'bad' or 'good'). They are purely instrumental – they are designed to enforce an image and an environment in which the purpose of control is to facilitate particular forms of behaviour and enjoyment of the facilities.

These kinds of measures are also used in other types of venues and enterprises, such as shopping centres and malls. They also feature prominently in the regulation of planned events, such as Schoolies Week. While the latter is not expressly oriented towards profit and consumption, the application of relevant techniques is intended to provide for and facilitate an event that is safe and socially controlled for the entertainment and benefit of members of the public generally (or, in some cases, specific segments of the population, such as teenagers).

By combining our knowledge of previous 'disorderly' events with knowledge of 'what works' to facilitate planned events, such as Schoolies Week, we can construct ideas of how we might plan for and intervene in problems such as gatecrashing. This is evident, for example, in the introduction of Party Safe Information Kits that are now promoted in most jurisdictions around the country. The kits include advice such as:

- Plan your party carefully beforehand.
- Make start and finish times.
- Have a strict invitation-only policy.
- Register the party with the police.
- Alert participants to the idea that police will patrol the party.
- Get other adults to help supervise.
- Advise neighbours in advance.
- Encourage parents to collect their children at the end of the party.

Strategic placement of the local police 'booze bus' in adjoining areas, monitoring of the internet to ascertain who is saying what about which venue, and assessment of dispersal and movement routes in relation to the party can also constitute low-level measures that contribute to safety and wellbeing.

Conclusion

The themes of this chapter have been the need to develop multipronged approaches that are inclusive of CPTED, situational and social prevention measures. Addressing crime and safety problems that arise in public spaces involves conscious decisions about what kind of public spaces we wish to foster, how best to regulate events and situations that may periodically become unruly or disruptive, and how we might negotiate the tensions associated with the ambiguities of public spaces. Whether it is graffiti, youth gangs, street violence or gatecrashing, measures can be taken that offer relatively benign ways in which to limit the extent of disorder and social harms associated with public spaces.

CASE STUDY 8.1 THE SOCIAL NORMS APPROACH TO ALCOHOL-RELATED ISSUES

There are systematic forms of school-based alcohol education that include different strategies and models. A social norm approach adopts what might be described as a positive strategy in order to reassure school students that sensible approaches to alcohol are in fact 'the norm'. The Social Norms Approach (SNAP) to schools-based alcohol education recognises the positive impact of peer groups, and the fact that healthy and protective behaviours are already present in most youthful populations (see Hughes 2008). The SNAP intervention is based on the idea that many young people have an inaccurate notion of how frequently and heavily their peers consume alcohol, that they base their own decisions and actions on what they believe most of their peers are doing and that they will be less likely to conform to a 'false norm' (e.g. most teenagers engage in lots of binge drinking) if repeatedly exposed to the 'true norm' (i.e. teenagers drink less, and less frequently, than the image). Process and impact evaluation of the SNAP showed that it is a 'theoretically informed and effective model for alcohol health promotion, which is compatible with the harm minimisation focus of the Australian drug and alcohol policy framework, and could usefully be applied to a range of other health and social issues' (Hughes et al., 2008a; Hughes 2008b, p. 2).

QUESTIONS

Questions for further exploration

1. Public space, including the street, is made up of multiple users and multiple uses. What are the implications of this observation for the development of programs to reduce crime and disorder in public spaces?

2. Why are some types of graffiti socially acceptable and other types not? Does this have any implication for how we might develop strategies to reduce graffiti?

3. What issues and factors should strategies to reduce the problem of youth gangs focus on?

4. In what sense is violence and alcohol use in Australia 'normalised'? What challenges does this present for the development of policy to reduce alcohol-related violence?

EXTENSION TOPICS AND REFERENCES

1. To what extent should policies to reduce crime and disorder in public spaces take account of the fact that public spaces are inherently ambiguous in regards to uses and users, with this a source of attraction and a potential mechanism of social exclusion/social inclusion? Discuss this with reference to young women's use of public spaces.

References

Hopkins, P. (2010) *Young people, place and identity*. London: Routledge.

White, R. (2012) 'The making, taking and shaking of public spaces', in E. Barclay, C. Jones & R. Mawby (eds), *The problem of pleasure: tourism, leisure and crime*. London: Routledge.

2. The night-time economy has revolutionised the nature and dynamics of inner-city public spaces. When, how and why did this occur, and what implications does this have for crime and crime prevention?

References

Graham, K. (2009) 'They fight because we let them! Applying a situational crime prevention model to barroom violence', *Drug and Alcohol Review*, vol. 28, no. 2, pp. 103–109.

Graham, K. & Homel, R. (2008) *Raising the bar: preventing aggression in and around bars, pubs and clubs*. Devon: Willan Publishing.

Mazerolle, L., White, G., Ransley, J. & Ferguson, P. (2012) 'Violence in and around entertainment districts: a longitudinal analysis of the impact of late-night lockout legislation', *Law & Policy*, vol. 34, no. 1, pp. 55–57.

Weisel, D.L. (2002) *Graffiti*. Problem-Oriented Guides for Police Series, No 9. Office of Community Oriented Policing Service, US Department of Justice, www.popcenter. org/problems/graffiti.

Winlow, S. & Hall, S. (2006) *Violent night: urban leisure and contemporary culture*. Oxford: Berg.

EMERGENT ISSUES FOR CRIME PREVENTION

Introduction

This chapter will discuss the following topics:

- cyber-crime and crime prevention directed at online activities
- crime prevention and counter-terrorism
- police and crime prevention
- environmental crime and crime prevention.

In this chapter we consider four areas in which significant events and technologies have emerged that are demanding societal responses of some kind or another and/or that are changing the face of crime control. The first two sections consider issues pertaining to cyber-crime and counter-terrorism. Following on from this, we briefly discuss the importance of new forms of policing to the overall crime prevention agenda. The final section examines environmental crimes and recent criminological responses to these threats.

Cyber-crime and cyber-safety

This section explores the nature and dynamics of cyber-crime and issues pertaining to cyber-safety. There is some overlap between these two issues, with each raising issues about the perils and pitfalls of new information technologies and phenomenon, such as the internet.

A variety of offences are associated with the use of information and communication technology. These offences are variously referred to as e-crime, cyber-crime, high-tech crime and computer crime. Three kinds of offences have been identified (Parliament of Australia Joint Committee 2004):

1. *An offence that is committed using the technology*

   e.g. conventional crime such as fraud committed by technological means, including identity fraud; grooming children in chat rooms by paedophiles that can end in actual contact with the child; and internet (bogus) banking, credit card fraud and money laundering.

2. *An offence that targets computers themselves, and seeks to destroy or alter stored information or data, with the intent also to interfere in processes that the data pertains to.*

   e.g. denial of service attacks, where internet ports or email of target computer systems are bombarded with data to prevent them from functioning (e.g. mass-mailing email systems); attempts to disrupt a city's water supply by interfering with the computers that control it. This interference can be conducted through a number of means, including attacks by hackers, worms, viruses and Trojans:

- hackers – people with sufficient technical ability to gain access to another person's computer or to a network through the use of stolen passwords, or interference technology that provides access to networks and individual computers
- worm – a self-replicating computer program that can delete files or send email documents
- virus – a piece of program code that copies itself and then attaches to the 'host' computer's operating system. They can be destructive by altering files or erasing information from disks, or can allow other third parties to gain access to a person's computer without authorisation
- trojan – a stand-alone program that must be transferred intentionally, such as through email. When opened it might alter or delete files on the machine, or access the user's email.

3. *An offence in which the computer is used as storage for information about an offence*

e.g. a drug offence in which supply records are kept on computer.

Other offences and offensive behaviours worth noting include:

- 'nuisance' emails and 'spam' (i.e. unsolicited commercial electronic messages)
- under-age access to material unsuitable for children
- illegal pornographic materials, such as that involving transmission of pornographic child sex imagery
- dissemination of hate or racist material online
- mishandling or ignoring of privacy provisions and illegitimate transfer of personal information
- cyber-bullying (see chapter 7).

To these we can add problems that have emerged with the expansion of new technologies, such as Bluetooth and mobile phone texting. These range from their impact on the safe driving of cars, to their use by street gangs to undertake illegal activity. A US study of current and former gang members in Fresno, Los Angeles and St Louis, for example, found that 71 per cent of those interviewed reported using a social networking site (Decker & Pyrooz 2011). From the point of view of offending, the study found that the gang members committed acts such as illegally downloading music, harassing or threatening someone online, and attacking another person because of events that occurred online.

Attention has not only been directed at computer offences, but at the wider issue of cyber-safety (Parliament of Australia 2010). Concerns here relate to the nature, prevalence, implications and level of risk associated with cyber-safety threats, such as:

- online child abuse (cyber-bullying, cyber-stalking and sexual grooming)
- exposure to illegal and inappropriate content
- inappropriate social and health behaviours (e.g. technology addiction and online promotion of anorexia, drug use, underage drinking and smoking)
- identity theft
- breaches of privacy.

We can add to this the phenomenon of gatecrashing, such as when the location of parties are posted on Facebook and hundreds of 'strangers' show up. Concern has also been expressed about particularly young people's use of social networking sites in relation to privacy, disclosure and breach of confidence; intellectual property rights, especially copyright infringement; defamation; and criminal laws, including harassment and offensive material (de Zwart et al. 2011). With regards to the latter, the issue of 'sexting' is especially relevant. Sexting is when someone sends inappropriate naked or sexual images or video footage of themselves or others by text message. This is increasing due to the availability of webcams, mobile phone cameras and video cameras. There is also increasing distribution due to availability and large-scale use of texting, YouTube, and Facebook. A recent problem has been the conviction of teenagers for 'child pornography' who participate in sexting.

Investigation of the intergenerational dynamics shaping attitudes towards and usage of social networking services and cyber-safety have attempted to re-focus attention on the ways in which young people themselves relate to new information technologies. These considerations are essential when it comes to crime prevention and harm reduction strategies involving new information and communication technologies.

Conventional approaches to promoting cyber-safety among young people tend to focus on risk management, typically through educational and regulatory approaches. Most cyber-safety programs are delivered through the school setting, which are typically removed from other settings (such as the family and work) and social relationships (with peers, parents and other adults) in which young people regularly engage (Third et al. 2010, p. 9). Thinking about the issues in this way means that responses to cyber-safety need to acknowledge young people's expertise in technology and the use of the internet (Third et al. 2010). The emphasis, therefore, should be less upon risk management and regulation focused on young people than on strategies that incorporate 'real world' experiences and knowledge acquisition. Third et al. (2010, p. 24), for example, argue that the following principles should guide the development of cyber-safety education models:

- Development must be undertaken in partnership with young people and adults in order that cyber-safety education can both be inclusive of young people's voices and expertise, and address adults' concerns and curiosities.
- Models for cyber-safety education must acknowledge the technical and social expertise of young people by positioning them as experts.
- Models must be experiential (i.e. they must engage parents in learning about the social, technical and cultural dimensions of SNS).
- The ideal model will combine face to face with online delivery.
- Models will have the scope to meet the specific technical skills needs of adults, as well as providing capacity for high-level conversations about the socio-cultural dimensions of young people's technology use.
- Approaches need to be flexible and iterative so that they can keep pace with the emergence of new online and networked media technologies and practices.

Rather than being top-down in orientation and reflecting generational assumptions and fears, such principles begin with the idea that young people are more knowledgeable than previously assumed when it comes to safety and security online.

Identity theft

A major concern for authorities is identity theft. The Australian Competition and Consumer Commission (undated) provides a Scam Watch information sheet on 'Identity theft'. It alerts the reader to the different types of identity theft:

- Sending an email in reply to a request that appears to originate from your banking or financial institution or telecommunications provider. Known as phishing, these emails aim to deceive you into disclosing your personal and banking details to scammers. Most work by including special links in the email to take you to a combination of genuine and bogus websites.
- Phoney fraud alerts are similar to phishing scams where scammers trick you into handing over your personal details. A common fraud alert involves the scammer pretending to be from your bank informing you that your credit card or account has been cancelled because of suspicious criminal activity (various excuses are used). They will then deceive you into providing account details to 'confirm' your identity.
- Bogus job opportunities on job websites. The scammer may use or sell your personal information provided in the job applications.

- Card skimming is the illegal copying of information from the magnetic strip of a credit or ATM card. This can create a fake or 'cloned' card.
- Spyware is software that traces the activity on your computer. For instance keyloggers record what keys you press on your keyboard. Scammers can use this information to steal online banking passwords or other personal information.

Newman and McNally (2005) posit that there are three stages to identity theft:

Stage 1: *Acquisition* of the identity through theft, computer hacking, fraud, trickery, force, or redirecting or intercepting mail, or even by legal means (e.g. purchase information on the Internet).

Stage 2: *Use* of the identity for financial gain (the most common motivation) or to avoid arrest or otherwise hide one's identity from law enforcement or other authorities (e.g. bill collectors). Crimes may include account takeover, opening of new accounts, use of debit or credit card details, sale of personal information on the street or black market, acquisition ('breeding') of additional identity-related documents (e.g. driver's licence, passport, visas and health cards), the filing of tax returns for large refunds or the commission of insurance fraud.

Stage 3: *Discovery*. While many misuses of credit cards are discovered quickly, the 'classic' identity theft involves a long time period prior to discovery, from six months to as long as several years. Evidence suggests that the time it takes to discover the theft is related to the amount of loss incurred by the victim (Newman & McNally 2005).

Identity theft is perpetrated by a range of offenders. There are organised criminal groups involved, as well as individual hackers. Three types of organised identity crime groups have been identified (Smith undated). They include traditional organised criminal groups that generate funds using ID crime, such as software piracy, credit card fraud, and card skimming (e.g. Japanese Yakuza, Asian triads and Eastern European gangs); organised groups with common objectives to perpetrate ID crime, such as carding, underground malware markets, and organised identity theft (e.g. Shadowcrew, Carderplanet, CardersMarket, Theft Services, DrinkOrDie, Rock-Phish, BotMaster and Mpack); and ideologically and politically motivated groups, such as terrorist groups who raise funds through ID crime for the financing of terrorism, fraud, money laundering and planned attacks (e.g. Imam Samudra (Bali) and Tariq Al-Daour (UK Al Qaeda cell).

From a crime prevention perspective it is essential people remain vigilant against becoming a victim of e-crime. There needs to be careful scrutiny of both computer hardware and incoming messages for anything that appears suspicious and 'out of the ordinary' in relation to email messages and computer updates. There need to be strong efforts to reduce the opportunities to commit crimes, as well as to reduce the rewards people can get from committing them (see McNally & Newman 2008). Less individualised and more systematic approaches to cyber-crime need to involve a wide range of stakeholders, constituencies and practices. For example, public police services (including international and regional networks, such as Interpol and Europol) engage in monitoring and enforcement activities in relation to crimes such as online grooming and the threat of paedophiles, child pornography, fraudsters and terrorist groups. In some instances, police services will engage in their own version of identity 'fraud' as part of law enforcement efforts. For example, US federal law enforcement agents have been using social networking sites – including Facebook, LinkedIn, MySpace and Twitter – to search for evidence and witnesses in criminal cases and in some instances to track suspects (Nasaw 2010). This has included FBI agents creating fake personalities in order to befriend suspects and lure them into revealing clues or confessing, and to access private information and map social networks. Such tactics have been used, as well, in relation to internet chatrooms in order to lure pornography traffickers and suspected sex predators.

Other actors are also involved in addressing cyber-crime and offensive behaviour on the internet. These range from internet users and user groups who can use moral censure to deal with certain types of online behaviour, through to corporations that may threaten the use of private and criminal prosecution. Some companies also combat hackers and crimes perpetrated by organised groups (including those supported by foreign governments) by tracking down the interlopers and employing their own forms of cyber-sabotage against them. Meanwhile, groups such as the Internet Watch Foundation not only raise awareness of cyber-crime, but compile reports of offending and pass them on to relevant authorities (Wall 2007, 2009). The complexities of cyber-crime require third parties to take a lead role in prevention because of the rapidly evolving uses of global telecommunications, with the threats to security it presents, being beyond the capacity of police or governments to address on their own. Responses, though, need to balance vigilance with the possibility of over-surveillance and potential abuse of rights (i.e. to privacy) that may accompany crime prevention efforts online.

Crime prevention and counter-terrorism

While there is no agreed definition of terrorism, it generally involves the calculated use of violence or the threat of violence to induce fear among particular populations (Schmid 2011). The definition of terrorism used by official agencies, such as the FBI in the US, is: 'The unlawful use of force or violence against persons or property to intimidate or coerce a Government, or the civilian population, or any segment thereof, in furtherance of political or social objectives' (Ronczkowski 2004, p. 18). The intent of terrorism is to coerce or intimidate governments or societies in the pursuit of goals that are generally political, religious or ideological (Crenshaw 1981; Schmid 2011). There are different types and forms of terrorism (Ronczkowski 2004; Schmid 2011). These include:

- *Political Terrorism*
  e.g. directed at bringing about political or policy change
- *Ecological Terrorism*
  e.g. designed to halt clearfelling of old growth forests
- *Agricultural Terrorism*
  e.g. use of chemicals to stop consumption of certain goods
- *Narco Terrorism*
  e.g. use of drug trade to fund terrorism
- *Biological Terrorism*
  e.g. use of biological or chemical agents to injure, maim or cause death
- *Cyber Terrorism*
  e.g. use of computer resources to disrupt service or destroy data.

The social profile of terrorists also has some bearing on the types of terrorist events evident around the world today and their underlying causes. For instance, there may be several different drivers of terrorism related to right-wing ideology (e.g. ultra-conservative or neo-fascist), fundamentalism (e.g. theological-based Christian, Muslim or Hindu), nationalism (independence movements) or criminal motivations (e.g. action of drug cartels) (see Ronczkowski 2004).

In the context of combating terrorism a deterrence-based model has tended to dominate policy responses that revolve around enhancing the powers of police and intelligence agencies to detain, question and monitor groups or individuals suspected of committing terrorism, or acting to support the commission of terrorism (Hocking 2004; Miller 2013; Pickering, McCulloch & Wright-Neville 2008). For example, key pieces of legislation have expanded the power of state and federal police to detain people for longer periods without charge, impose control orders and allow police agencies to intercept and collect people's personal information (e.g. the US *Patriot Act*; the UK *Terrorism Act 2000*; the Australian *Anti-Terrorism Act 2005* and *Criminal Code Amendment Act 2002 (No. 2)*). The overall aim has been to create a credible risk of detecting and pre-empting terrorism, with the latter becoming a key focus of counter-terrorism policies and laws (McCulloch & Pickering 2009). The problem, though, with the deterrence model is that like law and order, it draws on a narrow range of techniques and can have unintended consequences (Miller 2013), such as creating community backlash against counter-terrorism policies and laws and even generating support for terrorism itself (LaFree, Duga & Korte 2009; Pickering, McCulloch & Wright-Neville 2008).

The theory and approaches underpinning both social and environmental prevention have particular relevance to combating terrorism. For instance, the idea of early intervention and the principles of addressing risk and protective factors have relevance to strategies of de-radicalisation and countering violent extremism. Changing norms and values, similar to the aims of social crime prevention programs, dominate de-radicalisation programs aimed at terrorists and potential terrorists (Dalgaard-Nielsen 2013; Schmid 2013). Situational crime prevention theorists have argued that opportunity reduction is relevant to preventing terrorism (see Freilich & Newman 2009). This can include protecting vulnerable targets through target hardening or removal, and controlling access to weapons, tools or materials that can be used to commit terrorist acts. These responses aim to remove the conditions that make terrorist attacks possible. It has been pointed out by advocates of situational crime prevention that the targets of terrorism are not necessarily random or accidental, but rather are chosen for particular purposes due to their symbolic or strategic importance. Box 9.1 outlines some of these reasons under the acronym of EVIL DONE (Boba 2009).

Policy makers need to keep in mind that outside of the immediate need to prevent terrorist attacks, consideration needs to be given to how public authorities engage with communities over terrorism-related issues. For example, harsh counter-terrorism measures have the potential to undermine cooperation with police among particular communities (LaFree & Ackerman 2009). This point is worth exploring in greater detail because it has a bearing on a central feature of crime prevention: namely, community cooperation.

BOX 9.1: WHY ARE CERTAIN TARGETS SELECTED? EVIL DONE

- **E**xposed – targets are open and vulnerable.
- **V**ital – e.g. city infrastructure.
- **I**conic – target has symbolic value.
- **l**egitimate – target is justifiable in the minds of terrorists and supporters.
- **D**estructible – in the minds of the terrorists.
- **O**ccupied – there are many targets.
- **N**ear – target is within striking distance.
- **E**asy – target characteristics make certain types of attacks possible

---

It is recognised that community cooperation is central to mitigating the risks of terrorism (Pickering, McCulloch & Wright-Neville 2008; Jones & Libicki 2008). For example, the Australian Government Counter Terrorism white paper recognises that the community is a 'critical partner in protecting Australia from terrorism, and a valuable source of information regarding terrorist-related activity' (Department of the Prime Minister and Cabinet 2010). Events overseas highlight that an active citizenry is central to preventing terrorist attacks. For example, the detection and reporting by two street vendors of the Times Square car bomb in 2010 thwarted a potential terrorist attack in New York City. Further, of the 21 individuals convicted under anti-terrorism laws in Australia all had community attachments to friends, family and significant others (Porter & Kebbell 2011). These examples highlight that enhanced law enforcement and surveillance is limited when it comes to the domestic fight against terrorism. Studies show such tactics can in fact undermine the willingness of groups to cooperate with the police and defer to their authority and can create community backlash against counter-terrorism policing and laws (LaFree, Duga & Korte 2009; Neyroud 2007; Sun, Yuning & Poteyeva 2011).

In the domestic policing sphere, minority groups have been a key focus of counter-terrorism policing in Australia and abroad, whether defined by their religious (e.g. Muslim) or ethnic (e.g. Middle Eastern or Pakistani) affiliation or with radicalisation or terrorist attacks (e.g. the 9/11 attacks, Bali bombings or 7/7 London attacks). Among such populations counter-terrorism policies may be viewed as unjust because these groups feel they are used against them unfairly (Pickering, McCulloch & Wright-Neville 2008; Sun, Yuning & Poteyeva 2011). These issues are complex and require acknowledgement of and sensitivity to differences across various ethnic and religious groups (Dunn 2004; Field 2011). For instance, Muslims take very different positions towards terrorism – many actively and willingly support and work with police to counter it, others are hostile towards both Islamist terrorism and legal authorities, while others are at various points in between (Field 2011; Mubarak 2005). The position that different Muslim groups in Australia take when it comes to supporting counter-terrorism measures may be influenced by policy and practice in this area. For example, it is recognised that there are pockets of anger among Muslims communities in Australia resulting from their association, as conveyed in the media and through police intervention, with terrorist violence (Pickering, McCulloch & Wright-Neville 2008). This can have detrimental impacts on their support for community-based counter-terrorism efforts, and encourage a withdrawal from public cooperation as well as generating a mistrust of the police (Spalek & Imtoual 2007). Data in Australia and abroad already shows that Muslims (particularly young Muslims) have a deep mistrust of the police, and feel alienated as a result of counter-terrorism policies (Field 2011; Human Rights and Equal Opportunity Commission 2007; McDonald 2011; Poynting & Nobel 2004).

The policy challenge is that members of a religious or ethnic community may share political or religious viewpoints with those who commit acts of terrorism in ways that are not usually observed with ordinary criminal conduct (Dornschneider 2010; Tyler 2012; Wright-Neville & Smith 2009). The fact that key ethnic and religious identities (e.g. Muslims and Lebanese) have been demonised, stereotyped and singled out by media and political commentary on terrorism has activated resistance strategies among these groups, one of which is an increased sense of solidarity and enhanced feelings of responsibility for their collective image (Anne 2007; McDonald 2011; Rouseau & Jamil 2010). One consequence of this is that certain people may be unwilling to openly undermine terrorism and reject or challenge particular policies aimed at terrorism due to a sense of defiance that their community is being unfairly targeted (McDonald 2011; Rouseau & Jamil 2010; Sageman 2008). This can impact on their willingness to cooperate with the police and engage in activities supportive of crime prevention in this area.

As the counter-terrorism literature demonstrates, police have a vital role to play in the implementation of anti-terrorist strategies. Effective policing, in turn, though, relies upon the selection of the right approaches and techniques in order to maximise success in preventing terrorist and other criminal activities. Ensuring these policies do not simply alienate communities who need to be partners in efforts to combat terrorism has to be kept in mind.

Policing and crime prevention

As we define it, crime prevention is about preventing or reducing crime before it has actually occurred. The police have always had a major role in this process; however, now it is becoming more central to certain aspects of their work. One reason for this is that innovations such as community policing, problem-oriented policing, third-party policing and intelligence-led policing have resulted in police reassessing the effectiveness of traditional police practices, such as rapid response to calls for service, patrolling and criminal investigation (see Bullock & Tilley 2009; Mazerolle & Ransley 2005; Ratcliffe 2008). While such responses still dominate most police actions, the emphasis of innovations like problem-oriented policing, community policing and third-party policing has been for police to identify key targets and hot spots that require concentrated law enforcement efforts or other third-party interventions, and to establish strong links across agencies and within communities in order to enhance intelligence gathering, crime reduction and trust-building. The emphasis on external collaboration is vital to these police innovations.

While there is some overlap between intelligence-led policing, community policing, problem-oriented policing and third-party policing, there are also some key differences relating to the emphasis each places on partnerships with the community (see Table 9.1). From the point of view of crime prevention, the focus

Table 9.1 Innovations in policing and their role in crime prevention

Innovation	Definition	Crime prevention dimensions	Role of partnerships
Community policing	An organisational strategy that leaves setting priorities and the means of achieving them largely to residents and the police who serve in their neighborhoods (Skogan 2006).	Engagement and consultation with local communities to identify local crime problems.	Regarded as central to community policing in which police and residents work together to identify and solve community problems
Problem-oriented policing	An approach to policing in which discrete pieces of police business (e.g. burglary, alcohol-related violence and car theft) are subject to analysis, with the aim being to identify the key causes of the problem so as to develop a more effective strategy for dealing with it (Goldstein 1990; Spelman & Eck 1987).	Adopts a problem analysis (SARA – see Box 21) and identifies crime hotspots through crime mapping and is place-based, with an emphasis on the adoption of situational crime prevention approaches.	May involve partnerships with community groups or agencies, but can also simply involve a police-led response.
Third-party policing	Police efforts to persuade or coerce organisations or non-offending persons (e.g. public housing agencies, property owners, parents, health and building inspectors and business owners) to take some responsibility for preventing crime or reducing crime problems (Mazerolle & Ransley 2005).	Police engage with other organisations or individuals and use a range of civil, regulatory and administrative laws aimed at creating or enhancing the crime-control capacities of third parties.	Partnerships can range from one-way approaches in which police coerce third parties to take action against crime to collaborative multi-agency approaches.
Intelligence-led policing	A management philosophy/business model aimed at achieving crime reduction by disrupting offender activity (Ratcliffe 2008).	Combines crime analysis (e.g. data about the location of offences) with criminal intelligence (e.g. data about known offenders) and focuses police action on prolific offenders.	The main focus is on enhancing collaboration between different police units, through a top-down management approach so as to develop better crime intelligence.

is on anticipating risk and engaging in preemptive strategies to reduce or minimise crime. Broadly speaking, one can distinguish between 'bottom up' approaches and 'top down' approaches. Community policing, for example, provides an example of the former; intelligence-led policing the latter.

The benefits of community policing lie in the manner in which reciprocal trust relations can be built at the local community level with a wide variety of stakeholders. This can have the benefit of also feeding into the intelligence-gathering process, because residents can be more willing to pass on information to the police (Darcy 2005). However, for community policing to work effectively there has to be meaningful dialogue with local communities, in which the insights and experiences of local residents are taken into account – there cannot be a veneer of consultation: community engagement must lead to practical action that reflects the preferences of community groups (Murphy & Cherney 2011). As Darcy (2005 p. 153) points out, in highlighting the limitations of traditional coercive policing: 'in the absence of effective dialogue with local communities there is a real risk this form of policing can alienate the communities that most likely need our help'. Since the composition of the community is always changing, identification of community concerns requires constant dialogue with community representatives. This process demands analysis of the different social divisions and power distributions within a 'community'. It is also reflected in attempts to change the ethnic and racial composition of police agencies so they are more representative of a wider range of cultural backgrounds. Greater attention has also been given to the adoption of culturally sensitive training procedures and liaison officers to engage minority communities (Cherney & Chui 2010).

In some versions of community policing, crime control issues are determined and implemented entirely by the local community itself (see, for example, Airo-Farulla 1992). For instance, there are instances now across Australia where Aboriginal people are playing an increasing role in policing their own communities. This usually takes the form of Aboriginal Community Patrols, which are also known as Night Patrols, Street Patrols, Bare Foot Patrols, or Mobile Assistance Patrols, depending on the region (see Blagg & Valuri 2004a). The point of these patrols (which often involve women and community elders) is not to react and arrest, but for Indigenous people to act as effective place managers and intervene in community problems (e.g. public drinking, domestic violence and truancy) before they become serious enough to require a police response. Such initiatives draw upon principles of guardianship – a key component of situational crime prevention – and aim to tap into informal social control processes through organised, formal means by ensuring Indigenous people have a role in how their communities are policed.

While there is little doubt that strategies like community policing have led police to reassess their roles and functions, their implementation has not necessarily generated new forms of police practice or matched the ideals and intentions of advocates. For example, when it comes to community policing often the process of engagement with local communities has tended to be one-way and top-down, in that police have dictated the agenda (Bull & Stratta 1994; Skogan & Hartnett 1997). When it comes to problem-oriented policing, studies show that police still tend to rely on traditional and staple police responses, such as arrest or crackdowns, which fail to address the reasons why a location becomes a crime hotspot (Cordner & Biebel 2005). In the context of third-party policing, police can also tend to rely on a narrow range of coercive actions, with its adoption exacerbating the policing of disadvantaged communities (Desmond & Valdez 2013; Mazerolle & Ransley 2005). In the context of intelligence-led policing, police can likewise default to law enforcement responses and covert operations, which tend to only have a short-term impact on crime (Ratcliffe 2008). While this evidence calls into question police commitment to reforming their policies and practices, the innovations outlined in this section have nonetheless required police to re-think their role in crime prevention.

Eco-crime and crime prevention

In recent years there has been growing concern at local, regional, national and international levels about environmental issues, and the impacts of specific types of environmental harm, such as pollution, toxic waste and illegal logging. For criminologists, environmental considerations have generally been ignored or have garnered much less attention than traditional law and order and criminal justice concerns. This is now starting to change, as evidenced in a range of new research and scholarly discussions under the banner of 'green criminology' (Beirne & South 2007; White 2011; South & Brisman 2013).

Environmental crime prevention as a specific type of crime prevention encompasses a range of considerations. Different kinds of harm tend to require different kinds of responses. For example, generally speaking, environmental issues can be categorised according to three different domains: brown, green and white (see White 2008). *Brown* issues tend to be defined in terms of urban life and pollution (e.g. air quality), *green* issues mainly relate to wilderness areas and conservation matters (e.g. logging practices) and *white* issues refer to science laboratories and the impact of new technologies (e.g. genetically modified organisms). Conceptualising environmental issues in this way helps to demonstrate the link between environmental action (usually involving distinct types of community and environmental groups) and particular sites (e.g. urban centres, wilderness areas and seacoast regions). The salience of harms and threats associated with these sites resonate more with members of the public compared to others, while some environmental threats only emerge if an accident or disaster brings it to the fore. This also impacts on the levels of resources allocated to prevent certain environmental dangers or risks.

A key focus for criminological intervention has been the illegal trade in wildlife, and this, in turn, has tended to draw upon and reflect an interest in various crime prevention strategies. For instance, work over the past decade has been carried out in respect to:

- the illegal theft of and trade in reptiles in South Africa (Herbig 2010)
- fishing related crimes, including the poaching of abalone and lobster (Tailby & Gant 2002; McMullan & Perrier 2002)
- crime prevention and the illicit trade in endangered species involving many different kinds of animals (Wellsmith 2010; Schneider 2008, 2012)
- the illegal wildlife market in Africa (Warhol et al. 2003), in particular the trade in elephant ivory (Lemieux & Clarke 2009)
- the linkages between illicit markets involving trade in wildlife and drugs (South & Wyatt 2011).

One of the key lessons from these studies is that intervention ought to be based on a problem-solving approach. Specific problems demand particular kinds of responses. That is, general pronouncements about the nature of harm need to be accompanied by particular site or harm analysis. To illustrate this, we can consider the issue of illegal fishing.

First, we have to recognise that there are major variations in the specific nature of this type of criminal activity. Consider, for example, the following types of illegal fishing (see White 2008):

- commercial fishing that involves catches in excess of quota, false declarations, destruction of by-catch linked to marine pollution;
- recreational fishing that involves unlicensed fishing and fishing above allocated quotas;
- Indigenous fishing in traditional but foreign waters, and fishing without a permit
- large-scale illegal fishing, which also involves the overfishing of particular species, such as sharks
- specialist illegal fishing that is designed to exploit endangered species specifically for private fish collections or for medicinal purposes.

Illegal fishing differs depending upon location, and studies of particular types of illegal fishing (e.g. abalone, lobster and toothfish) show great variation in motives, techniques, local cultures and scale of operation (Tailby & Gant 2002; McMullan & Perrier 2002; Lugten 2005; Anderson & McCusker 2005). Environmental crime prevention thus has to address the specific nature of the phenomenon in question if it is to be appropriate to the circumstances. The making of such decisions can be guided by various crime prevention strategies.

In terms of *social crime prevention* methods, for example, children in schools can be exposed to programs that reshape their concepts of 'the environment', 'fish' and 'fishing'. This could include discussions of 'catch and release' as an imperative for recreational fishing, through to doing assignments on the effects of climate change on fish species. Young people who already, or who appear to be most likely to, degrade environments or abuse animals could be subjected to intensive programs aimed at changing attitudes and behaviour.

In terms of *environmental prevention*, boating enthusiasts and fishers generally can be advised how best to minimise their impact on fisheries, through measures such as knowledge of marine park boundaries, through to the use of suitable receptacles for waste products while at sea. Regular patrols of coastlines, and use of satellites, could facilitate surveillance and monitoring of fishing 'hot spots' and areas where environmental transgressions occur on a frequent basis.

Throughout this book our approach to crime prevention has emphasised the importance of undertaking preliminary analysis before developing an intervention plan. In this regard, Eck's (2003) model of crime prevention provides a useful starting point for investigation of the social processes associated with illegal fishing. This model can be used to guide assessment of the key relationships and agencies involved in shaping targets, places and offending as this occurs in a marine environment (see Figure 9.1).

Figure 9.1   A model of environmental crime prevention: factors relevant to illegal fishing

Place	Manager
Coastal waters	Fisheries, customs, quarantine, port authorities
High seas	Navy, fisheries
Marine parks	Park authorities, port authorities

Offender	Handler
Large-scale illegal operators	Buyers, market consumers
Small-scale traditional fishers	Communities, governments

Victim/Target	Guardian
Fish	Commercial and recreational fishers
Indigenous people	Communities, governments

Source: White, 2008

A wide range of crime prevention approaches can be drawn upon in relation to illegal fishing – that incorporate social developmental and communal-oriented measures as well as those that are situational and techniques oriented (White 2008; Lack 2007; Smith & Anderson 2004; Clarke 2008).

Considerable research has recently been carried out on the social processes associated with offending and the characteristics of offenders in regards to other specific types of animal-related crimes. For instance, in a landmark study that explores why people harm and kill animals, Nurse (2013) has developed a new typology of offender motivations, based upon five discrete, although not mutually exclusive, categories of offenders:

- *Traditional Criminals* – personal benefit from crimes such as wildlife trafficking
- *Economic Criminals* – employment-related crime (e.g., killing protected birds to ensure the safety of local game and habitats)
- *Masculinities Criminals* – exercise of stereotypical masculine nature (e.g., linked to sport and gambling)
- *Hobby Criminals* – collection and acquisition (e.g., egg collector)
- *Stress Offenders* – involved in animal harm as a result of their own stress or abuse (e.g., children who suffer abuse).

The relevance of this typology is not only that it provides more detailed knowledge about offenders. Nurse (2013) also observes that understanding different motivations has major implications for how we might respond to these kinds of animal harms. Specifically, he argues that calls for harsher penalties for animal cruelty are too simplistic and generally ineffective when translated into policy and practice. This is because such demands overlook the diverse motivations and circumstances surrounding animal-related crimes.

Similar observations and conclusions are evident in recent studies of poaching (see McMullan & Perrier 2002; Forsyth et al. 1998; Bell et al. 2007; Zhang et al. 2008; Green 2011; Pires & Clarke 2011; Kahler & Gore 2012). These studies indicate that people are engaged in poaching for a variety of reasons, and these reasons are partly related to immediate social context (e.g. exotic consumer products for the new middle classes in China, traditional hunting practices in Greece, community and commercial collusion in the taking of lobster in the Canadian Maritime provinces, and income supplementation in Bolivia). In some instances, poaching is perceived as a sort of 'folk crime' – something that everyone knows about, and that everyone allows to happen since it is not perceived to be criminal (unless certain informal protocols and boundaries are violated, such as being seen to be 'greedy', too 'commercially-oriented' or 'not leaving enough for other people'). Poaching therefore can exist with considerable community support in some locales and under some conditions (see White 2013c). This makes attempts to tackle poaching challenging because efforts can be undermined by informal processes or practices that allow poaching to be tolerated in some communities.

As this section has demonstrated, environmental crime prevention is both a burgeoning area of interest within criminology, and draws heavily upon many of the models and approaches described earlier in this book. The importance of specificity in analysis and in the interventions developed will ensure that crime prevention responses are tailored to the spectrum of activities related to pollution, illegal wildlife trade, illegal fishing and other environmental crimes.

Conclusion

This chapter has reviewed several areas where crime prevention thinking and practice is being called upon to deal with emerging types of crimes, risks and harms. Cyber-crime and cyber-safety, like terrorism and environmental crime, are multidimensional and constantly changing. Each of these areas is also beset by a sense of urgency that demands immediate responses. While the pressure on governments to react forcefully and decisively to incidents such as terrorism are understandable, they need to be tempered with the realisation that they can backfire and create more problems than they solve. The same conclusion applies to many of the crimes and threats covered in this chapter. Likewise, each area that we have surveyed is generating new, innovative and imaginative ways of thinking about crime prevention. Policing is also being reshaped in new ways, as has occurred under the guise of community policing, problem-oriented policing, third-party policing and intelligence-led policing. Importantly evidence shows that partnerships and collaborations are essential to addressing new emerging crimes and threats – which is a staple of good crime prevention work. This again confirms that good crime prevention is, ultimately, a collective exercise, and is not simply a matter of technique.

CASE STUDY 9.1 A MARKET REDUCTION APPROACH TO ENVIRONMENTAL CRIME

Another approach to dealing with illegal wildlife trade is to borrow ideas from crime prevention approaches that have been applied to burglary. In this instance, the emphasis is on adopting a Market Reduction Approach (MRA) to illegal wildlife trade (Schneider 2012). The MRA, as applied to the illicit endangered species trade, seeks to identify the routine patterns of those involved: hunters, poachers, handlers and consumers. It aims to identify those who hunt, transform, transport and buy the wildlife (the *likely offenders*); the precise wildlife being hunted, transformed, transported and purchased (the *suitable targets*); and those whose remit is to conserve and protect those species (i.e. the *capable guardians*) such as conservators, police, and customs and wildlife officers. Variables – such as country of origin (e.g. elephants in African nations); country of consumption (e.g. ivory sales in China); seasonality and mating season; and how things are harvested, processed and shipped – are all evaluated as part of this particular analytical approach. The aim is to find ways to disrupt markets in illegal wildlife trade by identifying features of such markets that can be subject to interventions.

QUESTIONS

Questions for further exploration

1. What is cyber-crime?

2. What makes digital crime different from ordinary crime, and what additional challenges does it pose for crime prevention?

3. How can social and environmental crime prevention approaches inform the development of strategies aimed at the prevention of terrorism?

4. What role should police play in crime prevention? Discuss in relation to particular innovations, such as community policing, problem-oriented policing, third-party policing or intelligence-led policing.

5. Pick any of the police innovations listed in Table 9.1. Undertake a literature search on the internet and identify what the research evidence indicates about its effectiveness in reducing crime and improving how police engage communities or external agencies.

6. The techniques of crime prevention are highly relevant in dealing with environmental crime. Discuss.

EXTENSION TOPICS AND REFERENCES

1. Terrorism takes many different forms and engages technologies and communities in varying ways. What are some of the key lessons to be learnt from crime prevention in developing appropriate counter-terrorism strategies?

References

Lum, C. & Kennedy, L.W. (eds) (2012), *Evidence-based counterterrorism policy*. New York: Springer.

McCulloch, J. (2002a) "'Either you are with us or you are with the terrorists'': the war's home front', in P. Scraton (ed.), *Beyond September 11: an anthology of dissent*. London: Pluto Press, pp. 54–59.

McCulloch, J. (2002b) 'War at home: national security arrangements post 11 September 2001', *Alternative Law Journal*, vol. 27, no. 2, pp. 87–91.

Pickering, S., Wright-Neville, D., McCulloch, J. & Lentini, P. (2007) *Counter-terrorism policing and culturally diverse communities*. Melbourne: Monash University.

2. Environmental crime demands specific interventions tailored to specific crimes. Provide examples of crime prevention in relation to environmental crimes, such as pollution offences, illegal fishing and illegal trade in wildlife.

References

Crofts, P., Morris, T., Wells, K. & Powell, A. (2010) 'Illegal dumping and crime prevention: a case study of Ash Road, Liverpool Council', *Public Space: The Journal of Law and Social Justice*, vol. 5, no. 4, pp. 1–23.

Pires, S. & Clarke, R.V. (2012) 'Are parrots CRAVED? An analysis of parrot poaching in Mexico', *Journal of Research in Crime and Delinquency*, vol. 49, no. 1, pp. 122–146.

Smith, R. & Anderson, K. (2004) 'Understanding non-compliance in the marine environment', *Trends & Issues in Crime and Criminal Justice*, no. 275.

Tailby, R. & Gant, F. (2002) 'The illegal market in Australian Abalone', *Trends & Issues in Crime and Criminal Justice*, no. 225.

Van Daele, S., Vander Beken, T. & Dorn, N. (2007) 'Waste management and crime: regulatory, business and product vulnerabilities', *Environmental Policy and Law*, vol. 37, no. 1, pp. 34–38.

10

PLANNING THE FUTURE

Introduction

Preceding chapters should have left readers in no doubt that we see crime prevention not just as a great *idea*, but a great *ideal*. They also make clear, however, that Western governments have had great difficulty translating this ideal into policy practice.

Of course, discrepancies between the ideals politicians articulate and measures they actually implement are hardly unusual. Nor are such disparities confined to the Western democracies or to the field of crime prevention. Less than three decades ago, even as nations like France, the US and Australia were beginning and ending their trials with prevention, another country – the former Soviet Union – was engaged in a much more ambitious experiment, that of glasnost. Mikhail Gorbachev, the architect of glasnost, won international acclaim, not just for his vision but for his endeavours to translate it into reforms that would render the USSR a more open society.

Implementing glasnost at the grassroots, however, proved an enormous challenge. One consequence was that Gorbachev's image among ordinary Soviet citizens differed vastly from his portrayal in Western media. Most people in the streets of the USSR did not revere Mikhail Gorbachev. On the contrary, the more glasnost progressed the more he became the object of ridicule and sarcasm. The following joke is typical:

> In the true spirit of *glasnost* and *perestroika* two friends, Ivan and Boris, are in a Moscow queue waiting to buy the week's bread for their families. It is Saturday, it is snowing, and they have been there for three hours. Still no sign of bread. Finally, Ivan snaps. 'I've had it! I don't care! I'm going to shoot Gorbachev!' He rushes off down the street, gesticulating and screaming. Boris says nothing. He stays in the queue. Three hours later, Ivan returns. Boris moves over. They continue to wait for bread. Finally, Boris breaks the silence: 'So, did you shoot Gorbachev?' 'I would have', says Ivan, 'but the shoot-Gorbachev queue was even longer than this one!'

Glasnost had its beginnings in the mid-1980s, when Gorbachev became general secretary of the USSR Communist Party Central Committee. By 1991 it had come to an end, its architect forced from office. For policy theorists and practitioners around the world, the demise of glasnost was an occasion to pause and reflect. Indeed, one of the present authors (the late Adam Sutton) made reference to it, when asked in 1991 to give a paper on crime prevention to a state conference of practitioners in Victoria.

He had been invited in the capacity of Director of South Australia's Together Against Crime strategy, launched just three years earlier and seen by some as cutting edge. No doubt, conference organisers expected an upbeat progress report. As the title of the address, 'Don't shoot the policy maker' – and its Gorbachev-inspired subheading – 'No need, someone else will do the job for you' – made clear, what they heard was different.

By mid-1991, when the paper was given, South Australia's program already was in difficulty (see chapter 6). By the end of the year Sutton had been replaced (Sutton 1997). Successors in that state have fared little better. Nowadays, crime prevention in South Australia enjoys little more than residual status. As chapter 6 has shown, other parts of Australia also have struggled to implement effective programs.

Has the decline of crime prevention in countries like France, the UK and Australia been inevitable? Is crime prevention doomed to be the capitalist democracies' minor version of glasnost: a policy whose ideals are incompatible with basic institutions and practices? We think not. As stated a number of times throughout this book, we are confident that – given the right combination of vision and expertise – local, state and federal authorities in most countries should be able to work together to develop, implement and assess prevention-based policies and programs that can compete with, and even eclipse, the 'law and order' paradigm. The fact that they have not yet done so merely confirms that the task is difficult – not that it is impossible.

Crime prevention will never disappear. Routine activity and situational theorists are correct when they argue that it always has been, and always will be, embedded in everyday life (chapter 4). The same is true of social prevention (chapter 3). The key to a successful crime prevention strategy, therefore, does not lie in adopting the UK Crime Reduction Programme approach, of first isolating 'what works', then finding ways to impose relevant practices on an unsuspecting, and possibly recalcitrant, public. Instead, it lies in central governments being prepared to initiate and sustain dialogues with local populations and communities. The underlying premise of such dialogue should be that 'ordinary' people and institutions will always possess the capacity to prevent crime.

However, governments can and should set priorities in relation to the approaches they will support (e.g. a preference for inclusive rather than exclusionary forms of social control), and acknowledge that structural and resource problems (e.g. poor design and management of the physical environment and lack of access to family support, jobs or education) may be making it difficult for many disadvantaged local communities to practice prevention effectively. Through dialogue, obstacles to effective prevention can be identified and overcome in ways that suit the interests and needs of both central and local stakeholders. For it to be initiated and sustained, however, all parties need to be honest and open about the contributions they will make to, and what they want to achieve from, crime prevention.

Governments need to initiate a process whereby both they and local stakeholders become more reflexive about what crime prevention is, and why it is important. Throughout this book we have emphasised that the process is not just technical: it must also involve an expression of values. To succeed, it must encompass some vision of the 'good society' as determined by and embedded in planners' conceptions of intervention. In our view, the vision ought to be premised on the notion of social inclusion; it should be based on a participatory model that allows for maximum liberty while promising safety and security for all. Our vision of crime prevention, therefore, is in contrast to, and in conflict with, the darker vision provided through law and order, since the latter focuses on coercive control, heightened surveillance and the discourse of fear. We see crime prevention as involving a less top-down, less coercive and less intrusive form of social regulation. We see crime prevention as ultimately about building positive community relationships. This requires considerable planning and social coordination.

Developing and implementing such policy, and persuading the public to accept it, inevitably will be a complex exercise involving a wide range of participants. Like all complex undertakings it can only succeed if guided and driven by strategic vision. When Boeing unveiled the 747 'jumbo jet' in 1970, it revolutionised approaches to large aircraft design and engineering. The wide-bodied 747 was the most risky project the company had ever attempted, demanding input and commitment from all its divisions. Ultimately, however, it was not just a technical accomplishment. Its success stemmed from a company president's vision and leadership and his capacity to convince Boeing's board of directors and its potential customers of a simple concept: that international commercial aircraft of the future must be capable of carrying specific payloads at specific speeds (Irving 1993).

Crime prevention can only succeed at a policy level in a democracy if political leaders can develop and communicate a similarly concise vision of, and values about, the type of society they want it to help produce. Crime prevention needs to be based on what Hughes (2007, p. 23) has termed 'utopian realism': realistic, research-based appreciation of the economic and political forces that constrain policy making combined with the capacity to think about the world normatively, as it should be. Criminology's tendency to portray prevention as the evidence-based, 'rational' alternative to law and order has made it difficult for the discipline to understand or discuss prevention policy in such imaginative ways. This has also made it difficult for crime prevention to gain leverage both politically and publicly.

To conclude, in this chapter we want to shrug off the rationalist straightjacket, and indulge in a little of Hughes' utopian realism. We want to give readers a sense of the ways prevention policy might be developed and implemented in an Australian city and state that had learnt from its past and was determined to make crime prevention part of its future. Our case study draws on, and combines, experience in a number of Australian state capitals. For convenience, we name it 'Metropolis City'.

Metropolis City

Planning for crime prevention and community safety has long been ingrained in Metropolis City. It began in the 1970s, when its urban planners discovered the work of Jane Jacobs and Oscar Newman (see chapter 4), and began to discuss and debate the type of city they wanted Metropolis to become.

It did not take long for them to agree that Metropolis should not pursue the path of many of the US's major cities. They did not want to allow its central zones to be dedicated solely to business and commercial activity: busy during the day, but deserted at night. Nor did they want it to become a Los Angeles style 'dispersed' city, whose development would be dictated by the preferences and needs of motor vehicle users.

Particularly influential in this debate in the 1970s was one individual: 'Bill Smith', who had only recently been recruited to the Planning Division. Before taking a job with Metropolis, Smith had spent a year backpacking around Europe and the US, consolidating knowledge and understanding accumulated in the course of his undergraduate degree in urban planning by living in a variety of cities and trying to understand what made the best ones great. As it turned out, Bill made Metropolis his home for more than four decades, eventually becoming head of urban design.

Smith's unwavering vision was of Metropolis as an inclusive focal point, not just for its local region, but for the entire state. During his time with the Planning Division he participated in the development and implementation of a series of five-year plans. The key themes were to ensure a mix of business and residential uses that would ensure that the inner city remained busy 24 hours a day, and would be perceived as a pleasant and safe place to be. Like other Metropolis planners, Smith kept abreast of CPTED theory as it was developed by successors to Oscar Newman. In accordance with CPTED principles, public and semi-public space throughout the city continued to be designed and managed in ways that provided subtle but consistent cues about how it was intended to be used. Adherence to these principles meant that not every possible user would feel welcome in every space (e.g. some spaces would present themselves as intended for use by older people rather than as recreational space for youngsters, and vice versa). Within Metropolis as a whole, however, there was designated space for all major groups – not just for the affluent consumers who patronised the businesses that generated tax income for the city.

Similar principles informed the granting of permits for the design and management of major private shopping complexes within the city. Over time, moreover, state government planning and development policy was influenced by the inclusive approach to urban design and management exhibited by its capital city. Many of the state government's senior planning staff had begun their professional careers with Metropolis City, and had imbibed the 'Metropolis culture'.

The philosophy that for decades had guided urban planning and design in Metropolis also had repercussions for broader social policy. Both at the city and at the state levels, the unstated working assumption or 'habitus' (Bourdieu 1977; Hughes 2007, pp. 85–86) informing the work of relevant professionals was an emphasis on social inclusion. It was hardly surprising, therefore, that when the state government announced in the late 1980s that it wanted to work with local authorities to develop and implement crime prevention programs, Metropolis City expressed interest.

Over the next decade it received state government funds to employ a series of community safety officers (CSOs) whose task was to develop and implement crime prevention and community safety projects. Initially the emphasis was on diversion programs for young people deemed 'at risk' in the Metropolis region. Later, CSOs broadened the scope of their activities to include negotiating codes of practice or 'accords' with licensed traders, aimed at reducing the incidence of alcohol-related violence within the city, and the coordination of environmental audits to assess and try to improve public perceptions of safety in key parts of the city. Safety officers generally reported to, and serviced, management committees chaired by local government, and also comprising senior representatives of police, other relevant state government authorities and business.

Despite the hard work of the safety officers, however, the state government's commitment to prevention eventually faded. Part of the problem was that it was never quite clear what its strategies and programs had been meant to achieve. A succession of initiatives had been announced, and at each launch the relevant state government minister stated that this strategy would be community-based, evidence-driven and embrace a 'whole-of-government' approach. With limited resources and authority, however, CSOs generally had difficulties matching these lofty ideals. Metropolis tried hard to support the CSO role, but there were no great regrets when the state wound back its commitment to crime prevention in the late 1990s. The city simply filled the gap by creating its own safety committee, serviced by its own planning, welfare and social development divisions, and also comprising representatives of police, key state government departments and the city's Chamber of Commerce. In context of this restructure, Metropolis quietly jettisoned the term 'crime prevention', which many grassroots staff were concerned had the potential to be stigmatising both for programs and for clients.

This was the situation until 2016 when a recently-elected state government approached the mayor of Metoropolis with renewed ideas about statewide crime prevention strategy in which the city could play a part. The state was concerned that while law and order had been politically successful, survey and police data indicated that crime victimisation had continued to increase. Rates of imprisonment were at record highs, and expenditure on police, courts and corrections at unprecedented levels. The need to contain budget expenditure was not the only issue, however. After decades of the 'tough on crime' approach, being sent to prison for a criminal offence had become almost a normal event – a 'rite of passage' into adulthood – for young men from Indigenous and grossly disadvantaged backgrounds. Research data indicated that once many of these young males emerged from gaol, their offending became even more frequent and serious. Senior government ministers had been briefed on these findings, and on evidence that social and environmental crime prevention could be cost-effective. This time around, they were determined to find a way to translate the knowledge base into policy.

Learning from the past

Senior staff from the Metropolis planning and social welfare divisions were given the go-ahead to discuss possible approaches with representatives of the state's Departments of Premier and Cabinet and of Justice. From the start, however, Metropolis City made it clear that prior to committing to specific programs and projects, it must reach agreement on basic principles with the state government.

The most important of these related to the overall goal for the proposed crime prevention initiative: what it was meant to achieve. Previous state and commonwealth programs had been strong on 'how-to' language ('evidence-based', 'whole-of-government', 'partnership driven', etc.), but weak in terms of strategic vision. In the absence of such vision, local stakeholders had interpreted crime prevention and community safety their own ways – only then to be accused of misapplying funds when central government ministers became dissatisfied with the projects put in place. Metropolis was not prepared to go down this path again.

Eventually, the state and Metropolis City concluded that social control and social ordering were key themes on which a shared strategic vision could be based. The state government had returned to crime prevention because it wanted to explore policy alternatives to criminal justice based 'law and order'. For Metropolis, developing and maintaining open and inclusive environments where people nonetheless felt themselves to be, and were, protected from criminal and other forms of victimisation and harm had long been core business.

Both parties agreed, however, that the vision of social control and social order that would provide the basis for their programs should not be a totally sanitising one, where all symptoms of surprise, difference and deviance were suppressed. Metropolis should be the sort of city that welcomed all users, even the most unconventional ones. The only exception would be those whose activities involved threat, loss or harm to others. Controls implemented in the context of the crime prevention and community safety strategy should allow individuals like Hobart's 'dancing man' (see chapter 8) to be not just tolerated but celebrated. This approach was highly consistent with principles that for decades had informed Metropolis City's approach to urban development. Its officials were satisfied that signing up to a statewide strategy based on such a vision would not compromise the city's own mission and goals.

The second principle informing the new partnership was dialogue and mutual respect. Previous attempts by state and national authorities to implement crime prevention had tended to work from an assumption that strategies should be designed and directed from the centre. In light of the UK's experience with the Crime Reduction Programme, the state had concluded that this approach no longer was feasible. From the outset, it was prepared to acknowledge that local government and community-based stakeholders also possessed relevant experience and expertise. This did not mean that expert theory and research would be disregarded; all parties to the development and implementation of crime prevention and community safety schemes should be prepared to acknowledge relevant science, and to explore its relevance to the specific problems they were dealing with. In the context of an open-minded commitment to problem identification and solving, however, no level of government should assume that it possessed a monopoly of knowledge about 'what works'.

Mutual respect would also extend to acknowledging concerns about terminology. For the central government it was important that prevention strategies be recognised as helping to reduce crime. In the absence of such recognition, relevant initiatives could not be presented as a viable alternative to police and other criminal justice responses, and consequently politicians would continue to be locked into the 'law and order' paradigm. For local government and other grassroots stakeholders, however, priorities differed. Their major concern was that attaching a crime prevention label to practices in fields as diverse as urban planning and design and early childhood education simply would result in the stigmatising of locations and participants.

In practical terms, this meant that in Metropolis and other locations the new crime prevention strategy would be developed and implemented through a series of two-year crime prevention plans, rather than taking the form of a series of discrete projects. A city-wide crime prevention planning process would allow funds to be allocated to mainstream institutions (such as preschools, schools and family support centres) whose work had demonstrated potential to help reduce offending. Only in the context of the overall plan, however, would these activities be theorised and celebrated as contributing to crime reduction. To avoid

Cambridge-Somerville effects, the city would avoid tagging specific social interventions as crime prevention.

Planning for the future

What sorts of activities formed part of Metropolis City's post-2016 crime prevention 'plans for the future'? They included a whole range, encompassing both environmental and social prevention. To ensure that prevention could present as a credible alternative to law and order, some initiatives were short-term, high-profile and visible. Others, however, particularly those that emphasised social prevention, were more unobtrusive. Plans included both situational measures – whose effects could be measured almost immediately – and social programs whose impacts on crime only become apparent after decades.

A key theme linking all crime prevention work was capacity-building. At the outset of the development of each two-year plan, key stakeholders reaffirmed their belief that Metropolis City already possessed institutional and community resources that could be mobilised in the cause of crime prevention and community safety. The key, however, was to keep expanding and modifying these resources to meet new challenges posed by changes in the physical and social environment. Through its crime prevention and community safety planning process, Metropolis City generated a constant stream of innovative programs, including schemes to reduce the incidence of crime at identified hot spots, schemes to improve guardianship and safety in public spaces, schemes to address entrenched problems (e.g. family violence) and programs to reduce economic and cultural marginalisation and ensure that the 'soft' disciplines of family and education extended to even the most disadvantaged groups.

Metropolis City's two-year planning process became a vehicle not just for translating research findings into ongoing programs, but for sustaining an ongoing discourse about crime prevention and community safety. At times, of course, this discourse became a source of tension between local and central authorities. As their knowledge about causes of crime grew – and, in particular, as they knew more about relationships between social inequality and violent and other crime (see chapter 3) – Metropolis City based politicians became more concerned and outspoken about the effects that state and federal government policies in fields such as education, employment and welfare might have for crime. Treasury officials sometimes were equivocal about the wisdom of encouraging city and other local stakeholders to become partners in the development of crime prevention strategies and programs. They argued that pointing out this had in fact reopened the door to demands for fundamental reassessments of budget priorities and values in a range of fields (see Case study 3.1, chapter 3). Nonetheless, at the end of the day, all agreed that the process was beneficial.

Conclusion

One aim of this book has been to introduce readers to the theories and techniques of crime prevention. In this last chapter, we have emphasised that crime prevention is also a social process. Inevitably, it will involve many different people and institutions, and many different sets of aims and objectives. At any phase of the crime prevention exercise, critical decisions will need to be made about who decides what, and why.

Throughout this book we have argued that good crime prevention needs to be based on explicit guiding values, progressive planning principles and extensive social participation. We have argued that strategic vision about what we want to achieve is essential to this task. Crime prevention plans must be based on local analysis and local collaborations, while drawing on general theories and on case studies from many different places and involving different kinds of issues and concerns. We have also emphasised that crime prevention initiatives must be subject to constant review and evaluation. Such evaluation does not, however, mean that crime prevention is a matter for experts only. Crime prevention is and ought to be seen not only as an everyday activity, but as something that is relevant to, and for, everyone. This does not simply relate to crimes that have traditionally dominated public and political attention – such as alcohol-related violence or juvenile offending – but is also pertinent to emerging crimes such as terrorism, environmental threats, and crimes linked to the proliferation of new technologies. This means that not only do policies need to draw on a range of third parties and partners, but also need to be mindful of their potentially negative impact on particular groups and communities. As such, how we actually 'do' crime prevention demands that transparency and accountability be built into the process.

From the outset we have said that ultimately crime prevention is also a matter of politics. It is about power and decision-making, resource allocation and budget priorities. We conclude with the observation that where we put our time, energy and money says a lot about the kind of society we live in now, and the kind of future we see for ourselves and our children. For us, crime prevention is integral to sustaining an exciting, pleasurable, safe and secure environment: one that opens up possibilities for human creativity, satisfaction and happiness.

GLOSSARY OF TERMS

affective results – the symbolic or expressive goals of crime prevention, such as reaffirming key social values, which need to be expressed as part of crime prevention policy and practice so they resonate with public perceptions, emotions and values.

audits – audits of a particular local environment that focus on examining and documenting the physical environment (identifying sites considered to be unsafe or threatening); the social environment (different users and uses of public space); the regulatory environment (the nature of police and security approaches); types of amenities (youth-specific and youth-friendly); and movements through public places (flows of people through particular areas). The purpose of such mapping exercises is to gain accurate information on how public spaces are used at different times and by different groups.

broken windows thesis – the argument that people constantly monitor spaces they move through for signs that order is being preserved. Lack of order-maintenance (e.g. failure to replace broken windows, repair vandalism and remove graffiti) will be read as evidence of community breakdown, and increase the likelihood that people avoid these areas; meanwhile, potential offenders may see the same physical symptoms as indicators of a lack of guardianship and conclude that the location offers ample opportunities for crime.

CCTV – closed-circuit television (CCTV) systems that are frequently installed in shopping malls and town centres as deterrents to anti-social and criminal behaviour.

community – a concept incorporating many different interests, groups, struggles, agendas, strategies and relationships to the state. Communities can be delineated by territorial boundaries that may include geography (local, regional or international), e.g. people living in the same area and power structures (federal, state; local government) defined by electoral boundaries; and services (transport line, school) defined by service providers such as local councils. The so-called 'bonds of community' can be conceived in terms of interconnected and deeply embedded institutional influences and interests (e.g. work, religion and communal associations), broader structural contexts (e.g. housing policy and employment opportunities) and social factors (e.g. gender, race and class).

community policing – a police strategy that focuses on developing closer links with groups in the community through methods of engagement and consultation, with the aim of improving police/community relations and tailoring police responses to local crime problems.

community safety – actual security and perceptions of safety felt by members of local communities; an indicator of general health and wellbeing.

community safety officers (CSO) – are specialised personnel who help drive the crime prevention process at the local level through developing plans and coordinating partnerships. One core role of CSOs is to enhance communication between state and local levels, helping to articulate a shared vision.

cost-benefit analysis – analysis that aims to measure the savings (either in monetary values or harms reduced) accrued from the implementation of a particular crime prevention approach. Cost-benefit analysis examines whether the effects produced by a crime prevention program (e.g. reductions in crime) exceed the resources spent on the program; that is, whether savings incurred by an intervention outweigh the costs of program inputs.

crime displacement – the displacement of crime due to the impact of particular situational and other direct environmental crime measures. Crime may be displaced geographically to another location (spatial displacement), offenders may substitute one type of crime for another (tactical displacement) or commit more serious crime.

crime hot spots – locations where crime is highly concentrated geographically due to the features of certain locations (e.g. the concentrations of bars and clubs) or characteristics of people who frequent, or are drawn to, such locations, leading to the coming together of motivated offenders and potential targets.

crime prevention – in the context of this book, attempts to prevent or reduce crime before it occurs; it does not directly include efforts to deal with offenders after the fact.

crime prevention partnerships – structured ways of working together to provide a more holistic response to crime. These can involve agencies such as police, schools, local government and businesses pooling resources, expertise and information to address crime problems. There are different types of partnership models, but the size of a crime prevention partnership will vary by the crime problem being addressed.

crime prevention through environmental design (CPTED) – CPTED focuses on the design and maintenance of built environments, including the manipulation of design relating to features of the built environment (e.g. housing, buildings, roads) and community amenities (e.g. gardens, nature strips) that can help enhance safety and security.

crime reduction – a concept that acknowledges that not all types of crimes can be prevented, but they can be minimised through targeted strategies and selection of appropriate techniques.

crime science – a field of research that draws on a range of scientific methods across the physical, social, biological and computer sciences that are seen as relevant to crime control. Central to this approach is the use of data, logic, evidence and rational thought. Such procedures are seen as providing the basis for the development of evidence-based policy.

crime triangle framework – an analytical framework that helps explain why crime occurs through the convergence of a motivated offender and a target in the absence of capable guardianship. The framework has also been adapted to incorporate how capable guardianship helps determine this convergence.

critical criminology – in the context of this book, the work of those theorists who argue that prevention policies need to be located in the context of broader economic and political forces reshaping late modern societies, such as shifts in forms of governance and in power relations between the state and the populations it seeks to govern.

cyber-crime – offences associated with the use of information and communication technology variously referred to as e-crime, cyber-crime, high-tech crime and computer crime. Offences include those committed using the technology (e.g. identity fraud), those that target the computers themselves and seek to destroy or alter information or data (e.g. hackers), and those in which the computer is used as storage for information about an offence (e.g. a drug offence in which supply records are kept on computer).

defensible space – the idea that architectural solutions can allow people to exert functional control by engendering a sense of territoriality and community among themselves (i.e. a desire to defend one's space and feelings of belonging) and facilitate responsibility for preserving a safe and well-maintained living environment. For example, through the use of physical and symbolic barriers,

space can be divided into four distinct categories: public, semi-public, semi-private (gardens) and private. Barriers can include hedges and walls between public and private areas, signboards (e.g. notices stating 'You are entering private property'), vegetation or changes in surfaces to create 'zones of transition' that give people cues that they are moving from public to private space.

developmental prevention – also known as 'early intervention', it aims to intervene early in the life course to alter the risk and protective factors in young people's lives that lead to crime (risk factors) or preclude the onset of offending (protective factors). The various stages, pathways, trajectories, phases and transitions over the life course are analysed so that suitable interventions are made at key stages throughout the life course and relevant 'protective' factors can be identified and strengthened.

distal – background factors, or the broader social context (including poverty, education, health and welfare, and employment) that can lead to crime. Addressing distal factors is usually associated with social prevention.

diversion – an approach that focuses on identifying individuals at risk of offending, and removing them from environments seen as contributing to crime. A central focus of preventive diversion is addressing factors likely to cause these individuals to drift into delinquency, such as low self-esteem, lack of self-discipline, weak attachment to family or school and low social or vocational skills. Diversion-based schemes tend to be one-off experiences (e.g. wilderness camps) and less systematic than developmental prevention.

environmental crime prevention – measures designed to reduce or prevent environmental crimes, such as illegal dumping of waste and illegal trade in wildlife.

environmental prevention – an approach addressing the target and guardianship aspects of crime. It aims to modify the physical (and, in the cyber era, virtual) contexts in which crimes can occur and potential offenders can operate – and, in particular, to minimise the extent to which such environments give rise to criminal opportunities. It encompasses broad-based planning and design and focused situational prevention.

evidence-based policy and practice – a term implying that policy and practice should be derived from systematic evidence about what works, rather than anecdote, popularism or program trends. What it means to be 'evidence-based' is highly contested.

experimental criminology – a field of criminology in which randomised control trials and meta-evaluations are seen as essential to the development of evidence-based crime prevention programs.

experimental methods – methods of evaluating crime prevention programs that involve randomly allocating people (i.e. members of the target population) to treatment and control groups, and comparing the two in relation to program outcomes pre and post the intervention period. Referred to as randomised control trials, the treatment group receives the intervention, while the control group does not. Based on the medical model, it is seen as the gold standard in evaluation design.

governmentality – an analysis that sees the resurgence of crime prevention policies and practices since the late 20th century as driven by a neo-liberal government agenda in which the state shifts responsibility for crime control to private citizens, commercial firms, community groups and agencies so they become active partners in the co-production of safety and security.

guardianship – defined in terms of both human actors and security devices (parents, security guards, store people, teachers, cameras and alarms) it can take the form of formal surveillance or more informal social controls (e.g. the presence of bystanders in a busy street).

impact evaluation – a type of evaluation, also known as 'outcome evaluation', concerned with examining the impact of the intervention (i.e. with answering the question 'Did it work?'). This relates to identifying whether an intervention led to a reduction in crime.

intelligence-led policing – an innovation in policing that emphasises the use of crime intelligence and criminal intelligence to identify prolific offenders and to undertake targeted preventative action through coordinated police action.

law and order – policies and practices that rely upon and emphasise coercive responses to crime, and that, accordingly, rely on punishment and on expanding police powers and numbers.

management protocols – protocols developed in relation to shopping centres in order to provide substantial guidance for managers, police, security, youth services and young people on how to deal with difficulties, such as conflicts between young patrons and security staff. Associated with these protocols there may also be a specific 'code of practice' for security personnel regarding engagement with young people and other users of such centres.

meta-evaluations – a systematic, statistically-based review of existing evaluations in order to establish which types of interventions reduce crime. Evaluations that adopt randomised control trials are seen as the most robust studies to select for a meta-review.

narrative reviews – reviews that aim to describe program components and processes (e.g. strategy implementation) but do not employ the statistical methods adopted in a meta-analysis. Narrative reviews can offer an overview of particular crime prevention approaches and indicate why they may constitute exemplary programs.

natural surveillance – an attempt to increase the number of 'eyes on the street'. This is achieved through planning (i.e. providing opportunities for people to exert social control in the course of their normal routine activities), and to ensuring that the design features of city buildings facilitate natural surveillance (e.g. by drawing people back to city centres through the establishment of mixed land uses and the provision of amenities such as shops, pubs, restaurants and parks and activities that draw people out of their homes and onto the streets during the day and at night).

primary prevention – prevention that addresses factors or conditions relevant to crime that can affect an entire populace, such as interventions with socioeconomically disadvantaged infants to improve their legitimate life opportunities in education and other fields. It can also include efforts to ensure that the built environment does not inadvertently include features that increase opportunities for crime.

problem-oriented policing – a police strategy that focuses on in-depth analysis of local crime problems that drain police resources (e.g. crime hotspots). The aim is to develop tailored responses based on data collection and analysis that are preventative in nature and do not rely on traditional police responses, such as arrest.

problem-solving – a perspective that views crime prevention as problem-oriented rather than practice-oriented, meaning that preconceived notions should not determine how to tackle the crime problem under investigation and that strategies need to be tailored to the specific nature of crime and safety problems in particular localities. Such a process should follow a systematic approach via in-depth collection of relevant data on the crime problem(s) and the selection of strategy objectives and interventions based upon this research, and accumulated evidence on what has been successful in reducing the particular crime problem.

process evaluation – evaluation that looks at the underlying mechanisms that drove the implementation of a strategy, and that assesses whether they hindered or facilitated its delivery. A process evaluation may focus on a broad range of factors relating to the roles of different agencies within a scheme, the decision-making processes underpinning policy formation and barriers encountered during strategy delivery.

proximal factors – immediate or foreground factors that can influence crime and have a bearing on the selection of crime prevention techniques. Proximate causes can relate to the roles of offenders, victims and guardians, and are closely associated with situational crime prevention.

punitiveness – a general policy and cultural attitude towards transgression in which arrest, imprisonment and other criminal justice based initiatives are favoured in efforts to deter and reduce offending.

responsibilisation – the idea that responsibility for crime prevention and safety is ultimately that of individuals and communities at the local level, rather than the state or society at large.

routine activity theory – the notion that crime is the product of three factors: the coming together at a particular time and place of a motivated offender, a potential target, and the absence of capable guardianship. It underpins the crime triangle framework.

secondary prevention – interventions in environments or with populations deemed 'at risk', with the aim of precluding the onset of offending. It can include situational interventions in locations

where crime is likely to occur (e.g. CCTV outside licensed premises and throughout entertainment districts) and measures to reduce the accessibility of certain targets (e.g. engine immobilisers in motor vehicles).

situational prevention – prevention that focuses on reducing opportunities for crime, rather than trying to change the disposition to offend, through direct and immediate techniques that reconfigure the environment so opportunities for crime are no longer available to motivated offenders, or are no longer seen as available by them.

social justice – a broad concern with matters of equality, respect and human dignity associated with policies that focus on equitable provision of health, welfare, education and other social goods and services.

social prevention – an approach that regards crime as the result of particular social deficits and considers that prevention should focus on aiding individuals, families and communities to act in ways that preclude crime. It aims to identify and address factors manifest in individual, family, peer, school, neighbourhood, community and other contexts that can affect whether people are likely to become involved in, or continue, offending.

tertiary prevention – targets known offenders, and environments already affected by crime, with the objective of reducing future offending and the re-victimisation of people or places. It can include prison-based treatment programs for convicted sex offenders and post-release schemes to help offenders resettle in the community.

third parties – individuals, families, businesses and communities that can have a role in reducing crime by changing how they behave or operate.

what works – instrumental efforts to ensure practical application and viability through evidence-based evaluation, with the key goal being to identify the most effective methods of crime reduction and to ensure that such knowledge guides policy and practice.

whole-of-government approach – an approach based upon the idea that strategies and programs to address crime are generally input from a range of agencies (e.g. education, human services, urban planning and police) located at different levels of government (e.g. both central and regional). Achievement of 'joined-up outcomes' around crime prevention therefore must involve more effective coordination between these levels of administration and spheres of specialisation.

CRIME PREVENTION: RELEVANT WEBSITES

Australia

Australian Bureau of Statistics – national criminal justice and correctional statistics

www.abs.gov.au

Australian Crime Commission

www.crimecommission.gov.au

Australian Crime Prevention Council

www.acpc.org.au

Australian Government – Crime prevention

www.crimeprevention.gov.au

Australian Government – Policing and organised crime

www.ag.gov.au

Australian Institute of Criminology – extensive criminological resources, publications and links

www.aic.gov.au

Australian Institute of Family Studies

www.aifs.gov.au

Australian Institute of Health and Welfare

www.aihw.gov.au

CrimNet – Information Network, Institute of Criminology, Sydney

http://mailman.sydney.edu.au/mailman/listinfo/law-crimnet

NSW Department of Attorney General and Justice – Crime prevention

www.crimeprevention.nsw.gov.au

Queensland – Crime and Misconduct Commission

www.cmc.qld.gov.au

Queensland – Crime Prevention Through Environmental Design

www.police.qld.gov.au/programs/cscp/safetyPublic

Queensland – Pathways to Prevention Program

www.griffith.edu.au/pathways-to-prevention

Tasmania – Department of Justice

www.justice.tas.gov.au

Victoria – Department of Justice – Community Crime Prevention

www.crimeprevention.vic.gov.au

Western Australia – Department of the Attorney General

www.dotag.wa.gov.au

International

Canada – International Centre for the Prevention of Crime

www.crime-prevention-intl.org

Canada – Public Safety Canada, National Crime Prevention Centre

www.publicsafety.gc.ca

Dutch Centre for Crime Prevention and Safety

www.hetccv.nl

European Crime Prevention Network

www.eucpn.org

International Society of Crime Prevention Practitioners

www.iscpp.org

Oxford Centre for Criminology

www.crim.ox.ac.uk/useful_links.php

Sweden – National Council for Crime Prevention

www.bra.se

The Campbell Collaboration

www.campbellcollaboration.org

The Netherlands Government – Crime Prevention

www.government.nl/issues/crime-and-crime-prevention

UK Government – Crime prevention

www.gov.uk/government/policies/reducing-and-preventing-crime—2

United Nations Crime and Justice Information Network

www.uncjin.org

United Nations Economic and Social Council

www.un.org/en/ecosoc

United Nations Interregional Crime and Justice Research Institute

www.unicri.it

United Nations Office on Drugs and Crime

www.unodc.org

US – Bureau of Justice Assistance

www.bja.gov

US – Centre for Problem-Oriented Policing

www.popcenter.org

US – National Crime Prevention Council

www.ncpc.org

United States – National Institute of Justice

www.nij.gov

REFERENCES

Ailard, T., Chrzanowski, A. & Stewart, A. (2012) 'Targeting crime prevention to reduce offending: identifying communities that generate chronic and costly offenders', *Trends & Issues in Crime and Criminal Justice*, no. 445, pp. 1–6.

Airo-Farulla, G. (1992) 'Community policing and self-determination', *Aboriginal Law Bulletin*, vol. 2, no. 54, pp. 8–9.

Allen, K. (2012) 'Off the radar and ubiquitous: text messaging and its relationship to "drama" and cyberbullying in an affluent, academically rigorus US high school', *Journal of Youth Studies*, vol. 15, no. 1, pp. 99–117.

Altman, J., Bek, H. & Roach, L. (1996) 'Use of wildlife by Indigenous Australians: economic and policy perspectives', in M. Bomford & J. Caughley (eds), *Sustainable use of wildlife by Aboriginal Peoples and Torres Strait Islanders*. Canberra: Bureau of Resource Sciences, Australian Government Publishing Service.

Anderson, J. & Homel, P. (2005) *Reviewing the New South Wales Local Crime Prevention Planning Process*. Canberra: Australian Institute of Criminology, www.aic.gov.au/publications/previous%20series/other/61–80.html.

Anderson, J. & Tresidder, J. (2008) *A review of the Western Australian community safety and crime prevention planning process: final report*. Canberra: Australian Institute of Criminology, www.aic.gov.au/publications/previous%20series/other/61–80.html.

Anderson, K. & McCusker, R. (2005) 'Crime in the Australian fishing industry: key issues', *Trends & Issues in Crime and Criminal Justice*, no. 297.

Armitage, R. (2000) 'An evaluation of Secured by Design Housing within West Yorkshire', Home Office Briefing Note 7/00, Policing and Reducing Crime Unit, Home Office Research, Development and Statistics Directorate, London.

Atkinson, R. (2006) 'Mob mentality: the threat to community sustainability from the search for safety', in P. Malpass & L. Cairncross (eds), *Building on the past: visions of housing futures*. Bristol: Policy Press, pp. 163–184.

Atkinson, R. & Blandy, S. (2005) *Housing Studies*, vol. 20, no. 2 (March) (special edition on gated communities).

—— (2006) *Gated communities*. London: Routledge.

Australian Bureau of Statistics (2002) *Crime and safety*, Canberra.

Australian Competition and Consumer Commission (undated) Scam Watch information sheet on 'Identity theft'. Canberra: ACCC, www.accc.gov.au, (accessed 1 March 2013).

Australian Institute of Criminology <www.aic.gov.au/research/cvp/topics/cpted.html#research> (accessed 27 February 2008).

Australian Institute of Criminology (2003) 'Measuring crime prevention program costs and benefits', *AIC Crime Reduction Matters*, no. 15.

—— (2008) *Australian crime facts and figures 2007*. Canberra: Australian Institute of Criminology.

—— (2010) 'Covert and cyber bullying', *Research in Practice*, no. 9 (February).

—— (2012) *National Crime Prevention Framework. Developed on behalf of the Australian and New Zealand Crime Prevention Senior Officers' Group 2012*. Canberra: Australian Institute of Criminology.

Barr, R. & Pease, K. (1990) 'Crime placement, displacement and deflection', in M. Tonry & N. Morris (eds), *Crime and Justice: Re Review of the Research*, vol. 12. Chicago: University of Chicago Press.

Becker, H. (1963) *Outsiders: studies in the sociology of deviance*. New York: The Free Press.

Beirne, P. & South, N. (eds) (2007) *Issues in green criminology: confronting harms against environments, humanity and other animals*. Devon: Willan Publishing.

Bell, S., Hampshire, K. & Topalidou, S. (2007) 'The political culture of poaching: a case study from northern Greece', *Biodiversity and Conservation*, vol. 16, no. 2, pp. 399–418.

Bell, W. (1991) 'The role of urban design in crime prevention: Adelaide city – a case study', *Australian Planner*, December, pp. 206–210.

Bennett, T., Holloway, K. & Farrington, D.P. (2006) 'Does Neighborhood Watch reduce crime? A systematic review and meta-analysis', *Journal of Experimental Criminology*, vol. 2, issue 4, pp. 437–458.

Berman, G. & Fox, A. (2010) *Trial and error in criminal justice reform: learning from failure*. Washington, DC: Urban Institute Press.

Bishop, D.M. (2006) 'Public opinion and juvenile justice policy: myths and misconceptions', *Criminology and Public Policy*, vol. 5, issue 4, pp. 653–664.

Blagg, H. & Valuri, G. (2003) *An overview of nght patrol services in Australia*. Canberra: Attorney-General's Department.

—— (2004a) 'Self-policing and community safety: the work of Aboriginal community patrols in Australia', *Current Issues in Criminal Justice*, vol. 15, no. 3, pp. 205–219.

—— (2004b) 'Aboriginal community patrols in Australia: self-policing, self-determination and security', *Policing & Society*, vol. 14, no. 4, pp. 313–328.

Blakely, E. & Snyder, M. (1999) *Fortress America: gated communities in the United States*. Washington, DC and Cambridge: Brookings Institution and Lincoln Institute of Land Policy.

Boba, R. (2009) 'Evil done', in J. D. Freilich & G.R. Newman (eds), *Reducing terrorism through situational crime prevention* (Crime Prevention Studies, no. 25) Monsey, New York: Criminal Justice Press, pp. 71–92.

Bonnemaison, G. (1983) *Confronting crime: prevention, repression and solidarity*. Paris: Documentation Francaise.

Bottoms, A. (1974) 'Defensible Space', *British Journal of Criminology*, vol. 14, no. 2, pp. 203–206.

Bourdieu, P. (1977) *Outline of a theory of practice*. Cambridge: Cambridge University Press.

Bourgois, P. (1995) *In search of respect: selling crack at El Barrio*. New York: Cambridge University Press.

Boyce, J. (2001) 'Crime prevention in a plains town – Moree'. Paper presented at 'The Character, Impact and Prevention of Crime in Regional Australia' conference, Townsville, August 2001.

Boyd, D. (2003) *Unnatural law: rethinking Canadian environmental law and policy*. Vancouver: UBC Press.

Boyle, S., Mortensen, L., Gronbaek, M. & Barefoot, J. (2007) 'Hostility, drinking pattern and mortality', *Addiction*, vol. 103, no. 1, pp. 54–59.

Braga, A.A. (2010) 'Setting a higher standard for the evaluation of problem-oriented policing initiatives', *Criminology & Public Policy*, vol. 9, no. 1, pp. 173–182.

Braga, A.A., Hureau, D. & Winship, C (2008) 'Losing faith? Police, black churches, and the resurgence of youth violence in Boston', *Ohio State Journal of Criminal Law*, vol. 6, pp. 141–172.

Braga, A., McDevitt, J. & Pierce, G.L. (2006) 'Understanding and preventing gang violence: problem analysis and response development in Lowell, Massachusetts', *Police Quarterly*, vol. 9, no. 1, pp. 20–46.

Braga, A.A. & Weisburd, D. (2010) *Policing problem places: crime hot spots and effective prevention*. New York: Oxford University Press.

Brain, K. (2000) 'Youth, alcohol, and the emergence of the Post-Modern Alcohol Order', Occasional Paper No. 1. London: Institute of Alcohol Studies.

Braithwaite, J. (1989) *Crime, shame and reintegration*. Cambridge: Cambridge University Press.

Branch, S., Freiberg, K. & Homel, R. (2010) 'Circles of care: the struggle to strengthen child developmental systems through the Pathways to Prevention project'. *Family Matters*, no. 84, pp. 28–34.

Branch, S., Homel, R. & Freiberg, K. (2012) 'Making the developmental system work better for children: lessons learned implementing an innovative programme', *Child & Family Social Work*. doi: 10.1111/j.1365–2206.2012.00845.x

Brantingham, P.J. & Brantingham, P.L. (1993) 'Nodes, paths and edges: considerations on the complexity of crime and the physical environment', *Journal of Environmental Psychology*, vol. 13, no. 1, pp. 3–28.

—— (1995) 'Criminality of place: crime generators and crime attractors', *European Journal on Criminal Policy and Research*, vol. 3, no. 3, pp. 1–26.

Brantingham, P.J. & Faust, F. (1976) 'A conceptual model of crime prevention', *Crime and Delinquency*, vol. 22, no. 3, pp. 284–296.

Brantingham, P.L., Brantingham, P.J. & Taylor, W. (2005) 'Situational crime prevention as a key component in embedded crime prevention', *Canadian Journal of Criminology and Criminal Justice*, vol. 42, no. 2, pp. 271–292.

Bricknell, S. (2008) 'Trends in violent crime', *Trends & Issues in Crimes and Criminal Justice*, no. 359.

Briscoe, S. & Donnelly, N. (2001a) *Temporal and regional aspects of alcohol-related violence and disorder*, Alcohol Studies Bulletin No. 1. Produced by the NSW Bureau of Crime Statistics and Research and the National Drug Research Institute of Curtin University.

—— (2001b) *Assault on Licensed Premises in Inner-Urban Areas*, Alcohol Studies Bulletin No. 2. Produced by the NSW Bureau of Crime Statistics and Research and the National Drug Research Institute of Curtin University.

Brown, D., Farrier, D., Egger, S. & McNamara, L. (2001) *Criminal laws: materials and commentary on criminal law and process in New South Wales*. Sydney: The Federation Press.

Bull, D. & Stratta, E. (1994) 'Police community consultation: an examination of its practice in selected constabularies in England and New South Wales, Australia', *Australian & New Zealand Journal of Criminology*, vol. 27, no. 3, pp. 237–249.

Bullock, K., Erol, R. & Tilley, N. (2006) *Problem-oriented policing and partnerships: implementing an evidence-based approach to crime reduction*. Cullompton, Devon: Willan Publishing.

Bullock, K. & Tilley, N. (2009) 'Evidence-based policing and crime reduction', *Policing*, vol. 3, no. 4, pp. 381–387.

Bushway, S.D. & Paternoster, R. (2013) 'Desistance from crime: a review and ideas for moving forward', in C.L. Gibson & M.D. Krohn (eds), *Handbook of life-course criminology: emerging trends and directions for future research*. New York: Springer, pp. 213–231.

Caldwell, L. & Smith, E. (2007) 'Leisure as a context for youth development and delinquency prevention', in A. France & R. Homel (eds), *Pathways and crime prevention: theory, policy and practice*. Cullompton, Devon: Willan Publishing.

Campbell Collaboration <www.aic.gov.au/campbellcj/> (accessed 26 February 2008).

Canada, National Crime Prevention Centre (1996) *Mobilizing political will and community responsibility to prevent youth crime*. Ottawa: National Crime Prevention Council.

—— (1998) *Building a safer Canada: a community based crime prevention manual*. Ottawa: Canadian Department of Justice.

Carcach, C. (1997) 'Youth as victims and offenders of homicide', *Trends & Issues in Crime and Criminal Justice*, no. 73.

Carrabine, E., Iganski, P., Lee, M., Plummer, K. & South, N. (2004) *Criminology: a sociological introduction*. London: Routledge.

Carson, W.G. (2004a) 'Is communalism dead? Reflections on the present and future practice of crime prevention: part 1', *Australian & New Zealand Journal of Criminology*, vol. 37, no. 1, pp. 1–21.

—— (2004b) 'Is communalism dead? Reflections on the present and future practice of crime prevention: part 2', *Australian and New Zealand Journal of Criminology*, vol. 37, no. 2, pp. 192–210.

Cashmore, J., Gilmore, L., Goodnow, J., Hayes, A., Homel, R., Lawrence, J. et al. (2001a) *Ending family violence? Programs for perpetrators* Canberra: Attorney-General's Department.

—— (2001b) *Pathways to prevention: developmental and early intervention approaches to crime in Australia (Appendices)*. Canberra: Attorney-General's Department.

Castellano, P. & Soderstrom, P. (1992) 'Therapeutic wilderness programmes and juvenile recidivism: A programme evaluation', *Journal of Offender Rehabilitation*, vol. 17, nos. 3–4, pp. 19–46.

Caughley, J., Bomford, M. & McNee, A. (1996) 'Use of wildlife by Indigenous Australians: issues and concepts', in M. Bomford & J. Caughley (eds), *Sustainable use of wildlife by Aboriginal Peoples and Torres Strait Islanders*. Canberra: Bureau of Resource Sciences, Australian Government Publishing Service.

Chatterton, P. & Hollands, R. (2003) *Urban nightscapes: youth cultures, pleasure spaces and corporate power*. London: Routledge.

Cherney, A. (2002) 'Beyond technicism: broadening the "what works" paradigm in crime prevention', *Crime Prevention and Community Safety: An International Journal*, vol. 3, no. 4, pp. 49–59.

—— (2004a) 'Contingency and politics: the local government community safety officer role', *Criminal Justice: The International Journal of Policy and Practice*, vol. 4, no. 2, pp. 115–128.

—— (2004b) 'A case study of crime prevention/community safety partnerships in Victoria', *Current Issues in Criminal Justice*, vol. 15, no. 3, pp. 237–252.

—— (2005) 'A letter from Australia: doing crime prevention research – a personal reflection', *Crime Prevention and Community Safety: An International Journal*, vol. 7, no. 1, pp. 53–62.

—— (2006a) 'Problem solving for crime prevention', *Trends & Issues in Crime and Criminal Justice*, no. 314.

—— (2006b) 'The role of local government in crime prevention: an overview', *Local Government Reporter*, vol. 5, nos. 3 & 4, pp. 25–28.

—— (2009) 'Exploring the concept of research utilisation: implications for evidence-based crime prevention', *Crime Prevention and Community Safety: An International Journal*, vol. 11, no. 4, pp. 243–257

Cherney, A. & Chui, W.H. (2010) 'Police auxiliaries in Australia: police liaison officers and the dilemmas of being part of the police extended family', *Policing and Society*, vol. 20, no. 3, pp. 280–297.

Cherney, A. & Head, B.W. (2011) 'Supporting the knowledge-to-action process: a systems-thinking approach', *Evidence & Policy*, vol. 7, no. 4, pp. 471–488.

Cherney, A. & Sutton, A. (2006) 'Crime prevention and reduction', in A. Goldsmith, M. Israel & K. Daly (eds), *Crime and justice in the 21st century: an Australian textbook in criminology*, 3rd edn. Sydney: Thomson/LBC, pp. 373–393.

—— (2007) 'Crime prevention in Australia: beyond what works', *Australian & New Zealand Journal of Criminology*, vol. 40, no. 1, pp. 65–81.

Chikritzhs, T., Catalano, P., Pascal, R. & Henrickson, N. (2007) *Predicting alcohol-related harms from licensed outlet density: a feasibility study*. Hobart: National Drug Law Enforcement Research Fund, Commonwealth of Australia.

Chikritzhs, T. & Stockwell, T. (2002) 'The impact of later trading hours for Australian public houses (hotels) on levels of violence', *Journal for the Study of Alcohol*, vol. 63, pp. 591–599.

Christensen, W. (2006) 'Nipped in the bud: a situational crime prevention approach to the prevention of bushfire arson', unpublished Masters thesis, School of Social Science, University of Queensland.

Clammer, J. (1997) 'Framing the other: criminality, social exclusion and social engineering in developing Singapore', *Social Policy and Administration*, vol. 31, no. 5, pp. 136–153.

Clancey, G. (n.d.) *Natural surveillance*, at http://garnerclancey.com/case_studies.php. (n.d.) *Promoting natural surveillance: balconies and patios*, at http://garnerclancey.com/case_studies php.

—— (n.d.) *Access control and territorial reinforcement*, at http://garnerclancey.com/case_studies.php.

—— (n.d.) *Promoting natural surveillance: balconies and patios*, at http://garnerclancey.com/case_studies.php.

—— (2011) 'Are we still "Flying Blind?" Crime data and local crime prevention in New South Wales', *Current Issues in Criminal Justice*, vol. 22, no. 3, pp. 492–500.

Clancey, G., Lee, M. & Crofts, T. (2012) '"We're not Batman" – roles and expectations of local government community safety officers in New South Wales', *Crime Prevention and Community Safety: An International Journal*, vol. 14, no. 4, pp. 235–257.

Clancey, G., Lee, M. & Fisher, D. (2012) 'Crime prevention through environmental design (CPTED) and the New South Wales crime risk assessment guidelines: a critical review', *Crime Prevention & Community Safety*, vol. 14, no. 1, pp. 1–15.

Clarke, R. (2008) 'Situational prevention', in R. Wortley & L. Mazerolle (eds), *Environmental criminology and crime analysis*. Devon: Willan Publishing.

Clarke, R. & Eck, J. (2005) *Crime analysis for problem solvers in 60 small steps*. Office of Community Oriented Policing Services, Centre for Problem Oriented Policing, US Department of Justice, www.cops.usdoj.gov/publications.

—— (2003) *Crime analysis for problem solvers in 60 small steps*. Office of Community Oriented Policing Services, Centre for Problem Oriented Policing, US Department of Justice.

Clarke, R.V. (1980) 'Situational crime prevention: theory and practice', *British Journal of Criminology*, vol. 20, no. 2, pp. 136–147.

—— (ed.) (1997) *Situational crime prevention: successful case studies*, 2nd edn, New York: Harrow & Heston.

—— (1998a) 'Defining police strategies: problem solving, problem oriented policing and community-oriented policing', in A. Grant & O. Shelley (eds), *Problem-oriented policing*, Police Executive Research Forum, Washington, DC, pp. 315–326.

—— (1998b) 'Theoretical background to crime prevention through environmental design (CPTED), and situational prevention'. Paper presented at the Australian Institute of Criminology Conference 'Designing out crime: crime prevention through environmental design (CPTED)', 16 June. Sydney, available at <www.aic.gov.au/conferences/cpted/clarke.html> (accessed 27 February 2008).

—— (1999) *Hot products: understanding, anticipating and reducing the demand for stolen goods*. London: HMSO.

—— (2005) 'Seven misconceptions of situational crime prevention', in N. Tilley (ed), *Handbook of crime prevention and community safety*. Devon: Willan Publishing, pp. 39–70.

Clarke, R.V. & Cornish, D.B. (eds) (1986) *The reasoning criminal: rational choice perspectives on offending*. New York: Springer-Verlag.

Clarke, R.V. & Felson, M. (eds) (1993) *Routine activity and rational choice: advances in criminological theory*. New Brunswick, New Jersey: Transaction.

Clarke, R.V. & Homel, R. (1997) 'A revised classification of situational crime prevention techniques', in S. Lab (ed.), *Crime prevention at a crossroads*, Cincinnati, Ohio: Anderson.

Clarke, R.V. & Weisburd, D. (1994) 'Diffusion of crime control benefits: observations on the reverse of displacement', in R.V. Clarke (ed.), *Crime Prevention Studies*, vol. 2. Monsey, New York: Criminal Justice Press, pp. 165–184.

Cohen, L.E. & Felson, M. (1979) 'Social change and crime rate trends: a routine activity approach', *American Sociological Review*, vol. 44, no. 4, pp. 588–608.

Cohen, M.A., Roland, T.R. & Steen, S. (2006) 'Prevention, crime control or cash? Public preferences towards criminal justice spending priorities', *Justice Quarterly*, vol. 23, no. 3, pp. 317–335.

Cohen, S. (1973) *Folk devils and moral panics*. London: Paladin.

Coleman, R. (2004) *Reclaim the streets: surveillance, social control and the city*. Cullompton, Devon: Willan Publishing.

Collin, P., Rahilly, K., Richardson, I. & Third, A. (2010) *The benefits of social networking services: literature review*. Melbourne: Cooperative Research Centre for Young People, Technology and Wellbeing.

Collins, A. (1998) 'Hip hop graffiti culture', *Alternative Law Journal*, vol. 23, no. 1, pp. 19–21.

Collins, J., Noble, G., Poynting, S. & Tabar, P. (2000) *Kebabs, kids, cops & crime: youth, ethnicity & crime*. Sydney: Pluto Press.

Colquhoun, I. (2004) *Design out crime: creating safe and sustainable communities*. Oxford: Elsevier Architectural Press.

Connell, J.P., Kubisch, A.C., Schorr, L.B. & Weiss, C.H. (1995) *New approaches to evaluating community initiatives, concepts, methods and contexts*. New York: Aspen Institute.

Connell, R. (1995) *Masculinities*. Sydney: Allen & Unwin.

—— (2000) *The men and the boys*. Sydney: Allen & Unwin.

Cook, T.D. & Campbell, D.T. (1979) *Quasi-experimentation*. Chicago: Rand McNally.

Coote, A., Allen, J. & Woodhead, D. (2004) *Finding out what works: understanding complex community-based initiatives*. London: Kings Fund.

Cordner, G. & Biebel, E.P. (2005) 'Problem-oriented policing practice', *Criminology & Public Policy*, vol. 4, no. 2, pp. 155–180.

Cozens, P.M., Hillier, D. & Prescott, G. (2001a) 'Crime and the design of residential property: exploring the theoretical background', *Property Management*, vol. 19, no. 2, pp. 136–164.

—— (2001b) 'Crime and the design of residential property: exploring the perceptions of planning professionals, burglars and other users part 2', *Property Management*, vol. 19, no. 4, pp. 222–248.

Cozens, P.M., Pascoe, T. & Hillier, D. (2004) 'The policy and practice of secured by design (SBD)', *Crime Prevention and Community Safety: an International Journal*, vol. 6, no. 1, pp. 13–29.

Cozens, P.M., Saville, G. & Hillier, D. (2005) 'Crime prevention through environmental design (CPTED): a review and modern bibliography', *Journal of Property Management*, vol. 23, no. 5, pp. 328–356.

Crane, P. (2000) 'Young people and public space: developing inclusive policy and practice', *Scottish Youth Issues Journal*, vol. 1, no. 1, pp. 105–124.

Crane, P. & Marston, G. (1999) *The Myer Centre Youth Protocol: a summary*. Brisbane: Brisbane City Council.

Crawford, A. (1994) 'The partnership approach to community crime prevention: corporatism at the local level?' *Social and Legal Studies*, vol. 3, no. 4, pp. 497–519.

—— (1997) *The local governance of crime: appeals to community and partnerships*. Oxford: Clarendon Press.

—— (1998) *Crime prevention and community safety: politics, policies and practices*. London and New York: Longman.

—— (1999) 'Questioning appeals to community within crime prevention and control', *European Journal on Criminal Policy and Research*, vol. 7, no. 4, pp. 509–530.

—— (2002) 'The growth of crime prevention in France as contrasted with the English experience: some thoughts on the politics of insecurity', in G. Hughes, E. McLaughlin & J. Muncie (eds), *Crime prevention and community safety: new directions*. London: Sage Publications in association with Open University Press, pp. 214–239.

—— (2009) 'Criminalizing sociability through anti-social behaviour legislation: dispersal powers, young people and the police', *Youth Justice*, vol. 9, no. 1, pp. 5–26.

Crawford, A. & Jones, M. (1995) 'Interagency crime prevention and community based crime prevention: some reflections on the work of Pearson and colleagues', *British Journal of Criminology*, vol. 35, no. 1, pp. 17–33.

Crawford, A. & Matassa, M. (2000), *Community safety structures: an international literature review*, Northern Ireland Officer, Statistics and Research Branch, Criminal Justice Policy Division, Massey House, Belfast.

Crenshaw, M. (1981) 'The causes of terrorism'. *Comparative Politics*, vol. 13, no. 4, pp. 379–399.

Crime Prevention Victoria (2003) *Safer design guidelines for Victoria*. Melbourne: Crime Prevention Victoria and Department of Sustainability and Environment.

Crofts, P., Morris, T., Wells, K. & Powell, A. (2010) 'Illegal dumping and crime prevention: a case study of Ash Road, Liverpool Council', *Public Space: The Journal of Law and Social Justice*, vol. 5, no. 4, pp. 1–23.

Cromwell, P. & Olson, J.N. (2004) *Breaking and entering: burglars on burglary*. Belmont, California: Wadsworth.

Crowe, T.D. (2000) *Crime prevention through environmental design: applications of architectural design and space management concepts*, 2nd edn. National Crime Prevention Institute.

Cullen, F.T., Vose, B.A., Lero Jonson, C.N. & Unnever, J.D. (2007) 'Public support for early intervention: is child saving a "habit of the heart"?', *Victims & Offenders*, vol. 2, no. 2, pp. 109–124.

Cunneen, C., Findlay, M., Lynch, R. & Tupper, V. (1989) *Dynamics of collective conflict: riots at the Bathurst Bike Races*. Sydney: Law Book Company.

Cunneen, C., Fraser, D. & Tomsen, S. (1997) 'Introduction: defining the Issues', in C. Cunneen et al. (eds), *Faces of hate: hate crime in Australia*. Sydney: Hawkins Press.

Cunneen, C. & White, R. (2007) *Juvenile justice: youth and crime in Australia*. Melbourne: Oxford University Press.

Currie, E. (1988) 'Two visions of community crime prevention', in T. Hope & M. Shaw (eds), *Communities and crime reduction*. London: HMSO.

—— (2013) *Crime and punishment in America*. New York: Picador.

Dalgaard-Nielsen, A. (2013) 'Promoting exit from violent extremism: themes and approaches', *Studies in Conflict & Terrorism*, vol. 36, no. 2, pp. 99–115.

Darcy, D. (2005) 'Policing the socially disadvantaged, the value of rekindling community policing in Woolloomooloo – a police commander's perspective', *Current Issues in Criminal Justice*, vol. 17, no. 1, pp. 144–153.

Darke, S. (2011) 'The enforcement approach to crime prevention', *Critical Social Policy*, vol. 31, no. 3, pp. 410–430.

Davids, C. (1995) 'Understanding the significance and persistence of Neighbourhood Watch in Victoria', *Law in Context*, vol. 13, no. 1, pp. 57–80.

Davies, J. (1995) 'Less Mickey Mouse, more Dirty Harry: property, policing and the postmodern metropolis', *Polemic*, vol. 5, no. 2, pp. 63–69.

Davis, M. (1990) *City of quartz: excavating the future in Los Angeles*. London: Verso.

Davis, P. (2004) 'Is evidence-based government possible?' Jerry Lee Lecture Presented at the 4th Annual Campbell Collaboration Colloquium, Washington; DC, 18 February, available at

<www.policyhub.gov.uk/downloads/JerryLeeLecture1202041.pdf> (accessed 27 February 2008).

Dearden, J. (2009) 'Alcohol and homicide in Australia' (PowerPoint display). National Homicide Monitoring Program. Canberra: Australian Institute of Criminology.

Dearden, J. & Payne, J. (2009) 'Alcohol and homicide in Australia', *Trends & Issues in Crime and Criminal Justice*, no. 371.

Decker, S. & Pyrooz, D. (2011) 'Leaving the gang: logging off and moving on', Council on Foreign Relations at <www.cfr.com> (accessed 30 March 2012).

Decker, S.H. (1996) 'Collective and normative features of gang violence', *Justice Quarterly*, vol. 13, no. 2, pp. 243–64.

De Liege, M.P. (1988) 'The fight against crime and fear: a new initiative in France', in T. Hope & M. Shaw (eds), *Communities and crime reduction*. London: HMSO, pp. 254–259.

—— (1991) 'Social developments and prevention of crime in France', in F. Heidenson & M. Farrell (eds), *Crime in Europe*. London: Routledge, pp. 121–132.

Department of Prime Minister of Cabinet (2010) *Counter-terrorism White Paper: Securing Australia – Protecting our Community*. Canberra: Deparment of Prime Minister and Cabinet.

Desmond, M. & Valdez, N. (2013) 'Unpolicing the urban poor consequences of third-party policing for inner-city women', *American Sociological Review*, vol. 78, no. 1, pp. 117–141.

de Zwart, M., Lindsay, D., Henderson, M. & Phillips, M. (2011) 'Randoms vs Weirdos: teen use of social networking sites and perceptions of legal risk', *Alternative Law Journal*, vol. 36, no. 3, pp. 153–157.

Dhiri, S. & Brand, S. (1999) 'Analysis of costs and benefits: guidance for evaluators', Crime Reduction Program Guidance Note 1, London: Home Office.

Diacon, D. (ed.) (1999) *Building safer urban environments: the way forward*. Leicestershire: Building and Social Housing Foundation.

Dishion, T.J., McCord, J. & Poulin, F. (1999) 'When interventions harm: peer groups and problem behavior', *American Psychologist*, vol. 54, no. 9, pp. 755–764.

Dixon, D. (2005) 'Why don't the police stop crime?', *Australian & New Zealand Journal of Criminology*, vol. 38, no. 1, pp. 4–24.

Dornschneider, S. (2010) 'Belief systems and action inferences as a source of violence in the name of Islam'. *Dynamics of Asymmetric Conflict*, vol. 3, no. 3, pp. 223–247.

Dunn, K. (2004) 'Islam in Sydney: contesting the discourse of absence', *Australian Geographer*, vol. 35, no. 3, pp. 333–353.

Durkheim, E. (1912) [1995] *The elementary forms of religious life*. New York: Free Press.

—— (1969) [1893] 'Types of law in relation to social solidarity', from The Division of Labour in Society (trans. G. Simpson, Free Press of Glencoe, 1964, New York), in V. Aubert (ed.), *Sociology of law: selected readings*. Penguin: Harmondsworth, pp. 17–29.

—— (1984) *The division of labour in society* (trans. W.D. Halls). New York: Free Press.

Eck, J.E. (2002a) 'Preventing crime at places', in L.W. Sherman, D.P. Farrington, B.C. Welsh & D.L. MacKenzie (eds), *Evidence-based crime prevention*. New York: Routledge, pp. 241–294.

—— (2002b) 'Learning from experience in problem orientated policing and situational prevention: the positive functions of weak evaluations and the negative functions of strong ones', in

N. Tilley (ed.), *Evaluation for crime prevention* (Crime Prevention Studies, vol. 14). Monsey, New York: Criminal Justice Press, pp. 93–117.

—— (2003) 'Police problems: the complexity of problem theory, research and evaluation', in J. Knuttsson (ed.), *Problem oriented policing: from innovation to mainstream* (Crime Prevention Studies, vol. 15). Monsey, New York: Criminal Justice Press, pp. 79–113.

—— (2005) 'Evaluation for lesson learning', in N. Tilley (ed.), *Handbook of crime prevention and community safety*. Cullompton, Devon: Willan Publishing, pp. 699–733.

—— (2006) 'When is a bologna sandwich better than sex? A defence of small-n case study evaluations', *Journal of Experimental Criminology*, vol. 2, no. 3, pp. 345–362.

Eck, J.E., Clarke, R.V. & Guerette, R. (2007), *Risky facilities: crime concentration in homogeneous sets of facilities* (Crime Prevention Studies, vol. 21). Monsey, New York: Criminal Justice Press.

Eck, J.E. & Spelman, W. (1988) *Problem solving: problem-oriented policing in Newport News*. US Department of Justice, National Institute of Justice, Washington, DC.

Eck, J.E. & Weisburd, D. (eds) (1995) *Crime and place (Crime Prevention Studies, vol. 4)*. Monsey, New York: Criminal Justice Press.

Eckersley, R. & Reeder, L. (2008) *Violence in public places: explanations and solutions. A report on an expert roundtable for Victoria Police*. Canberra: Australia 21.

Ekblom, P. (1987) 'Crime prevention in England: themes and issues', in D. Challinger (ed.), *Preventing property crime*. Canberra: Australian Institute of Criminology.

—— (1994) *Proximal circumstances: a mechanism-based classification of crime prevention*, Crime Prevention Studies, vol. 2. Monsey, New York: Criminal Justice Press, pp. 185–232.

—— (2000) 'The conjunction of criminal opportunity: a tool for clear, joined up thinking about community safety and crime reduction', in S. Ballintyne, K. Pease & V. McLaren (eds), *Secure foundations: key issues in crime prevention, crime reduction and community safety*. London: Institute of Public Policy Research, pp. 30–66.

—— (2002) *From the source to the mainstream is uphill: the challenge of transferring knowledge of crime prevention through replication, innovation and anticipation*, Crime Prevention Studies, vol. 13, Monsey, New York: Criminal Justice Press, pp. 131–203.

—— (2010) *Crime prevention, security and community safety using the 5Is framework*. Basingstoke: Palgrave Macmillan.

—— (2011) 'Deconstructing CPTED … and reconstructing it for practice, knowledge management and research', *European Journal on Criminal Policy and Research*, vol. 17, no. 1, pp. 7–28.

Elliot, D.S. (2013) 'Crime prevention and intervention over the life course', in C.L. Gibson & M.D. Krohn (eds), *Handbook of life-course criminology: emerging trends and directions for future research*. New York: Springer, pp. 297–315.

Fagan, A., Brooke-Weiss, B., Cady, R. & Hawkins, D.J. (2009) 'If at first you don't succeed … keep trying: strategies to enhance coalition/school partnerships to implement school-based prevention programming', *Australian & New Zealand Journal of Criminology*, vol. 42, no. 3, pp. 387–405.

Fagan, A.A. & Catalano, R.F. (2013) 'What works in youth violence prevention: a review of the literature', *Research on Social Work Practice*, vol. 23, no. 2, pp. 141–156.

Farrell, G. (2010) 'Situational crime prevention and its discontents: rational choice and harm reduction versus "cultural criminology"', *Social Policy & Administration*, vol. 44, no. 1, pp. 40–66.

Farrell, G., Bowers, K.J. & Johnson, S.D. (2005) 'Cost-benefit analysis for crime science: making cost-benefit analysis useful through a portfolio of outcomes', in M.J. Smith & N. Tilley (eds), *Crime science: new approaches to preventing and detecting crime*. Cullompton, Devon: Willan Publishing, pp. 56–81.

Farrell, G. & Roman, J. (2006) 'Crime as pollution: proposal for market-based incentives to reduce crime externalities', in K. Moss & M. Stephens (eds), *Crime reduction and the law*. London: Routledge, pp. 135–155.

Farrington, D.P. (1995) 'The development of offending and antisocial behaviour from childhood: key findings from the Cambridge Study in Delinquent Development', *Journal of Child Psychology and Psychiatry*, vol. 36, no. 6, pp. 929–964.

—— (2000) 'Explaining and preventing crime: the globalization of knowledge – The American Society of Criminology 1999 Presidential Address', *Criminology*, vol. 38, no. 1, pp. 1–24.

Farrington, D.P. & Petrosino, A. (2001) 'The Campbell Collaboration crime and justice group', *The Annals of the American Academy of Political and Social Science*, vol. 578, no. 1, pp. 35–44.

Farrington, D.P., Weisburd, D. & Gill, C.E. (2011) 'The Campbell Collaboration Crime and Justice Group: a decade of progress', in C. J. Smith, S. X. Zhang & R. Barberet (eds), *Routledge handbook of international criminology*. New York: Routledge, pp. 53–63.

Farrington, D.P. & Welsh, B.C. (2003) 'Family-based prevention of offending: a meta-analysis', *Australian and New Zealand Journal of Criminology*, vol. 36, no. 2, pp. 127–151.

—— (2007) *Saving children from a life crime: early risk factors and effective interventions*. New York: Oxford University Press.

Feins, J.D., Epstein, J.C. & Widom, R. (1997) *Solving crime problems in residential neighbourhoods. Comprehensive changes in design, management and use*. Washington, DC: National Institute of Justice Issues and Practices, US Department of Justice.

Field, C.D. (2011) 'Young British Muslims since 9/11: a composite attitudinal profile', *Religion, State and Society*, vol. 39, nos. 2–3, pp. 159–175.

Freilich, J.D. & Newman, G.R. (eds) (2009) *Reducing terrorism through situational crime prevention* (Crime Prevention Studies, vol. 25). Monsey, New York: Criminal Justice Press.

Felson, M. (1995) *Those who discourage crime*, Crime Prevention Studies, vol. 4. Monsey, New York: Criminal Justice Press, pp. 53–66.

—— (2002) *Crime and everyday life*, 3rd edn. Thousand Oaks, California: Sage Publications.

—— (2006) *Crime and nature*. Thousand Oaks, California: Sage Publications.

Ferrell, J. (1997) 'Youth, crime and cultural space', *Social Justice*, vol. 24, no. 4, pp. 21–38.

Fitzgerald, J. (1999) *Women in prison: the criminal court perspective*, Crime and Justice Statistics Bureau Brief. Sydney: NSW Bureau of Crime Statistics and Research.

Flaspoher, P., Duffy, J., Wandersman, A., Stillman, L. & Maras, M.A. (2008) 'Unpacking prevention capacity: an intersection of research-to-practice models and community-centred models', *American Journal of Community Psychology*, vol. 41, pp. 182–196.

Fleming, J. (2005) '"Working together": Neighbourhood Watch, reassurance policing and the potential of partnerships'. *Trends & Issues in Crime and Criminal Justice*, no. 303.

—— (2008) *Rules of engagement: policing anti-social behaviour and alcohol-related violence in and around licensed premises.* Sydney: NSW Bureau of Crime Statistics and Research.

Forrester, L. (1993) 'Youth-generated cultures in Western Sydney', in R. White (ed.), *Youth subcultures: theory, history and the Australian experience.* Hobart: National Clearinghouse for Youth Studies.

Forsyth, C., Gramling, R. & Wooddell, G. (1998) 'The game of poaching: folk crimes in southwest Louisiana', *Society & Natural Resources: an international journal*, vol. 11, no. 1, pp. 25–38.

Foucault, M. (1991) 'Governmentality', in G. Burchell, C. Gordon & P. Miller (eds), *The Foucault effect: studies in governmentality with two lectures by, and an interview with, Michel Foucault.* Chicago: University of Chicago Press.

France, A., Freiberg, K. & Homel, R. (2010) 'Beyond risk factors: towards a holistic prevention paradigm for children and young people', *British Journal of Social Work*, vol. 40, no. 4, pp. 1192–1210.

France, A. & Homel, R. (2006) 'Societal access routes and developmental pathways: putting social structure and young people's voice into the analysis of pathways into and out of crime', *Australian & New Zealand Journal of Criminology*, vol. 39, no. 3, pp. 296–309.

—— (2007) *Pathways and crime prevention: theory, policy and practice.* Cullompton, Devon: Willan Publishing.

Freiberg, A. (2001) 'Affective versus effective justice: instrumentalism and emotionalism in criminal justice', *Punishment and Society*, vol. 3, no. 2, pp. 256–278.

Freiberg, K. & Homel, R. (2011) 'Preventing the onset of offending', in A. Stewart, T. Allard & S. Dennison (eds), *Evidence-based policy and practice in juvenile justice.* Sydney: Federation Press, pp. 320–233.

Freiberg, K., Homel, R. & Lamb, C. (2007) 'The pervasive impact of poverty on children: tackling family adversity and promoting child development through the Pathways to Prevention Project', in A. France & R. Homel (eds), *Pathways and crime prevention: theory, policy and practice.* Cullompton, Devon: Willan Publishing, pp. 226–246.

Fung, A. (2004) *Empowered participation: reinventing urban democracy.* Princeton, New Jersey: Princeton University Press.

Gabor, T. (1990) 'Crime displacement and situational crime prevention: toward the development of some principles', *Canadian Journal of Criminology*, vol. 32, pp. 41–74.

Garland, D. (1996) 'The limits of the sovereign state: strategies of crime control in contemporary society', *British Journal of Criminology*, vol. 36, no. 4, pp. 445–471.

—— (1999) 'The common place and the catastrophic: interpretations of crime in late modernity', *Theoretical Criminology*, vol. 3, no. 3, pp. 353–364.

—— (2000) 'Ideas, institutions and situational crime prevention', in A. Von Hirsch, D. Garland & A. Wakefield (eds), *Ethical and social perspectives on situational crime prevention.* Oxford: Hart Publishing, pp. 1–16.

—— (2001) *The culture of control: crime and social order in contemporary society.* Oxford: Oxford University Press.

Gastman, R., Rowland, D. & Sattler, T. (2006) *Freight train graffiti.* London: Thames and Hudson.

Geason, S. & Wilson, P. (1990) *Preventing graffiti and vandalism.* Canberra: Australian Institute of Criminology.

Gelb, K. (2003) 'Women in prison – why the rate of incarceration is increasing'. Paper presented at the Evaluation in Crime and Justice: Trends and Methods Conference, Australian Institute of Criminology and Australian Bureau of Statistics, Canberra, 24–25 March.

George A.L. & Bennett, A. (2005) *Case studies and theory development in the social sciences.* Cambridge, Massachusetts: MIT Press.

Giddens, A. (1991) *Modernity and self-identity: self and society in the late modern age.* Cambridge: Polity Press.

Gilling, D. (1996) *Problems with the problem orientated approach*, Crime Prevention Studies, vol. 5. Monsey, New York: Criminal Justice Press, pp. 7–23.

—— (1997) *Crime prevention: theory, policies and politics.* London: UCL Press.

Gilling, D. & Hughes, G. (2002) 'The community safety profession: towards a new expertise in the governance of crime, disorder and safety in the UK?', *Community Safety Journal*, vol. 1, no. 1, pp. 4–12.

Glenorchy City Council (2003) *Face the challenge, take the risk, enjoy the ride: a local government guide to youth participation.* Glenorchy City, Hobart: Tasmania Department of Education, Tasmania Office of Youth Affairs.

Goldblatt, P. & Lewis, C. (1998) *Reducing offending: an assessment of research evidence on ways of dealing with offending behaviour*, Home Office Research Study No. 187. London: Home Office.

Goldson, B. (ed.) (2011) *Youth in crisis? 'Gangs', territoriality and violence.* London: Routledge.

Goldstein, H. (1990) *Problem-oriented policing.* New York: McGraw-Hill.

Goode, E. & Ben-Yehuda, N. (1994) *Moral panics: the social construction of deviance.* Oxford: Blackwell.

Goodnow, J.J. (2006) 'Adding social contexts to developmental analysis of crime prevention', *Australian & New Zealand Journal of Criminology*, vol. 39, no. 3, pp. 327–8.

Gordon, R. (2000) 'Criminal business organizations, street gangs and "wanna-be" groups: a Vancouver perspective', *Canadian Journal of Criminology*, vol. 39, pp. 42–60.

Gottfredson, M. & Hirschi, T. (1990) *A general theory of crime.* Stanford, California: Stanford University Press.

Grabosky, P. & James, M. (eds) (1995) *The promise of crime prevention: leading crime prevention programs.* Canberra: Australian Institute of Criminology.

Graham, J. & Bennett, T. (1995) *Crime prevention strategies in Europe and North America.* Helsinki: European Institute for Crime Prevention and Control.

Graham, K. (2009) '"They fight because we let them!" Applying a situational crime prevention model to barroom violence', *Drug and Alcohol Review*, vol. 28, no. 2, pp. 103–109.

Graham, K. & Homel, R. (2008) *Raising the bar: preventing aggression in and around bars, pubs and clubs.* Devon: Willan Publishing.

Grant, F. & Grabosky, P. (eds) (2000) *The promise of crime prevention: leading crime prevention programs*, 2nd edn. Canberra: Australian Institute of Criminology.

Gray, D., Shaw, G., d'Abbs, P., Brooks, D., Stearne, A., Mosey, A. & Spooner, C. (2006) *Policing, volatile substance misuse, and Indigenous Australians.* National Drug Law Enforcement Research Fund,

Monograph Series No. 16. Canberra: Australian Government Department of Health and Ageing.

Green, E. (2011) 'Telephoning fish: an examination of the creative deviance used by wildlife violators in the United States', *International Journal of Rural Criminology*, vol. 1, no, 1, pp. 23–39.

Green, L. (1996) *Policing places with drug problems*. Thousand Oaks, California: Sage Publications.

Guerette, R.T. (2005) Migrant death and the border safety initiative: an application of situational crime prevention to inform policy and practice, unpublished dissertation, Rutgers University.

—— (2009a) *Analyzing crime displacement and diffusion*. US Department of Justice, Office of Community Oriented Policing Services, www.popcenter.org/tools/displacement.

—— (2009b) *The pull, push and expansion of situational crime prevention evaluation: an appraisal of thirty-seven years of research*, Crime Prevention Studies, vol. 24, pp. 29–58.

Guerette, R.T. & Bowers, K.J. (2009) 'Assessing the extent of crime displacement and diffusion of benefits: a review of situational crime prevention evaluations', *Criminology*, vol. 47, no. 4, pp. 1331–1368.

Hagedorn, J. (ed.) (2007) *Gangs in the global city: alternatives to traditional criminology*. Chicago: University of Illinois Press.

—— (2008) *A world of gangs: armed young men and gangsta culture*. Minneapolis, Minnesota: University of Minnesota Press.

Haggerty, K.D. (2007) 'The novelty of crime science', *Policing and Society*, vol. 17, no. 1, pp. 83–88.

Halsey, M. (2001), 'An aesthetic of prevention', *Criminal Justice*, vol. 1, no. 4, pp. 385–420.

Halsey, M. & Young, A. (2002) 'The meanings of graffiti and municipal administration', *Australian & New Zealand Journal of Criminology*, vol. 35, no. 2, pp. 165–186.

—— (2006) '"Our desires are ungovernable": writing graffiti in urban space', *Theoretical Criminology*, vol. 10, no. 3, pp. 275–306.

Halstead, B. (1992) 'Traffic in flora and fauna', *Trends & Issues in Crime and Criminal Justice*, no. 41.

Hamilton-Smith, N. (2002) 'Anticipating consequences: developing a strategy for the targeted measurement of displacement and diffusion of benefits', in N. Tilley (ed.), *Evaluation for crime prevention* (Crime Prevention Studies, vol. 14). Monsey, New York: Criminal Justice Press, pp. 11–52.

Hanmer, J., Griffiths, S. & Jerwood, D. (1999) *Arresting evidence: domestic violence and repeat victimisation*. Police Research Series Paper 104. London: Home Office Research, Development and Statistics Directorate.

Hardin, G. (1968) 'The tragedy of the commons', *Science*, vol. 162, no. 3859, pp. 1243–1248.

Hauber, A., Hofstra, B., Toornvliet, L. & Zandbergen, A. (1996) 'Some new forms of functional social control in the Netherlands and their effects', *British Journal of Criminology*, vol. 36, no. 2, pp. 199–219.

Hauck, M. (2007) 'Non-compliance in small-scale fisheries: a threat to security?', in P. Beirne & N. South (eds), *Issues in green criminology: confronting harms against environments, humanity and other animals*. Cullompton, Devon: Willan Publishing.

Hawkins, J.D. (1999) 'Preventing crime and violence through communities that care', *European Journal on Criminal Policy and Research*, vol. 7, pp. 443–458.

Hawkins, J.D., Arthur, M.W. & Catalano, R.F. (1995) 'Preventing substance abuse', in M. Tonry & D.F. Farrington (eds), *Building a safer society: strategic approaches to crime prevention*, Chicago: University of Chicago Press, pp. 343–427.

Hawkins, J.D. & Catalano, R.F. (1992) *Communities that care: action for drug abuse prevention.* San Francisco: Jossey-Bass.

Hawkins, J. D., Catalano, R. F. & Arthur, M. (2002) 'Promoting science-based prevention in communities', *Addictive Behaviors*, vol. 27, no. 6, pp. 951–976.

Hawkins, J.D. & Catalano, R.F. et al. (1999) 'Preventing adolescent health-risk behaviours by strengthening protection during childhood', *Archives of Paediatrics and Adolescent Medicine*, vol. 153, no. 3, pp. 226–243.

Hayward, K. (2002) 'The vilification and pleasures of youthful transgression', in J. Muncie, G. Hughes & E. McLaughlin (eds), *Youth justice: critical readings.* London: Sage Publications.

Healey, K. (ed.) (1996) *Youth gangs.* Sydney: Spinney Press.

Hedderman, C. & Williams, C. (2001) 'Making partnerships work: emerging findings from the Reducing Burglary Initiative', Home Office Briefing Note 1/01, Policing and Reducing Crime Unit. London: Home Office Research, Development and Statistics Directorate, London.

Henderson, M., Henderson, P. & Associates Pty Ltd (2001) *Preventing repeat residential burglary.* Canberra: Attorney-General's Department.

Herbig, J. (2010) 'The illegal reptile trade as a form of conservation crime: a South African criminological investigation', in R. White (ed.), *Global environmental harm: criminological perspectives.* Devon: Willan Publishing.

Hesseling, R.B.P. (1994) 'Displacement: a review of the empirical literature', in R.V. Clarke (ed.), *Situational crime prevention: successful case studies*, vol. 3, Monsey, New York: Criminal Justice Press, pp. 197–230.

Heywood, P. & Crane, P. with Egginton, A. & Gleeson, J. (1997) *Young people in major centres: a policy investigation and development project for Brisbane City Council* – Draft 1: Planning & Management Guidelines, Brisbane City Council.

—— (1998) *Out and about: in or out? Better outcomes from young people's use of public and community space in the City of Brisbane – Vol. 2: Policies, Implementation Strategies and Tools.* Community Development Team West, Brisbane City Council.

Hil, R. (1999), 'Beating the developmental path: critical notes on the pathways to prevention report', *Youth Studies Australia*, vol. 18, no. 4, pp. 49–50.

Hill, I. & Pease, K. (2002) 'The wicked issues: displacement and sustainability', in S. Ballintyne, K. Pease & V. McLaren (eds), *Secure foundations: key issues in crime prevention, crime reduction and community safety.* London: Institute of Public Policy Research, pp. 131–141.

Hinduja, S. & Patchin, J. (2012) 'Preventing cyberbullying: top ten tips for teens', Cyberbullying Research Centre, www.cyberbullying.us (accessed 16 April 2013).

Hirsch, V.A., Garland, D. & Wakefield, A. (eds) (2000) *Ethical and social perspectives on situational crime prevention.* Oxford: Hart Publishing.

Hocking, J. (2004) *Terror laws, ASIO, counter-terrorism and the threat to democracy.* Sydney: University of New South Wales Press.

Hoefnagels, P. (1997) *The prevention pioneers: history of the Hein Roethof Prize 1987–1996*. The Hague: Ministry of Justice, the Netherlands.

Hofstra, B. & Shapland, J. (1997) 'Who is in control?', *Policing and Society*, vol. 6, pp. 265–281.

Hollis-Peel, M.E., Reynald, D.M. Bavel, M.V., Elffers, H. & Walsh, B.C. (2011) 'Guardianship for crime prevention: a critical review of the literature', *Crime, Law and Social Change*, vol. 56, no. 1, pp. 53–70.

Homel, P. (2004) The whole of government approach to crime prevention, *Trends & Issues in Crime and Criminal Justice*, no. 287.

—— (2005) 'A short history of crime prevention in Australia', *Canadian Journal of Criminology and Criminal Justice*, vol. 47, no. 2, pp. 355–368.

—— (2006) 'Joining up the pieces: what central agencies need to do to support effective local crime prevention', in J. Knutsson & R. V. Clarke (eds), *Putting theory to work: implementing situational crime prevention and problem-oriented policing* (Crime Prevention Studies, vol. 20). Monsey, New York: Criminal Justice Press, pp. 111–138.

—— (2009a) 'Lessons for Canadian crime prevention from recent international experience', *Revue de l'IPC/IPC Review*, vol. 3 (March), pp. 13–39.

—— (2009b) 'Improving crime prevention knowledge and practice', *Trends & Issues in Crime and Criminal Justice*, no. 385, pp. 1–6.

—— (2010) 'Delivering effective local crime prevention: why understanding variations in municipal governance arrangements matters', in M. Idriss et al. (eds), *2010 International report on crime prevention and community safety: trends and prospects*. Montreal: International Centre for the Prevention of Crime, pp. 118–119.

Homel, P., Nutley, S., Tilley, N. & Webb, B. (2005) *Making it happen from the centre: managing for the regional delivery of local crime reductions outcomes*, Home Office Online Report 54/04. London: Home Office.

Homel, P., Nutley, S., Webb, B. & Tilley N. (2004) *Investing to deliver: reviewing the implementation of the UK Crime Reduction Programme*. London: Home Office Research Study 281.

Homel, R. (2005a) 'Developmental crime prevention', in N. Tilley (ed.), *Handbook of crime prevention and community safety*. Devon: Willan Publishing, pp. 71–106.

—— (2005b) 'Moving developmental prevention from "Success in miniature" to mainstream practice that improves outcomes: Can it be done?' Paper presented at the Australian Institute of Criminology 'Delivering Crime Prevention: Making the Evidence Work' conference, Sydney, 21–22 November 2005.

Homel, R. et al. (1999) *Pathways to prevention: developmental and early intervention approaches to crime*. Canberra: Attorney-General's Department.

Homel, R., Freiberg, K., Lamb, C., Leech, M., Batchelor, S., Carr, A. et al. (2006a) 'The Pathways to Prevention Project: doing developmental prevention in a disadvantaged community', *Issues in Crime & Criminal Justice*, no. 323. Canberra: Australian Institute of Criminology.

Homel, R., Freiberg, K., Lamb, C., Leech, M., Hampshire, A., Hay, I. et al. (2006b) *The Pathways to Prevention Project: the first five years, 1999–2004*. Sydney: Griffith University and Mission Australia.

Homel, R. & Homel, P. (2012) 'Implementing crime prevention: good governance and a science of implementation' in B. Welsh & D. Farrington (eds), *The Oxford handbook on crime prevention.*, Oxford: Oxford University Press.

Homel, R., Lamb, C. & Freiberg, K. (2006) 'Working with the Indigenous community in the Pathways to Prevention Project', *Family Matters*, no. 75, pp. 36–41.

Homel, R. & McGee, T. (2012) 'Community approaches to preventing crime and violence: the challenge of building prevention capacity', in R. Loeber & B.C. Welsh (eds) *The Future of Criminology*. Oxford: Oxford University Press, pp. 172–177.

Hope, T. (2001) 'Community crime prevention in Britain: a strategic overview', *Criminal Justice*, vol. 1, no. 4, pp. 421–439.

—— (2003) 'The reducing burglary initiative and how scientific crime prevention got it wrong'. Paper presented at the 17th Annual Australian and New Zealand Society of Criminology Conference, Controlling Crime Risks and Responsibilities, 1–3 October, Sydney.

—— (2004) 'Pretend it works: evidence and governance in the evaluation of the reducing burglary initiative', *Criminal Justice*, vol. 4, no. 3, pp. 287–308.

—— (2005) 'Sustainability in crime prevention: a nautical tale'. Address to the 10th Anniversary Colloquium of the International Centre for the Prevention of Crime, Paris, 1–2 December 2004 (copy obtained from the author).

—— (2011) 'Official Criminology and the New Crime Science', in M. Bosworth & H. Caroyln (eds), *What is criminology?* Oxford: Oxford University Press, pp. 456–474.

Hope, T. & Karstedt, S. (2003) 'Towards a new social prevention', in H. Kury & J. Obergfell-Fuchs (eds), *Crime prevention: new approaches*. Weisser Ring, Mainz: Mainzer Schriften zur Situation von Kriminalitaetsopfern, pp. 461–489.

Hope, T. & Murphy, D.J.I. (1983) 'Problems of implementing crime prevention: the experience of a demonstration project', *The Howard Journal of Criminal Justice*, vol. 22, nos. 1–3, pp. 38–50.

Hope, T. & Shaw, M. (eds) (1988) *Communities and crime reduction*. London: HMSO.

Hope, T. & Sparks, R. (2000) 'For a sociological theory of situations (or how useful is pragmatic criminology?)', in A. Von Hirsch, D. Garland & A. Wakefield (eds), *Ethical and social perspectives on situational crime prevention*. Oxford: Hart Publishing, pp. 175–191.

Hopkins, P. (2010) *Young people, place and identity*. London: Routledge.

Hough, M. (2004) 'Modernization, scientific rationalism and the crime reduction programme', *Criminal Justice*, vol. 4, no. 3, pp. 239–253.

—— (2006) *Not seeing the wood for the trees: mistaking tactics for strategy in crime reduction initiatives* (Crime Prevention Studies, vol. 2). Monsey, New York: Criminal Justice Press, pp. 139–162.

—— (2011) 'Criminology and the role of experimental research', in M. Bosworth & H. Caroyln (eds), *What is criminology?* Oxford: Oxford University Press, pp. 198–208.

Hough, M. & Tilley, N. (1998) 'Auditing crime and disorder: guidance for local partnerships', Crime Detection and Prevention Series Paper 91, Home Office, London.

Howell, J. (2000) 'Youth gang programs and strategies: summary', US Department of Justice, Office of Justice Programs, Office of Juvenile Justice and Delinquency Prevention, Washington, DC.

Hughes, C. (2008) *The Social Norms Analysis Project: results, insights and future priorities.* Briefing Paper No. 7. Hobart: Tasmanian Institute of Law Enforcement Studies, University of Tasmania.

Hughes, C., Julian, R., Richman, M., Mason, R. & Long, G. (2008a) 'Harnessing the power of perception: reducing alcohol-related harm among rural teenagers', *Youth Studies Australia*, vol. 27, no. 2, pp. 26–35.

—— (2008b) *Trialling 'Social Norms' strategies for minimising alcohol-related harm among rural youth (Social Norms Analysis Project): final report to the Alcohol Education and Rehabilitation Foundation.* Hobart: Tasmanian Institute of Law Enforcement Studies.

Hughes, G. (1998) *Understanding crime prevention: social control, risk and late modernity.* Buckingham: Open University Press.

—— (2002a) 'Crime and disorder reduction partnerships: the future of community safety', in G. Hughes, E. McLaughlin & J. Muncie (eds), *Crime prevention and community safety: new directions.* London: Sage Publications in association with Open University Press, pp. 123–142.

—— (2002b) 'Plotting the rise of community safety: critical reflections on research, theory and politics', in G. Hughes & A. Edwards (eds), *Crime control and community: the new politics of public safety.* Cullompton, Devon: Willan Publishing, pp. 20–45.

—— (2004) 'Straddling adaptation and denial: crime and disorder reduction partnerships in England and Wales', *Cambrian Law Review*, vol. 35, pp. 1–22.

—— (2007) *The politics of crime and community.* Houndsmill: Palgrave Macmillan.

Hughes, G. & Edwards, A. (2001) 'Defining community safety expertise', *Crime Justice Matters*, no. 45, Autumn, pp. 4–5.

Hughes, G. & Gilling, D. (2004) 'Mission impossible? The habitus of the community safety manager and the new expertise in local partnership governance of crime and safety', *Criminal Justice: The International Journal of Policy and Practice*, vol. 4, no. 2, pp. 129–149.

Hughes, K., Anderson, Z., Morleo, M. & Bellis, M. (2007) 'Alcohol, nightlife and violence: the relative contributions of drinking before and during nights out to negative health and criminal justice outcomes', *Addiction*, vol.103, no 1, pp. 60–65.

Human Rights and Equal Opportunity Commission (1991) *Racist violence.* Canberra: AGPS.

—— (2007), *Unlocking doors: Muslim communities and police tackling racial and religious discrimination together.* Human Rights and Equal Opportunity Commission.

Indermaur, D. (1996) 'Violent crime in Australia: interpreting the trends', *Trends & Issues in Crime and Criminal Justice*, no. 61.

International Center for Alcohol Policies (2008) *Alcohol and violence: exploring patterns and responses.* Washington, DC: ICAP.

International CPTED Association <www.cpted.net/default.html> (accessed 27 February 2008).

Irving, C. (1993) *Wide-body: the triumph of the 747.* New York: W. Morrow.

Iveson, K. (2000) 'Beyond designer diversity: planners, public space and a critical politics of difference', *Urban Policy and Research*, vol. 18, no. 2, pp. 219–238.

Jackson-Jacobs, C. (2004) 'Taking a beating: the narrative gratifications of fighting as an underdog', in J. Ferrell, K. Hayward, W. Morrison & M. Presdee (eds), *Cultural criminology unleashed*. London: Glasshouse Press.

Jacobs, J. (1961) *The death and life of great American cities*. New York: Sage Random House.

Jacobson, M. & Lindblad T.B. (eds) (2003) *Overground: 9 Scandinavian graffiti writers*. Stockholm: Dokument Forlag.

James, M. & Carcach, C. (1998) Homicide between intimate partners in Australia, *Trends & Issues in Crime and Criminal Justice*, no. 90.

Jill Dando Institute of Crime Science <www.jdi.ucl.ac.uk/> (accessed 27 February 2008).

Johnson, S.D. & Bowers, K.J. (2003) 'Opportunity is in the eye of the beholder: the role of publicity in crime prevention', *Criminology & Public Policy*, vol. 23, no. 3, pp. 497–524.

Jones, S.G. & Libicki, M.C. (2008) *How terrorist groups end: lessons for countering al Qa'ida*. Arlington, Virginia: RAND.

Jordan, B. (1996) *A theory of poverty and social exclusion*. Cambridge: Polity Press.

Kahler, J. & Grove, M. (2012) 'Beyond the cooking pot and pocket book: factors influencing noncompliance with wildlife poaching rules', *International Journal of Comparative and Applied Criminal Justice*, iFirst, pp. 1–18.

Katz, J. (1988) *The seductions of crime*. New York: Basic Books.

Kelman, S., Hong, S. & Turbitt, I. (2012) 'Are there managerial practices associated with the outcomes of an interagency service delivery collaboration? Evidence from British Crime and Disorder Reduction Partnerships', *Journal of Public Administration Research and Theory*. First published online 30 October 2012 doi:10.1093/jopart/mus038.

King, M. (1988) *How to make crime prevention work: the French experience*. London: NACRO.

Kitchen, T. (2002) 'Crime prevention and the British planning system: new responsibilities and older challenges', *Planning Theory & Practice*, vol. 3, no. 2, pp. 155–172.

Klein, M.W. (1995) *The American street gang*. New York: Oxford University Press.

—— (2002) 'Street gangs: a cross-national perspective', in R. Huff (ed.), *Gangs in America*, 3rd edn. Thousand Oaks, California: Sage Publications.

Klein, M., Kerner, H.J., Maxon, C. & Weitekamp, E. (eds) (2001) *The Eurogang paradox: street gangs and youth groups in the US and Europe*. Dordrecht: Kluwer Academic Publishers.

Knutsson, J. (ed.) (2003) *Problem oriented policing: from innovation to mainstream* (Crime Prevention Studies, vol. 15). Monsey, New York: Criminal Justice Press.

—— (2009) 'Standards of evaluations in problem-oriented policing projects: good enough?', in J. Knutsson & N. Tilley (eds), *Evaluating crime reduction initiatives*. Monsey, New York: Criminal Justice Press.

Koch, B.C.M. (1998) *The politics of crime prevention*. Aldershot: Ashgate.

Koehler, J. Losel, F. Akoensi, T.D. & Humphreys, D.K. (2013) 'A systematic review and meta-analysis on the effects of young offender treatment programs in Europe', *Journal of Experimental Criminology*, vol. 9, no. 1, pp. 19–43.

KPMG (2008) *Evaluation of the Temporary Late Night Entry Declaration: final report*. Melbourne: Department of Justice, Victorian Government.

Kraft, E. & Wang, J. (2009) 'Effectiveness of cyber bullying prevention strategies: a study on students' perspectives', *International Journal of Cyber Criminology*, vol. 3, no. 2, pp. 513–535.

Kruttschnitt, C., Gartner, R. & Hussemann, J. (2008) 'Female violent offenders: moral panics or more serious offenders?', *Australian & New Zealand Journal of Criminology*, vol. 41, no. 1, pp. 9–35.

Lack, M. (2007) *Catching on? Trade-related Measures as a fisheries management tool*. Cambridge: TRAFFIC International.

LaFree, G. & Ackerman, G. (2009) 'The empirical study of terrorism: social and legal research', *Annual Review of Law and Social Science*, vol. 5, pp. 347–374.

LaFree G., Duga, L. & Korte, R. (2009) 'The impact of British counterterrorist strategies on political violence in Northern Ireland: comparing deterrence and backlash models', *Criminology*, vol. 47, no. 1, pp. 17–45.

Laub, J.H. (2004) 'The life course of criminology in the United States', *Criminology*, vol. 42, no. 1, pp. 1–26.

Laub, J.H., Nagin, D.S. & Sampson, R.J. (1998) 'Trajectories of change in criminal offending: good marriage and the desistance process', *American Sociological Review*, vol. 63, no. 2, pp. 225–238.

Laub, S.P. (2013) *Crime prevention: approaches, practices, and evaluations*. 8th edn. Waltham, Massachusetts: Anderson Publishing.

Law Reform Commission (1994) *Equality before the law: justice for women*. Report No. 69, Part I. Canberra: Commonwealth of Australia.

Laycock, G. (2001) *Scientists or politicians: who has the answer to crime?* Jill Dando Institute of Crime Science, School of Public Policy, University College London, at <www.jdi.ucl.ac.uk> (accessed 27 February 2008).

—— (2002) 'Methodological issues in working with policy advisors and practitioners', in N. Tilley (ed.), *Analysis for crime prevention* (Crime Prevention Studies, vol. 13). Monsey, New York: Criminal Justice Press, pp. 205–237.

—— (2005a) 'Defining crime science', in M.J. Smith & N. Tilley (eds), *Crime science: new approaches to preventing and detecting crime*. Cullompton, Devon: Willan Publishing, pp. 3–24.

—— (2005b) 'Deciding what to do', in N. Tilley (ed.), *Handbook of crime prevention and community safety*. Cullompton, Devon: Willan Publishing, pp. 674–698.

—— (2006) 'Implementing crime reduction measures: conflicts and tensions', in J. Knutsson & R.V. Clarke (eds), *Putting theory to work: implementing situational crime prevention and problem-oriented policing* (Crime Prevention Studies, vol. 20). Monsey, New York: Criminal Justice Press, pp. 65–88.

Laycock, G. & Webb, B. (2003) 'Conclusions: the role of the centre', in K. Bullock & N. Tilley (eds), *Crime reduction and problem-oriented policing*. Cullompton, Devon: Willan Publishing, pp. 285–301.

Lee, M. (2006) 'Public dissent and governmental neglect: isolating and excluding Macquarie Fields', *Current Issues in Criminal Justice*, vol. 18, no. 1, pp. 32–50.

Lee, M. & Herborn, P. (2003) 'The role of place management in crime prevention: some reflections on governmentality and government strategies', *Current Issues in Criminal Justice*, vol. 15, no. 1, pp. 26–39.

Lemieux, A.M., & Clarke, R.V. (2009) 'The international ban on ivory sales and its effects on elephant poaching in Africa', *British Journal of Criminology*, vol. 49, no. 4, pp. 451–471.

Livingston, M. (2008) 'Alcohol outlet density and assault: a spatial analysis', *Addiction*, vol. 103, no. 4,, pp. 619–628.

Livingston, M. & Room, R. (undated) 'Research into alcohol availability' (PowerPoint display). The AER Centre for Alcohol Policy Research. Melbourne: Turning Point Alcohol & Drug Centre.

Lockwood, D. (1997) *Violence among middle school and high school students: analysis and implications for prevention*. National Institute of Justice, Research in Brief. Washington, DC: Office of Justice Programs, US Department of Justice.

Loeber, R., Farrington, D., Stouthamer-Loeber, M. et al. (2003) 'The development of male offending: key findings from fourteen years of the Pittsburgh Youth Study', in T. P. Thornberry & M. Krohn (eds), *Taking stock of delinquency: an overview of findings from contemporary longitudinal studies*. New York: Kluwer, pp. 93–130.

Low, S. (2003) *Behind the gates: life, security and the pursuit of happiness in Fortress America*. London: Routledge.

Lugten, G. (2005) 'Big fish to fry – international law and deterrence of the toothfish pirates', *Current Issues in Criminal Justice*, vol. 16, no. 3, pp. 307–321.

Lum, C. & Kennedy, L.W. (eds) (2012) *Evidence-based counterrorism policy*. New York: Springer.

Lum, C. & Yang, S.N. (2005) 'Why do researchers in crime and justice choose non-experimental methods', *Journal of Experimental Criminology*, vol. 1, no. 2, pp. 191–213.

Madjulla Incorporated (2004) *A report of the Derby/West Kimberley Project: working with adolescents to prevent domestic violence*. Canberra: Attorney-General's Department.

Maguire, M. (2004) 'The crime reduction programme in England and Wales: reflections on the vision and the reality', *Criminal Justice*, vol. 4, no. 3, pp. 213–237.

Makkai, T. (1998) 'Alcohol and disorder in the Australian community: part II – perpetrators', *Trends & Issues in Crime and Criminal Justice*, no. 77.

Makkai, T. & MacAllister, I. (1998) *Patterns of drug use in Australia*. Canberra: National Drug Strategy.

Malone, K. (1999) 'Growing up in cities as a model of participatory planning and "place-making" with young people', *Youth Studies Australia*, vol. 18, no. 2, pp. 17–23.

Malone, K. & Hasluck, L. (2002) 'Australian youth: aliens in a suburban environment', in L. Chawla (ed.), *Growing up in an urbanising world*. London: Earthscan.

Manning, M., Homel R., & Smith, C. (2006) 'Economic evaluation of a community based early intervention program implemented in a disadvantaged urban area of Queensland', *Economic Analysis and Policy*, vol. 36, no. 1/2, pp. 99–130.

Martin, S. (1996) 'Investigating hate crimes: case characteristics and law enforcement responses', *Justice Quarterly*, vol. 13, no. 3, pp. 455–480.

Matassa, M. & Newburn, T. (2003) 'Problem-oriented evaluation: evaluating problem oriented policing initiatives', in K. Bulluck & N. Tilley (eds), *Crime reduction and problem oriented policing*. cullompton, devon: Willan Publishing, pp. 183–216.

Mawby, R. (1977) 'Defensible space: a theoretical and empirical appraisal', *Urban Studies*, vol. 14, no. 2, pp. 169–179.

Maxson, C.L. & Klein, M.W. (1989) 'Street gang violence', in N. Warner & M. Wolfgang (eds), *Violent crime, violent criminals*. Newbury Park, California: Sage Publications.

Mayhew, P. (1979) 'Defensible space: the current status of crime prevention theory', *Howard Journal of Criminal Justice*, vol. 18, no. 3, pp. 150–159.

Mazerolle, L., Price, J. & Roehl, J. (2000) 'Civil remedies and drug control: a randomized field trial in Oakland, California', *Evaluation Review*, vol. 24, no. 2, pp. 212–241.

Mazerolle, L. & Ransley, J. (2005) *Third party policing*. Cambridge: Cambridge University Press.

Mazerolle, L., Soole, D. & Rombouts, S. (2006) 'Street-level drug law enforcement: a meta-analytical review', *Journal of Experimental Criminology*, vol. 2, no. 4, pp. 409–435.

Mazerolle, L., White, G., Ransley, J. & Ferguson, P. (2012) 'Violence in and around entertainment districts: a longitudinal analysis of the impact of late-night lockout legislation', *Law & Policy*, vol. 34, no. 1, pp. 55–79.

Mazerolle, L.M., Wickes, R.L. & McBroom, J. (2010) 'Community variations in violence: the role of social ties and collective efficacy in comparative context', *The Journal for Research in Crime and Delinquency*, vol. 47, no. 1, pp. 3–30.

McCamley, P. (2002) 'Minimising subjectivity: a new risk assessment model for CPTED', *CPTED Journal: The Journal of International Crime Prevention through Environmental Design Association*, vol. 1, no. 1, pp. 25–35.

McCord, J. (2003) 'Cures that harm: unanticipated outcomes of crime prevention programs', *Annals of the American Academy of Political and Social Science*, vol. 587, no. 1, pp. 16–30.

McCord, N. & McCord, J. (1959) *Origins of crime: a new evaluation of the Cambridge-Somerville Study*. New York: Columbia University Press.

McCulloch, J. (2002a) '"Either you are with us or you are with the terrorists": the war's home front', in P. Scraton (ed.), *Beyond September 11: an anthology of dissent*. London: Pluto Press, pp. 54–59.

—— (2002b) 'War at home: national security arrangements post 11 September 2001', *Alternative Law Journal*, vol. 27, no. 2, pp. 87–91.

McCulloch, J. & Pickering, S. (2009) 'Pre-crime and counter-terrorism: imagining future crime in the "War on Terror"', *British Journal of Criminology*, vol. 49, no. 5, pp. 628–645.

McDonald, K. (1999) *Struggles for subjectivity: identity, action and youth experience*. Cambridge: Cambridge University Press.

McDonald, L.Z. (2011) 'Security identities, resisting terror: Muslim youth work in the UK and its implications for security', *Religion, State and Society*, vol. 39, nos. 2–3, pp. 177–189.

McIlwain, G. & Homel, R. (2009) *Sustaining a reduction of alcohol-related harms in the licensed environment: a practical experiment to generate new evidence*. Brisbane: Key Centre for Ethics, Law, Justice and Governance, Griffith University.

McLaughlin, E. (2002) 'Same beds, different dreams: postmodern reflections on crime prevention and community safety', in G. Hughes & A. Edwards (eds), *Crime control and community: the new politics of public safety*. Cullompton, Devon: Willan Publishing, pp. 46–62.

McLaughlin, E., Muncie J. & Hughes, G. (2001) 'The permanent revolution: new labour, new public management and the modernization of criminal justice', *Criminal Justice: International Journal of Policy and Practice*, vol. 1, no. 3, pp. 301–318.

McMullan, J. & Perrier, D. (2002) 'Lobster poaching and the ironies of law enforcement', *Law & Society Review*, vol. 36, no. 4, pp. 679–720.

McNallay, M. & Newman, G.R. (eds) (2008) *Perspectives on identity theft*. Cullompton, Devon; New York: Criminal Justice Press.

Measham, F. (2006) 'The new policy mix: alcohol, harm minimisation, and determined drunkenness in contemporary society', *International Journal of Drug Policy*, vol. 17, no. 4, pp. 258–268.

Measham, F. & Brain, K. (2005) '"Binge" drinking, British alcohol policy and the new culture of intoxication', *Crime, Media, Culture*, vol. 1, no. 3, pp. 262–283.

Memmott, P., Stacy, R., Chambers, C. & Keys, C. (2001) *Violence in Indigenous communities*. Canberra: Attorney-General's Department.

Merry, S. (1981) 'Defensible space undefended: social factors in crime prevention through environmental design', *Urban Affairs Quarterly*, vol. 16, no. 3, pp. 397–422.

Merton, R.K. (1938) 'Social structure and anomie', *American Sociological Review*, vol. 3, no. 5, pp. 672–682.

Messerschmidt, J. (1986) *Capitalism, patriarchy and crime*. New Jersey: Rowman & Littlefield.

—— (1997) *Crime as structured action: gender, race, class, and crime in the making*. London: Sage Publications.

Miller, D. (2013) 'Terrorist decision making and the deterrence problem', *Studies in Conflict & Terrorism*, vol. 36, no. 2, pp. 132–151.

Miller, L. (2001) *The politics of community crime prevention: implementing Operation Weed and Seed in Seattle*. Burlington, Vermont: Ashgate.

Miller, L.L. (2008) *The perils of federalism: race, poverty, and the politics of crime control*. Oxford: Oxford University Press.

Miller, W.B. (1992) *Crime by youth gangs and groups in the United States*. Washington, DC: US Department of Justice, Office of Justice Programs, Office of Juvenile Justice and Delinquency Prevention.

Minnery, J. & Lim, B. (2005) 'Measuring crime prevention through environmental design', *Journal of Architectural and Planning Research*, vol. 22, no. 4, pp. 330–341.

Moffitt, T.E. (1993) 'Adolescent-limited and life-course persistent antisocial behaviour: A developmental taxonomy', *Psychological Review*, vol. 100, no. 4, pp. 674–701.

Moore, D. (2000) 'Risking Saturday night: regulating student alcohol use through "common sense"', *Theoretical Criminology*, vol. 4, no. 4, pp. 411–428.

Morgan, J. (1991) *Safer communities: the local delivery of crime prevention through the partnership approach*. Standing Conference on Crime Prevention. London: Home Office.

Moss, K. & Pease, K. (2004) 'Data sharing in crime prevention: how and why', *Crime Prevention and Community Safety: An International Journal*, vol. 6, no. 1, pp. 7–12.

Mouzos, J. (1999) 'Mental disorder and homicide in Australia', *Trends & Issues in Crime and Criminal Justice*, no. 133.

—— (2000) *Homicidal encounters: a study of homicide in Australia, 1989–1999*. Research and Public Policy Series no. 28. Canberra: Australian Institute of Criminology.

—— (2002) *Homicide in Australia: 2000–2001* (National Homicide Monitoring Program annual report). Canberra: Australian Institute of Criminology.

Mouzos, J. & Thompson, S. (2000) 'Gay-hate related homicide: an overview of major findings in NSW' *Trends & Issues in Crime and Criminal Justice*, no. 155.

Mubarak, H. (2005) 'Young and Muslim in Post-9/11 America', *The Review of Faith & International Affairs*, vol. 3, no. 2, pp. 41–43.

Murphy, K. & Cherney, A. (2011) 'Fostering cooperation with the police: how do ethnic minorities in Australia respond to procedural justice-based policing?' *Australian and New Zealand Journal of Criminology*, vol. 44, no. 2, pp. 235–257.

Nagin, D.S. (2001) 'Measuring the economic benefits of developmental prevention programs', in M. Tonry (ed.), *Crime and justice: a review of research*, vol. 28. Chicago: University of Chicago Press, pp. 347–384.

Nagin, D. S., Piquero, A. P., Scott, E. S. & Steinberg, L. (2006) 'Public preferences for rehabilitation versus incarceration of juvenile offenders: evidence from a contingent valuation survey', *Criminology and Public Policy*, vol. 5, no. 4, pp. 627–651.

Nasaw, D. (2010) 'FBI using Facebook in fight against crime', *The Guardian*, 16 March.

National Motor Vehicle Theft Reduction Council (2005) 'Target thefts impacted by immobilizers', *Theft Matters Bulletin*, October 2005 Melbourne: National Motor Vehicle Theft Reduction Council, Mat <www.carsafe.com.au> (accessed 27 February 2008).

—— (2006) *Annual report: the benefits of theft-reform*. Melbourne: National Motor Vehicle Theft Reduction Council, at <www.carsafe.com.au> (accessed 27 February 2008).

Netherlands Ministry of Justice (1985) *Society and crime: a policy plan for The Netherlands*. The Hague: Ministry of Justice.

New Zealand Crime Prevention Unit (1994) *The New Zealand Crime Prevention Strategy*. Department of the Prime Minister and Cabinet, Parliament Buildings. Wellington: Crime Prevention Unit.

New Zealand Ministry of Justice (2003) *Review of the Safer Community Council Network: future directions*. Wellington.

—— (2005) *National guidelines for crime prevention through environmental design in New Zealand*, Part 2 Implementation Guide, at <www.justice.govt.nz/pubs/reports/2005/cpted-part-2/index.html> (accessed 27 February 2008).

Newman, G. & McNally, M. (2005) *Identity theft literature review*. Washington, DC: US Department of Justice.

Newman, O. (1972) *Defensible space: people and design in the violent city*. London: Architectural Press.

—— (1975) 'Reactions to the "Defensible Space" study and some further readings', *International Journal of Mental Health*, vol. 4, no. 3, pp. 48–70.

—— (1996) *Creating defensible space*. Washington, DC: US Department of Housing and Urban Development Office of Policy Development and Research.

Nicholas, R. (2008) *Understanding and responding to alcohol-related social harms in Australia: options for policing*. Hobart: National Drug Law Enforcement Research Fund, Commonwealth of Australia.

NSW Department of Urban Affairs & Planning (1999) *Urban design guidelines with young people in mind*. Sydney: Department of Urban Affairs and Planning.

NSW Police Service (2001) 'Safer by Design: evaluation document one', NSW Police Service <www.police.nsw.gov.au/community_issues>(accessed 27 February 2008).

NSW Shopping Centre Protocol Project (2005) *Creating the dialogue: a guide to developing a local youth shopping centre protocol*. Sydney: Attorney General's Crime Prevention Division.

Neyroud, P. (2007) 'Policing terrorism', *Policing*, vol. 1, no. 1, pp. 5–8.

Nurse, A. (2013) *Animal harm: perspectives on why people harm and kill animals*. Surrey: Ashgate.

Nutley, S. & Homel, P. (2006) 'Delivering evidence-based policy and practice: lessons from the implementation of the UK Crime Reduction Program', *Evidence and Evaluation*, vol. 2, no. 1, pp. 5–26.

Nutley, S., Walter, I. & Davies, H. (2007) *Using evidence: how research can inform public services*. Bristol: Policy Press.

Olds, D. (2013) 'Moving toward evidence-based preventive interventions for children and families', in R.D. Krugman & J.E. Korbin (eds) *C. Henry Kempe: a 50 year legacy to the field of child abuse and neglect child maltreatment*, vol. 1. New York: Springer, pp. 165–173.

Olds, D., Henderson, C., Cole, R., Eckenrode, J., Kitzman, H., Luckey, D., Pettitt, L., Sidora, K., Morris, P. & Powers, J. (1998) 'Long-term effects of nurse home visitation on children's criminal and anti-social behaviour: 15-year follow up of a randomized controlled trial', *Journal of the American Medical Association*, vol. 14, October, pp. 1238–1244.

Olds, D., Henderson, C., Kitzman, H., Eckenrode, J., Cole, R. & Tatelbaum, R. (1999) 'Prenatal and infancy home visitation by nurses: recent findings', *The Future of Children, Home Visiting: Recent Program Evaluations*, vol. 9, no. 1 (Summer/Spring), pp. 44–65.

Olds, D.L. (2002) 'Prenatal and infancy home visiting by nurses: from randomized trials to community replication', *Prevention Science*, vol. 3, no. 3, pp. 153–172.

Olds, D.L., Hill, P.L. & O'Brian, R. et. al. (2003) 'Taking preventive intervention to scale: the nurse–family partnership', *Cognitive and Behavioral Practice*, vol. 10, no. 4, pp. 278–290.

Olweus, D. (1993) *Bullying at school: what we know and what we can do*. Cambridge: Blackwell.

O'Malley, P. (1994) 'Responsibility and crime prevention: a response to Adam Sutton, *Australian & New Zealand Journal of Criminology*, vol. 27, no. 1, pp. 21–24.

O'Malley, P. & Sutton, A. (eds) (1997) *Crime prevention in Australia: issues in policy and research*. Sydney: Federation Press.

Ontario, Government of (2008) *The Review of the Roots of Youth Violence: volume 2 – Executive Summary*. Toronto: Queen's Printer for Ontario.

Painter, K. (1992) 'Different worlds: the spatial, temporal and social dimensions of female victimization', in D. Evans, N. Fyfe & D. Herbert (eds), *Crime, policing and place: essays in environmental criminology*. London: Routledge.

Painter, K. & Farrington, D. P. (1997) 'The crime reducing effect of improved street lighting: the Dudley Project', in R.V. Clarke (ed.), *Situational crime prevention: successful case studies*. New York: Harrow & Hestor.

Paneth, N. (2004) 'Assessing the contributions of John Snow to epidemiology: 150 years after removal of the Broad Street pump handle', *Epidemiology*, vol. 15, no. 5, pp. 514–516.

Panton, S. (1998) The Local Crime Prevention Committee Program, Evaluation Report, Crime Prevention Unit, Attorney General's Department, South Australia.

Pappas, C. (2001) *US gangs: their changing history and contemporary solutions*. Youth Advocate Program International Resource Paper. Washington, DC: Youth Advocate Program International.

Parliament of Australia (2010) *Joint Select Committee on Cyber-safety*. Canberra: Parliament House.

Parliament of Australia Joint Committee (2004) *Cybercrime*. Canberra.

Parmar, A. & Sampson, A. (2006) 'Evaluating domestic violence initiatives', *British Journal of Criminology*, vol. 47, no. 4, pp. 671–691.

Parramatta Local Government Area (2001) *Draft community safety and crime prevention plan 2001–2004*. Parramatta City Council, NSW.

Pavlich, G. (1999) 'Preventing crime: "social" versus "community" governance in Aotearoa/New Zealand', in R. Smandych (ed.), *Governable places: readings on governmentality and crime control*. Dartmouth: Ashgate, pp. 103–131.

Pawson, R. (2002) 'Evidence-based policy: in search of a method', *Evaluation*, vol. 8, no. 2, pp. 157–181.

—— (2003) 'Nothing as practical as a good theory', *Evaluation*, vol. 9, no. 4, pp. 471–490.

—— (2006) *Evidence-based policy: a realist perspective*. London: Sage Publications.

Pawson, R. & Tilley, N. (1997) *Realistic evaluation*. London: Sage Publications.

Payne, A.A. & Eckert, R. (2010) 'The relative importance of provider, program, school, and community predictors of the implementation quality of school-based prevention programs', *Prevention Science*, vol. 11, no. 2, pp. 126–141.

Pease, K. (2001) 'Distributive justice and crime', *European Journal of Criminal Policy and Research*, vol. 9, no. 4, pp. 413–425.

Perrone, S. & White, R. (2000) 'Young people and gangs', *Trends & Issues in Crime and Criminal Justice*, no. 167.

Petrosino, A., Petrosino, C.T. & Buehler, J. (2003) '"Scared Straight" and other juvenile awareness programs for preventing juvenile delinquency' (updated C2 Review), in *The Campbell Collaboration Reviews of Intervention and Policy Evaluations (C2-RIPE)*, November 2003. Philadelphia, Pennsylvania: Campbell Collaboration.

Petrosino, A. & Soydan, H. (2005) 'The impact of program developers as evaluators on criminal recidivism: results from meta-analysis of experimental and quasi-experimental research', *Journal of Experimental Criminology*, vol. 1, no. 4, pp. 435–50.

Phillips, C. (2002) 'From voluntary to statutory status: reflecting on the experience of three partnerships established under the *Crime and Disorder Act 1998*', in G. Hughes, E. McLaughlin & J. Muncie (eds), *Crime prevention and community safety: new directions*. London: Sage Publications, pp. 163–181.

Phoenix, J. & Kelly, K. (2013) 'You Have To Do It For Yourself': responsibilization in youth justice and young people's situated knowledge of youth justice', *British Journal of Criminology*, vol. 53, no. 3, pp. 419–437.

Pickering, S., McCulloch, J. & Wright-Neville, D. (2008) *Counter-terrorism policing: community, cohesion and security*. New York: Springer.

Pickering, S., Wright-Neville, D., McCulloch, J. & Letini, P. (2007) *Counter-terrorism policing and culturally diverse communities*. Melbourne: Monash University.

Piquero, A.R., Cullen, F.T., Unnever, J.D. Piquero, N.L & Gordon, J.A. (2010) 'Never too late: public optimism about juvenile rehabilitation', *Punishment & Society*, vol. 12, no. 2, pp. 187–207.

Pires, S. & Clarke, R. (2011) 'Sequential foraging, itinerant fences and parrot poaching in Bolivia', *The British Journal of Criminology*, vol. 51, no. 2, pp. 314–335.

—— (2012) 'Are parrots CRAVED? An analysis of parrot poaching in Mexico', *Journal of Research in Crime and Delinquency*, vol. 49, no. 1, pp. 122–146.

Polk, K. (1994) *When men kill: scenarios of masculine violence*. Melbourne: Cambridge University Press.

—— (1997) 'A community and youth development approach to youth crime prevention', in P. O'Malley & A. Sutton (eds), *Crime Prevention in Australia: issues in policy and research*. Sydney: Federation Press.

Porter, L.E. & Kebbell, M.R. (2011) 'Radicalization in Australia: examining Australia's convicted terrorists', *Psychiatry, Psychology and Law*, vol. 18, no. 2, pp. 212–231.

Posavac, E.J. & Carey, R.C. (1997) *Program evaluation: methods and case studies*. Englewood Cliffs, New Jersey: Prentice-Hall.

Poyner, B. (1983) *Design against crime: beyond defensible space*. London: Butterworths.

—— (1997) 'Situational prevention in two parking facilities', in R.V. Clarke (ed.), *Situational crime prevention: successful case studies*. Monsey, New York: Criminal Justice Press, pp. 157–166.

—— (2006) *Crime free housing in the 21st century*. London: UCI Jill Dando Institute of Crime Science. London: University College London.

Poynting, S. & Noble, G. (2004) *Living with racism: the experience and reporting by Arab and Muslim Australians of discrimination, abuse and violence since 11 September 2001*. Report to the Human Rights and Equal Opportunity Commission, Australia.

Poynton, S., Donnelly, N., Weatherburn, D., Fulde, G. & Scott, L. (2005) 'The role of alcohol in injuries presenting to St Vincent's Hospital Emergency Department and the associated short-term costs', *Alcohol Studies Bulletin*, no. 6. Produced by the Alcohol Education and Rehabilitation Foundation and the NSW Bureau of Crime Statistics and Research, Sydney.

Prenzler, T. (2009) 'Strike Force Piccadilly: a public–private partnership to stop ATM ram raids', *Policing: An International Journal of Police Strategies & Management*, vol. 32, no. 2, pp. 99–119.

Presdee, M. (2000) *Cultural criminology and the carnival of crime*. London: Routledge.

Presdee, M. & Walters, R. (1998) 'The perils and politics of criminological research and the threat to academic freedom', *Current Issues in Criminal Justice*, vol. 10, no. 2, pp. 156–167.

Price, M. & Dalgleish, J. (2010) 'Experiences, impacts and coping strategies as described by Australian young people'. *Youth Studies Australia*, vol. 29, no. 2, pp. 51–59.

Putt, A.D. & Springer, J.F. (1998) *Policy research: concepts, methods and applications*. Englewood Cliffs, New Jersey: Prentice-Hall.

Quah, J. (1992) 'Crime prevention Singapore style', *Asian Journal of Public Administration*, vol. 14, no. 2, pp. 149–185.

Queensland Government (2007) *Crime Prevention Through Environmental Design (CPTED) Guidelines for Queensland*. Brisbane: Queensland Police Service.

Queensland Police Service (2006) *Crime Prevention through Environmental Design: an Introduction to CPTEWD Guidelines for Queensland*. Brisbane: Queensland Police Service in partnership with the Queensland Department of Communities and Department of Local Government, Planning, Sport and Recreation.

Ratcliffe, J. (2003) 'Intelligence-led policing', *Trends & Issues in Crime and Criminal Justice*, no. 248.

——— (2008) 'Intelligence-led policing', in R. Wortley & L. Mazerolle (eds), *Environmental criminology and crime analysis*. Devon: Willan Publishing.

Ray, J., Moineddin, R., Bell, C., Thiruchelvam, D., Creatore, M, Gozdyra, P. et al. (2008) 'Alcohol sales and risk of serious assault', *PLoS Medicine*, vol. 5, no. 5: e104.

Reynald, D.M. (2011) 'Translating CPTED into crime preventive action: a critical examination of CPTED as a tool for active guardianship', *European Journal on Criminal Policy and Research*, vol. 17, no. 1, pp. 69–81.

Rigby, K. (2002) *A meta-evaluation of methods and approaches to reduce bullying in pre-schools and early primary school in Australia*. Canberra: Attorney-General's Department.

——— (2003) 'Addressing bullying in schools: theory and practice', *Trends & Issues in Crime and Criminal Justice*, no. 259.

Robinson, C. (2000) 'Creating space, creating self: street-frequenting youth in the city and suburbs', *Journal of Youth Studies*, vol. 3, no. 2, pp. 429–443.

Roche, A., Bywood, P., Borlagdan, J., Lunnay, B., Freeman, T., Lawton, L., Toveli, A. & Nicholas, R. (2008) *Young people and alcohol: the role of cultural influences*. Melbourne: DrinkWise Australia Ltd.

Rodger, J.J. (2008) *Criminalising social policy: anti-social behaviour and welfare in a de-civilised society*. Devon: Willan Publishing.

Ronczkowski, M. (2004) *Terrorism and organized hate crime: intelligence gathering, analysis and investigations*. Boca Raton, Florida: CRC Press/Taylor & Francis.

Room, R. & Rossow, I. (2001) 'The share of violence attributable to drinking', *Journal of Substance Use*, vol. 6, no. 4, pp. 218–228.

Rosenbaum, D. (1987) 'The theory and research behind Neighbourhood Watch: is it a sound fear and crime reduction strategy?', *Crime & Delinquency*, vol. 33, no. 1, pp. 103–134.

Roth, J. (1994a) *Understanding and preventing violence. Research in Brief*. Washington, DC: National Institute of Justice, US Department of Justice.

——— (1994b) *Psychoactive substances and violence. Research in Brief*. Washington, DC: National Institute of Justice, US Department of Justice.

Royal Commission into Aboriginal Deaths in Custody (1991) National Report (vol. 1, by Commissioner Elliott Johnston) Canberra: Australian Government Publishing Service.

Sageman, M. (2008) *Leaderless jihad: terror networks in the twenty-first century*. Philadelphia: University of Pennsylvania Press.

Salvadori, I. (1997) 'A dragon in the neighbourhood: city planning with children in Milan, Italy', *Social Justice*, vol. 24, no. 3, pp. 192–202.

Sampson, R. & Laub, J. (2003) 'Life-course desisters? Trajectories of crime among delinquent boys followed to age 70', *Criminology*, vol. 41, no. 3, pp. 555–592.

Sampson, R.J. (1997) 'Neighbourhoods and violent crime: a multilevel study of collective efficacy', *Science*, vol. 277, no. 5328, pp. 918–925.

Sandercock, L. (1983) 'Who gets what out of public participation?', in L. Sandercock & M. Berry (eds), *Urban political economy: the Australian case*. Sydney: George Allen & Unwin.

—— (1997) 'From main street to fortress: the future of malls as public spaces – or – "shut up and shop"', *Just Policy*, vol. 9, no. 9, pp. 27–34.

Sansfacon, D. & Waller, I. (2001) 'Recent evolution of governmental crime prevention strategies and implications for evaluation and economic analysis', in B.C. Welsh, D. Farrington & L.W. Sherman (eds), *Costs and benefits of preventing crime*. Boulder, Colorado: Westview Press, pp. 225–247.

Sargeant, E., Wickes, R. & Mazerolle, L. (2013) 'Policing community problems: exploring the role of formal social control in shaping collective efficacy', *Australian & New Zealand Journal of Criminology*, vol. 46, no. 1, pp. 70–87.

Sarre, R. & Prenzler, T. (2005) *The law of private security in Australia*. Pyrmont, NSW: Thomson/LBC.

Saville, G. & Cleveland, G. (1997) '2nd Generation CPTED: an Antidote to the Social Y2K Virus of Urban Design'. Paper presented at the 2nd Annual International CPTED Conference, Orlando, Florida, 3–5 December.

—— (2003a) 'An introduction to 2nd generation CPTED: Part 1', *CPTED Perspectives*, vol. 6, no. 1, pp. 7–9.

—— (2003b) 'An introduction to 2nd generation CPTED: Part 2', *CPTED Perspectives*, vol. 6, no. 2, pp. 4–8.

Schinkel, W. (2004) 'The will to violence', *Theoretical Criminology*, vol. 8, no. 1, pp. 5–31.

Schmid, A.P. (ed.) (2011) *The Routledge handbook of terrorism research*. New York: Taylor & Francis.

—— (2013) 'Radicalisation, de-radicalisation, counter-radicalisation: a conceptual discussion and literature review'. The Hague: ICCT, at www.icct.nl/download/file/ICCT-Schmid-Radicalisation-De-Radicalisation-Counter-Radicalisation-March-2013.pdf

Schneider, J. (2008) 'Reducing the illicit trade in endangered wildlife: the market reduction approach', *Journal of Contemporary Criminal Justice*, vol. 24, no. 3, pp. 274–295.

—— (2012) *Sold into extinction: the global trade in endangered species*. New York: Praeger.

Schneider, R.H. & Kitchen, T. (2002) *Planning for crime prevention: a transatlantic perspective*. London: Routledge.

Schweinhart, L.J. (1993) *Significant benefits: the High/Scope Perry Preschool Study through Age 27* (Monographs of the High/Scope Educational Research Foundation, no. 10). Ypsilanti: High/Scope Press.

Schweinhart, L.J., Montie, J., Xiang, Z., Barnett, W.S., Belfield, C.R. & Nores, M. (2005) *Lifetime effects: the High/Scope Perry Preschool Study through Age 40* (Monographs of the High/Scope Educational Research Foundation, no. 14). Ypsilanti: High/Scope Press.

Scott, L., Donnelly, N., Poynton, S. & Weatherburn, D. (2007) 'Young adults' experience of responsible service practice in NSW: an update', *Alcohol Studies Bulletin*, no. 9. Produced by Alcohol Education and Rehabilitation Foundation and the NSW Bureau of Crime Statistics and Research.

Shaftoe, H. & Read, T. (2005) 'Planning out crime: the appliance of science or an act of faith', in N. Tilley (ed.), *Handbook of crime prevention and community safety*. Cullompton, Devon: Willan Publishing, pp. 245–265.

Shapland, J. (2000) 'Situational prevention: social values and social viewpoints', in A. Von Hirsch, D. Garland & A. Wakefield (eds), *Ethical and social perspectives on situational crime prevention*. Oxford: Hart Publishing, pp. 113–124.

Shaw, G., Biven, A., Gray, D., Mosey, A., Stearne, A. & Perry, J. (2004) *An evaluation of the Comgas Scheme: they sniffed it and they sniffed it – but it just wasn't there*. Canberra: Australian Government Department of Health and Ageing.

Shaw, M. (2001) *The role of local government in community safety*. Montreal, Canada: International Centre for the Prevention of Crime.

—— (2009) 'International models of crime prevention', in A. Crawford (ed.), *Crime prevention policies in comparative perspective*. Devon: Willan Publishing.

Shearing, C. & Stenning, P. (1992) 'From the Panopticon to Disneyworld: the development of discipline', in R. Clarke (ed.), *Situational crime prevention: successful case studies*. New York: Harrow and Heston.

Sherman, L.W. (2006) 'To develop and test: the inventive difference between evaluation and experimentation', *Journal of Experimental Criminology*, vol. 2, no. 3, pp. 393–406.

—— (2011) 'Criminology as invention', in M. Bosworth and H. Caroyln (eds), *What is criminology?* Oxford: Oxford University Press, pp. 423–439.

Sherman, L.W., Farrington, D.P., Welsh, B.C. & MacKenzie, D.L. (2002) *Evidence-based crime prevention*. London & New York: Routledge.

—— (2006) 'Preventing crime', in L.W. Sherman, D.P. Farrington, B.C. Welsh & D.L. MacKenzie (eds), *Evidence-based crime prevention*, rev. edn. London & New York: Routledge.

Sherman, L.W., Gottfredson, D., MacKenzie, D., Eck, J., Reuter, P. & Bushway, S. (1997) *Preventing crime: what works, what doesn't, what's promising*. Washington, DC: Office of Justice Programs, US Department of Justice.

Sherman, L.W. & Strang, H. (2004) '"Verdicts of interventions"? Interpreting results from randomised controlled experiments in criminology', *American Behavioural Scientist*, vol. 47, no. 5, pp. 575–607.

Simon, D. (2000) 'Corporate environmental crimes and social inequality: new directions for environmental justice research', *American Behavioral Scientist*, vol. 43, no. 4, pp. 633–645.

Singh, J. (2000) *Crime prevention: the Singapore Approach*, (Resource Material Series, no. 56). Tokyo: UNAFEI.

Skogan, W.G. (1988) 'Community organisations and crime', in M. Tonry & N. Morris (eds), *Crime and justice: a review of research*. Chicago: University of Chicago Press, pp. 39–78.

—— (1990) *Disorder and decline*. Berkeley and Los Angeles: University of California Press.

—— (2006) 'The promise of community policing', in D. Weisburd & A. A. Bragga (eds), *Police innovation: contrasting perspectives*. Cambridge: Cambridge University Press, pp. 27–43.

Skogan, W.G. & Hartnett, S.M. (1997) *Community policing: Chicago style*. New York: Oxford University Press.

Smith, M. (1996) *Crime prevention through environmental design in parking facilities*. National Institute of Justice, Research in Brief, April 1996, US Department of Justice, Office of Justice Programs, Washington, DC.

—— (1998) *Ecologism: towards ecological citizenship*. Minneapolis: University of Minnesota Press.

Smith, M.J. & Tilley, N. (eds) (2005) *Crime science: new approaches to preventing and detecting crime*. Cullompton, Devon: Willan Publishing.

Smith, R. (undated) 'Organised identity crime in a global perspective'. Paper presented at the International Serious and Organised Crime Conference. Canberra: Australian Institute of Criminology.

Smith, R. & Anderson, K. (2004) 'Understanding non-compliance in the marine environment', *Trends & Issues in Crime and Criminal Justice*, no. 275.

South, N. & Brisman, A. (eds) (2013) *The Routledge international handbook of green criminology*. New York: Routledge.

South, N. & Wyatt, T. (2011) 'Comparing illicit trades in wildlife and drugs: an exploratory study', *Deviant Behaviour: An Interdisciplinary Journal*, vol. 132, no. 6, pp. 538–561.

South Australian Attorney-General's Department (1989) *Confronting crime: the South Australian Crime Prevention Strategy*. Adelaide: Attorney-General's Department.

South Australian Crime Prevention Unit (2007) 'Crime Prevention and Community Safety Grants Program: guidelines 2007', Attorney-General's Department, at Adelaide <www.cpu.sa.gov.au> (accessed on 6 June 2007).

South Australian Department of Planning and Urban Transport (2004) *Designing out crime: design solutions for safer neighbourhoods*. Adelaide: South Australia Department of Planning and Urban Transport.

Spalek, A. & Imtoual, A. (2007) 'Muslim communities and counter-terror responses: "hard" approaches to community engagement in the UK and Australia', *Journal of Muslim Minority Affairs*, vol. 27, no. 2, pp. 185–202.

Spelman, W. & Eck, J.E. (1987) *Problem-oriented policing*. US Department of Justice, National Institute of Justice. Washington, DC.

Spencer, L., Ritchie, J., Lewis, J. & Dillon, L. (2003) *Quality in qualitative evaluation: a framework for assessing research evidence*. London: National Centre for Social Research, Cabinet Office.

Spergal, I. & Grossman, S. (1997) 'The Little Village Project: a community approach to the gang problem', *Social Work*, vol. 42, pp. 456–470.

Stenson, K. (2005) 'Sovereignty, biopolitics and the local government of crime in Britain', *Theoretical Criminology*, vol. 9, no. 3, pp. 265–287.

Step Back Think (2008) *Who is Step Back Think?* Melbourne.

Stockwell, T., Masters, L., Philips, M., Daly, A., Gahegan, M., Midford, R. et al. (1998) 'Consumption of different alcoholic beverages as predictors of local rates of night-time assault and acute alcohol-related morbidity', *Australian and New Zealand Journal of Public Health*, vol. 22, pp. 237–242.

Stummvoll, G. (2012) 'Governance through norms and standards: the normative force behind design-led crime prevention', *Criminology and Criminal Justice*, vol. 12, no. 4, pp. 377–396.

Sun, I.Y., Yuning. W. & Poteyeva, M. (2011) 'Arab Americans' opinion on counterterrorism measures: the impact of race, ethnicity, and religion', *Studies in Conflict & Terrorism*, vol. 34, no. 7, pp. 540–555.

Sutton, A. (1991) 'The Bonnemaison Model: theory and application', in B. Halstead (ed.), *Youth crime prevention: proceedings of a policy forum held 28th & 29th August 1990*. Canberra: Australian Institute of Criminology.

—— (1994a) 'Community crime prevention: a national perspective', in D. Chappell & P. Wilson (eds), *The Australian criminal justice system: the mid-1990s*. Melbourne: Butterworths, pp. 213–234.

—— (1994b) 'Crime prevention: promise or threat?', *Australian & New Zealand Journal of Criminology*, vol. 27, no. 1, pp. 3–20.

—— (1996) 'Taking out the interesting bits? Problem solving and crime prevention', *Crime Prevention Studies*, vol. 5, pp. 57–74.

—— (1997) 'Crime prevention: policy dilemmas – a personal account', in P. O'Malley & A. Sutton (eds), *Crime prevention in Australia: issues in policy and research*. Sydney: Federation Press, pp. 12–37.

—— (2000a) 'Crime prevention: a viable alternative to the justice system?', in D. Chappell & P. Wilson (eds), *Crime and the criminal justice system in Australia: 2000 and beyond*. Melbourne: Butterworths, pp. 316–331.

—— (2000b) 'Drugs and dangerousness: perception and management of risk in the neo-liberal era', in M. Brown & J. Pratt (eds), *Dangerous offenders: punishment and social order*. London: Routledge, pp. 165–180.

Sutton, A. & Cherney, A. (2002) 'Prevention without politics: the cyclical progress of crime prevention in an Australian state', *Criminal Justice: International Journal of Policy and Practice*, vol. 2, no. 3, pp. 325–344.

—— (2003) 'Crime prevention and community safety: some grassroots perspectives'. Paper presented at the Crime Prevention Victoria Conference, Crime Prevention for a Safer Victoria: A Consultative Symposium, 29–30 September 2003, Melbourne.

Sutton, A., Cherney, A. & White, R. (2008) *Crime prevention: principles, policies and practices*. Melbourne: Cambridge University Press.

Sutton, A. & Wilson, D. (2004) 'Open-street CCTV in Australia: the politics of resistance and expansion', *Surveillance and Society*, vol. 2, nos 2/3, pp. 310–322, at <www.surveillance-and-society.org/cctv.htm> (accessed 27 February 2008).

Tailby, R. & Gant, F. (2002) 'The illegal market in Australian abalone', *Trends & Issues in Crime and Criminal Justice*, no. 225.

Taylor, R. & Gottfredson, S. (1986) 'Environmental design, crime and prevention: an examination of community dynamics', in A. Reiss & M. Tonry (eds), *Crime and Justice: A Review of Research*, vol. 8. Chicago: University of Chicago Press, pp. 387–416.

Third, A., Richardson, I., Collin, P., Rahilly, K. & Bolzan, N. (2010) *Intergenerational attitudes towards social networking and cybersafety: a Living Lab Research Report*. Melbourne: Cooperative Research Centre for Young People, Technology and Wellbeing.

Tierney, J.P., Grossman, J.B. & Resch, N.L. (1995) *Making a difference: an impact evaluation of Big Brothers, Big Sisters*. Philadelphia: Public/Private Ventures.

Tilley, N. (2001) 'Evaluation and evidence led crime reduction policy and practice', in R. Matthews & J. Pitts (eds), *Crime disorder and community safety*. London: Routledge, pp. 81–97.

—— (2002) 'The rediscovery of learning: crime prevention and scientific realism', in G. Hughes & A. Edwards (eds), *Crime control and community: the new politics of public safety*. Devon: Willan Publishing, pp. 63–85.

—— (2004a) 'Karl Popper: a philosopher for Ronald Clarke's situational crime prevention', *Israel Studies in Criminology: Tradition and Innovation in Crime and Criminal Justice*, vol. 8. Whitby, Ontario: de Sitter Publications.

—— (2004b) 'Applying theory-driven evaluation to the British Crime Reduction Programme: the theories of the programme and its evaluation', *Criminal Justice*, vol. 4, no. 3, pp. 255–276.

—— (2005) 'Driving down crime at motorway service areas', in M.J. Smith & N. Tilley (eds), *Crime science: new approaches to preventing and detecting crime*. Devon: Willan Publishing, pp. 104–125.

—— (2006) 'Knowing and doing: guidance and good practice in crime prevention', in J. Knutsson & R.V. Clarke (eds), *Putting theory to work: implementing situational crime prevention and Problem-oriented Policing* (Crime Prevention Studies, vol. 20). Monsey, New York: Criminal Justice Press, pp. 217–252.

—— (2010) 'Whither problem-oriented policing', *Criminology & Public Policy*, vol. 9, no. 1, pp. 183–195.

Tilley, N. & Laycock, G. (2000) 'Joining up research, policy and practice about crime', *Policy Studies*, vol. 21, no. 3, pp. 214–227.

Tillyer, M.S. & Eck, J.E. (2011) 'Getting a handle on crime: a further extension of routine activities theory', *Security Journal*, vol. 24, no. 2, pp. 179–193.

Tomsen, S. (1997) 'Youth violence and the limits of moral panic', *Youth Studies Australia*, vol. 16, no. 1, pp. 25–30.

—— (1997a) 'A top night: social protest, masculinity and the culture of drinking violence', *The British Journal of Criminology*, vol. 37, no. 1, pp. 90–102.

—— (2001) 'Hate crime and masculinity: new crimes, new responses and some familiar patterns'. Paper presented at the 4th National Outlook Symposium on Crime in Australia, 'New Crimes or New Responses', Australian Institute of Criminology, Canberra.

—— (2005) '"Boozers and bouncers": masculine conflict, disengagement and the contemporary governance of drinking-related violence and disorder', *The Australian & New Zealand Journal of Criminology*, vol. 38, no. 3, pp. 283–297.

—— (2009) *Violence, prejudice and sexuality*. New York: Routledge.

Tonry, M. & Farrington, D.P. (1995), 'Strategic approaches to crime prevention', in M. Tonry & D.P. Farrington (eds), *Building a safer society: strategic approaches to crime prevention*. Chicago and London: University of Chicago Press, pp. 1–22.

Toohey, P. (2008) 'After the binge', *Weekend Australian*, 29 November.

Toumbourou, J.W. (1999) 'Implementing communities that care in Australia: a community mobilisation approach to crime prevention', *Trends & Issues in Crime and Criminal Justice*, no. 122, at <www.aic.gov.au> (accessed 27 February 2013).

Tremblay, R. & Craig, W. (1995) 'Building a safer society: strategic approaches to crime prevention', *Crime and Justice*, vol. 19, pp. 151–236.

Trench, S., Tanner, O. & Tiesdell, S. (1992) 'Safer cities for women: perceived risks and planning measures', *Town Planning Review*, vol. 63, no. 3, pp. 279–295.

Treno, A.J., Johnson, F.W., Remer, L.G. & Grunewald, P.J. (2007) 'The impact of outlet densities on alcohol-related crashes: a spatial panel approach', *Accident Analysis & Prevention*, vol. 39, no. 5, pp. 894–901.

Tulloch, J., Lupton, D., Blood, W., Tulloch, M., Jennett, C. & Enders, M. (1998a) *Fear of crime: audit of the literature and programs*. Canberra: Attorney-General's Department.

—— (1998b) *Fear of crime: the fieldwork research*. Canberra: National Campaign Against Violence and Crime.

Tyler, T. (2012) 'Toughness vs. fairness: police policies and practices for managing the risk of terrorism', in C. Lum & L.W. Kennedy (eds), *Evidence-based counterterrorism policy*. New York: Springer.

UK National Strategy for Neighbourhood Renewal (2000) *Report of Policy Action Team 8: anti-social behaviour*. London: Home Office.

US Bureau of Justice Assistance (1997) *Addressing community gang problems: a model for problem solving*. Washington, DC: Office of Justice Programs, US Department of Justice.

—— (1998) *Addressing community gang problems: a practical guide*. Washington, DC: Office of Justice Programs, US Department of Justice.

US Department of Health & Human Services (2013) 'Prevent cyberbullying', at www.stopbullying. gov/cyberbullying/prevention (accessed 16 April 2013).

van Andel, H. (1988) *Crime prevention that works: the care of public transport in the Netherlands*. The Hague: Ministry of Justice Research and Documentation Centre.

—— (1992) 'The care of public transport in the Netherlands', in R.V. Clarke (ed.), *Situational crime prevention: successful case studies*. New York: Harrow & Heston, pp. 151–163.

van Daele, S., Vander Beken, T. & Dorn, N. (2007) 'Waste management and crime: regulatory, business and product vulnerabilities', *Environmental Policy and Law*, vol. 37, no. 1, pp. 34–38.

van de Bunt, H.G. & van de Schoot, C.R.A. (2003) *Prevention of organised crime: a situational approach*. The Hague, the Netherlands: Boom Juridische Uitgevers.

Van Dijk, J. (1995) 'In search of synergy: coalition-building against crime in the Netherlands', *Security Journal*, vol. 6, pp. 7–11.

Van Dijk, J. & de Waard, J. (1991) 'A two-dimensional typology of crime prevention projects: with a bibliography', *Criminal Justice Abstracts*, vol. 23, no. 3, pp. 483–503.

Van Dijk, J.J. M. & Junger-Tas, J. (1988) 'Trends in crime prevention in the Netherlands', in T. Hope & M. Shaw (eds), *Communities and crime reduction*. London: HMSO.

van Swaaningen, R. (2002) 'Towards a replacement discourse on community safety: Lessons from the Netherlands', in G. Hughes, E. McLaughlin & J. Muncie (eds), *Crime prevention and community safety: new directions*. London: Sage Publications in association with Open University Press, pp. 260–278.

Victoria, Parliament of (2008) *Inquiry into strategies to prevent high volume offending and recidivism by young people: discussion paper*. Melbourne: Drugs and Crime Prevention Committee, Parliament of Victoria.

Victorian Drugs and Crime Prevention Committee (2012) *Inquiry into locally based approaches to community safety and crime prevention. Final report*. Melbourne: Drugs and Crime Prevention Committee, Parliament of Victoria, www.parliament.vic.gov.au/dcpc/inquiries/article/1842.

Vinson, T. (2004) *Community adversity and resilience: the distribution of social disadvantage in Victoria and New South Wales and the mediating role of social cohesion*. Richmond, Victoria: The Ignatius Centre for Social Policy and Research, Jesuit Social Services.

Vinson, T. & Baldry, E. (1999) 'The spatial clustering of child maltreatment: are micro-social environments involved?' Paper presented at the Children and Crime: Victims and Offenders Conference, Australian Institute of Criminology, Brisbane, 17–18 June.

Vinson, T. & Homel, R. (1975) *Indicators of community well-being*. Canberra: Australian Government Publishing Service.

Von Hirsch, A., Garland, D. & Wakefield, A. (eds) (2000) *Ethical and social perspectives on situational crime prevention*. Oxford: Hart Publishing.

WA Office of Crime Prevention <www.crimeprevention.wa.gov.au> (accessed 27 February 2008).

Wacquant, L. (2008) *Urban outcasts: a comparative sociology of advanced marginality*. Cambridge: Polity Press.

Walker, L. (1998) 'Chivalrous masculinity among juvenile offenders in Western Sydney: a new perspective on working class men and crime', *Current Issues in Criminal Justice*, vol. 9, no. 3, pp. 279–293.

Walker, L., Butland, D. & Connell, R. (2000) 'Boys on the road: masculinities, car culture and road safety education', *Journal of Men's Studies*, vol. 2, no. 8, pp. 153–166.

Wall, D. (2007) *Cybercrimes: the transformation of crime in the information age*. Cambridge: Polity Press.

—— (2009) 'Cybercrime', in A. Wakefield & J. Fleming (eds), *The Sage dictionary of policing*. London: Sage Publications.

Waller, I. (1988) *Current trends in European crime prevention including France, England and the Netherlands: towards national commitment, local inter-agency involvement and support of effective crime prevention*. Ottawa: Department of Justice.

Walmsley, R. (2003) *World prison population list*, 4th edn. London: Home Office Research, Development and Statistics Directorate.

Walters, R. (2003) *Deviant knowledge: criminology, politics and policy*. Cullompton, Devon: Willan Publishing.

Warchol, G., Zupan, L. & Clack, W. (2003) 'Transnational criminality: an analysis of the illegal wildlife market in Southern Africa', *International Criminal Justice Review*, vol. 13, no. 1, pp. 127.

Weatherburn, D. (2002) 'Law and order blues', *Australian & New Zealand Journal of Criminology*, vol. 35, no. 2, pp. 127–144.

—— (2004) *Law and order in Australia: rhetoric and reality*. Sydney: Federation Press.

Weatherburn, D. & Holmes, J. (2010) 'Re-thinking Indigenous over-presentation in prison', *Australian Journal of Social Issues*, vol. 45, no. 4, pp. 559–576.

Weatherburn, D. & Lind, B. (1998) 'Poverty, parenting, peers and crime-prone neighbourhoods', *Trends & Issues in Crime and Criminal Justice*, no. 85

—— (2001) *Delinquent-prone communities.* Cambridge: Cambridge University Press.

Weber, M. (1991) 'Science as a vocation', in H.H. Gerth & C. Wright Mills (eds), *From Max Weber: essays in sociology.* London: Routledge.

Weekend Australian (2007) 'Petrol sniffing scourge defeated', 17–18 March, pp. 1–2.

Weisburd, D., Groff, E.R., & Yang, S.M. (2012) *The criminology of place: street segments and our understanding of the crime problem.* New York: Oxford University Press.

Weisburd, D., Telep, C.W., Hinkle, J.C. & Eck, J.E. (2010) 'Is problem-oriented policing effective in reducing crime and disorder?', *Criminology & Public Policy*, vol. 9, no. 1, pp. 139–172.

Weisburd, D., Wyckoff, I.A., Ready, J., Eck, J.E., Hinkle, J.C. & Gajewski, F. (2006) 'Does crime just move around the corner? A controlled study of spatial displacement and diffusion of crime control benefits', *Criminology*, vol. 44, no. 3, pp. 549–592.

Weisel, D.L. (2002) *Graffiti.* Problem-oriented guides for police series, no 9. Office of Community Oriented Policing Service, US Department of Justice, at www.popcenter.org/problems/graffiti.

Weiss, C.H. (1995) 'Nothing as practical as good theory: exploring theory-based evaluation for comprehensive community initiatives for children and families', in J.P. Connell, A.C. Kubisch, L.B. Schorr & C.H. Weiss (eds), *New approaches to evaluating community initiatives, concepts, methods and contexts.* Washington, DC: Aspen Institute.

Wellsmith, M. (2010) 'The applicability of crime prevention to problems of environmental harm: a consideration of illicit trade in endangered species', in R. White (ed.), *Global environmental harm: criminological perspectives.* Devon: Willan Publishing.

Welsh, B.C. (2012) 'The case for early crime prevention.' *Criminology & Public Policy*, vol. 11, pp. 259–264.

Welsh B.C. & Farrington, D.P. (1998) 'Assessing the effectiveness and economic benefits of an integrated developmental and situational crime prevention programme', *Psychology, Crime and Law*, vol. 4, no. 4, pp. 281–308.

—— (1999) '"Value for money": A review of the costs and benefits of situational crime prevention', *British Journal of Criminology*, vol. 39, no. 3, pp. 345–368.

—— (2000) 'Monetary costs and benefits of crime prevention programs', in M. Tonry (ed.), *Crime and justice: a review of research,* vol. 27. Chicago: University of Chicago Press, pp. 305–361.

—— (2001) 'Towards an evidence-based approach to preventing crime', *Annals of the American Academy of Political and Social Science*, vol. 578, no. 1, pp. 158–173.

—— (2002) *Crime prevention effects of closed television: a systematic review,* Home Office Research Study 252. London: Home Office.

—— (2004) 'Surveillance for crime prevention in public space: results and policy choices in Britain and America', *Criminology and Public Policy*, vol. 3, no. 3, pp. 497–526.

—— (2006) 'Closed-circuit television surveillance', in B.C. Walsh & D.P. Farrington (eds), *Preventing crime: what works for children, offenders, victims, and places.* New York: Springer, pp. 193–208.

—— (eds) (2008) *Preventing crime: what works for children, offenders, victims and places?* Dordrecht, the Netherlands: Springer, pp. 193–208.

—— (2011) 'Evidence-based crime policy', in M. Tonry (ed.), *The Oxford handbook of crime and criminal justice.* New York: Oxford University Press, pp. 60–92.

—— (2012a) 'Science, politics and crime prevention: towards a new crime policy', *Journal of Criminal Justice*, vol. 40, no. 1, pp. 128–133.

—— (eds) (2012b) *The Oxford handbook of crime prevention.* New York: Oxford University Press.

Welsh, B.C., Farrington, D.P. & Sherman, L.W. (eds) (2001) *Costs and benefits of preventing crime.* Boulder, Colorado: Westview Press.

West, A., Lewis, J. & Currie, P. (2009) 'Students' Facebook "friends": public and private spheres', *Journal of Youth Studies*, vol. 12, no. 6, pp. 615–627.

West, D. J. (1973) *Who becomes delinquent?* London: Heinemann.

Western Australian Planning Commission (2006) *Designing out crime: planning guidelines.* Perth: Western Australian Planning Commission.

Whelan, J. (2001) 'The dynamics of community reputation: a case study', Sociology Honours thesis, School of Sociology and Social Work, University of Tasmania, Hobart.

White, R. (1990) *No space of their own: young people and social control in Australia.* Melbourne: Cambridge University Press.

—— (1998) *Public spaces for young people: a guide to creative projects and positive strategies.* Sydney: Australian Youth Foundation and National Campaign Against Violence and Crime.

—— (1999a) 'Public spaces, social planning and crime prevention', *Urban Policy and Research*, vol. 17, no. 4, pp. 301–308.

—— (1999b) *Hanging out: negotiating young people's use of public space.* Canberra: National Crime Prevention, Attorney General's Department.

—— (2001) 'Graffiti, crime prevention and cultural space', *Current Issues in Criminal Justice*, vol. 12, no. 3, pp. 253–268.

—— (2006a) 'Youth gang research in Australia', in J. Short & L. Hughes (eds) *Studying youth gangs.* Walnut Creek, California: AltaMira Press.

—— (2006b) 'Swarming and the dynamics of group violence', *Trends & Issues in Crime and Criminal Justice*, no. 326.

—— (2007a) *Seniors in shopping centres: preliminary report of findings.* Brisbane: National Seniors Productive Ageing Centre.

—— (2007b) *Anti-Gang Strategies and Interventions*, ARACY Gangs Briefing Paper No. 2. Perth: Australian Research Alliance for Children and Youth.

—— (2007c) 'Green criminology and the pursuit of social and ecological Justice', in P. Beirne & N. South (eds), *Issues in green criminology: confronting harms against environments, humanity and other animals.* Devon: Willan Publishing.

—— (2007d) 'Fishing for the future: exploring the ambiguities of environmental harm', The Criminology Public Lecture, James Cook University, Townsville, 22 May.

—— (2008) *Crimes against nature: environmental criminology and ecological justice.* Devon: Willan Publishing.

—— (2011) *Transnational environmental crime: toward an eco-global criminology*. London: Routledge.

—— (2012) 'The making, taking and shaking of public spaces', in E. Barclay, C. Jones & R. Mawby (eds), *The problem of pleasure: tourism, leisure and crime*. London: Routledge.

—— (2013a) 'Doing evaluation research', in M. Walter (ed) *Social research methods: an Australian perspective*, 3rd edn. Melbourne: Oxford University Press.

—— (2013b) *Youth gangs, violence and social respect: exploring the dynamics of provocations and punch-ups*. London: Palgrave Macmillan.

—— (2013c) *Environmental harm: an eco-justice perspective*. Bristol: Policy Press.

White, R. with Aumair, M., Harris, A. & McDonnel, L. (1997) *Any which way you can: youth livelihood, community resources and crime*. Sydney: Australian Youth Foundation.

White, R. & Coventry, G. (2000) *Evaluating community safety: a guide*. Melbourne: Department of Justice.

White, R., Kosky, B. & Kosky, M. (2001) *MCS Shopping Centre Project: a youth-friendly approach to shopping centre management*. Hobart: Australian Clearinghouse for Youth Studies.

White, R. & Mason, R. (2006) 'Youth gangs and youth violence: charting the key dimensions', *Australian and New Zealand Journal of Criminology*, vol. 39, no. 1, pp. 54–70.

White, R. & Perrone, S. (2001) 'Racism, ethnicity and hate crime', *Communal/Plural*, vol. 9, no. 2, pp. 161–181.

—— (2005) *Crime and social control: an introduction*. Melbourne: Oxford University Press.

—— (2010) *Crime, criminality and criminal justice*. Melbourne: Oxford University Press.

White, R. & Sutton, A. (1995) 'Crime prevention, urban space and social exclusion', *Australian and New Zealand Journal of Sociology*, vol. 31, no. 1, pp. 82–99.

—— (2001) 'Social planning for mall redevelopment: an Australian case study', *Local Environments*, vol. 6, no. 1, pp. 65–80.

White, R. & Wyn, J. (2013) *Youth and society: exploring the social dynamics of youth experience*. Melbourne: Oxford University Press.

Wickes, R.L. (2010) 'Generating action and responding to local issues: collective efficacy in context,' *Australian & New Zealand Journal of Criminology*, vol. 43, no. 3., pp. 423–443.

Wikstrom, P.O.H. (2007) 'Doing without knowing: common pitfalls in crime prevention', in G. Farrell, K. Bowers, S. Johnson & M. Townsley (eds), *Imagination for crime prevention: essays in honour of Ken Pease* (Crime Prevention Studies, vol. 21). Monsey, New York: Criminal Justice Press, pp. 59–80.

Wikstrom, P.O.H. & Torstensson, M. (1999) 'Local crime prevention and its national support: organisation and direction', *European Journal of Criminal Policy and Research*, vol. 7, no. 4, pp. 459–481.

Wiles, P. (2002) 'Criminology in the twenty-first century: public good or private interest', *Australian & New Zealand Journal of Criminology*, vol. 35, no. 22, pp. 238–252.

Wiles, P. & Pease, K. (2000) 'Crime prevention and community safety: Tweedledum and Tweedledee?', in S. Ballintyne, K. Pease & V. McLaren (eds), *Secure foundations: key issues in crime prevention, crime reduction and community safety*. London: Institute of Public Policy Research, pp. 21–29.

Wilkinson, R.G. (2005) *The impact of inequality: how to make sick societies healthier.* New York: New Press.

Willemse, H. 1994 *Developments in Dutch crime prevention,* Crime Prevention Studies, vol. 2. Monsey, New York: Criminal Justice Press, pp. 33–47.

Wilson, D. & Sutton, A. (2003) *Open street CCTV in Australia: a comparative study of establishment and operation* (Report on a Criminology Research Council Funded Project). Melbourne: Department of Criminology, University of Melbourne.

Wilson, D.B. (2001) 'Meta-analytical methods for criminology', *Annals of the American Academy of Political and Social Science,* vol. 578, no. 1, pp. 71–89.

Wilson, J.Q. & Kelling, G.L. (1982) 'Broken windows: the police and neighbourhood safety', *Atlantic Monthly,* March, pp. 29–38.

Wilson, P. (1982) *Black death, white hands.* Sydney: George Allen & Unwin.

Wilson, P. & Wileman B. (2005) 'Developing a safe city strategy based on CPTED research: an Australian case study', *Journal of Architectural and Planning Research,* vol. 22, no. 4, pp. 319–329.

Winlow, S. & Hall, S. (2006) *Violent night: urban leisure and contemporary culture.* Oxford: Berg.

Wolverhampton Crime & Disorder Co-ordination Group (2001) *Wolverhampton Youth Safety Strategy: building safer communities,* Wolverhampton City Council.

Wood, J. & Bradley, D. (2009) 'Embedding partnership policing: what we've learned from the Nexus policing project', *Police Practice and Research: An International Journal,* vol. 10, no. 2, pp. 133–144.

World Corporal Punishment Research (corpun) (2007) 'Singapore: judicial and prison caning', at <www.corpun.com> (accessed on 17 June 2007).

Worpole, K. & Greenhalgh, L. (1996) *The freedom of the city.* London: Demos.

Wortley, R. (2002) *Situational prison control: crime prevention in correctional institutions.* Cambridge: Cambridge University Press.

Wortley, R., & Mazerolle, L. (eds) (2012) *Environmental criminology and crime analysis.* Cullompton, Devon: Willan Publishing.

Wortley, R. & McFarlane, M. (2011) 'The role of territoriality in crime prevention: a field experiment', *Security Journal,* vol. 24, no. 2, pp. 149–156.

Wright-Neville, D. & Smith, D. (2009) 'Political rage: terrorism and the politics of emotion', *Global Change, Peace & Security,* vol. 21, no. 1, pp. 85–98.

Wynne, B. (1996) 'May the sheep safely graze? A reflexive view of the expert–lay knowledge divide', in S. Lash (ed.), *Risk, environment and modernity.* New York: Sage Publications, pp. 44–83.

Yin, R.K. (2003) *Case study research: design and methods.* Thousand Oaks, London and New Delhi: Sage Publications.

Zedner, L. (2010) 'Security, the state, and the citizen: the changing architecture of crime control', *New Criminal Law Review,* vol. 13, no. 2, pp. 379–403.

Zhang, L., Hua, N. & Sun, S. (2008) 'Wildlife trade, consumption and conservation awareness in southwest China', *Biodiversity Conservation,* vol. 17, pp. 1493–1516.

INDEX

factors for reduction of, 37
outcome evaluation, 85–86

Party Safe Information Kits,
188
Pathways to Prevention project
(Aust.), 46, 93
Perry Preschool Project (US),
34, 35, 36, 37, 38, 44,
93
petrol sniffing, 66
phishing, 196
poaching, 208
policing, 4, 17, 35
aggressive, 7
bottom-up, 204
community, 202, 204–205,
209
crime prevention and,
202–205
external collaboration and,
202
high-profile, 128
intelligence-led, 202, 204,
205, 209
local, 42
privatisation of, 8, 10
problem-oriented, 87, 202,
205, 209
third-party, 202, 209
top-down, 204, 205
traditional, 202, 204
zero-tolerance, 42
primary prevention, 23,
38, 39
problem-solving methodology,
25–29
process evaluation, 95–97
public housing, 68–69
public space, 55, 142
ambiguities of, 164–168
definition, 167
mass privatisation of, 165
mundane, 166
people watching and, 167
pleasures of, 167
predictability and, 167
social dynamics of, 10
urban, balancing spontaneity
and civility in, 143–144,
148

uses of, 165
youth and, 167–168
punishment, 4, 19, 24, 41, 63,
104, 128
affective dimension of, 41

quasi-experimental evaluation,
88–89, 98, 133
Queensland Pathways project,
101

randomised control trials, 86,
87, 97–98
rational choice theory, 65
responses to alcohol-related
violence, 181
control of licensed premises,
183
Don't Turn a Night Out into
a Nightmare campaign
(Aust.), 184
education programs,
183–184
enforcement of existing
consumption laws,
181–183
integrated approaches to,
184–186
Safer Bars Programme
(Can.), 185
Step Back Think program
(Aust.), 184
responsibilisation, 6, 8, 16
risk index, 74
routine activity theory, 18–19,
30, 56, 65

Safe Cities program (UK), 121
Safer Bars Programme (Can.),
185
Safer Cities and Shires strategy
(Vic.), 96, 126
Safer Suburbs program (Aust.),
126
Scared Straight program (US),
91, 99
Schoolies Week, 186, 188
SCP (situational crime
prevention), 53
anticipatory benefits and, 64
as a commodity, 63

compared to CPTED, 54–55
crime science paradigm and,
61, 62
critiques of, 60–64
diffusion of benefits and, 64
guardianship and, 66
key techniques of, 58–59, 58
opportunity and, 56, 62, 64
promotion of innovative
thinking and, 64
specialisation and, 60–61
transferability of, 60
Seattle Social Development
Project (US), 35, 38
secondary prevention, 23,
38, 39
Secured by Design strategy
(UK), 72
security differentials, 140
security services,
commodification of,
10, 141
self-transcendence, 170
sexting, 195
See also texting
Sherman report, 91
shoplifting, 153
shopping centres and public
malls, 4, 10, 65, 67, 112,
137, 144–145, 188
Brisbane City Council, 145
characteristics of tenancy
and, 152
exclusionary crime
prevention and, 148
Festival Faire shopping
centre (Qld), 152–155
inclusionary crime
prevention and, 148
inclusive planning processes
and, 145
informal rules of non-
engagement and, 148
management protocols for,
145–146
MCS Shopping Centre Youth
Project (Aust.), 151–155
Myer Centre Youth Protocol
(Qld), 146
Netherlands approach to,
118, 146–147

Lightning Source UK Ltd.
Milton Keynes UK
UKOW05f0726090417
298657UK00020B/694/P